AMERICA: WALLETS, BULLETS AND ROSES

By: N S ABDOU

ALSO CHECK: **THE BARBED –FENCE ROSE**

e-mail:abdounagueh@yahoo.com

TWEETER: NAGUEH ABDOU

FB: NAGUEH ABDOU

An-eye-for an-eye-for-an-eye…ends making everybody blind.

Mahatma Gandhi.

"We are one, after all, you and I; together we suffer, together exist, and forever recreate one another."

Pierre Teilhard de Chardin.

1

TABLE OF CONTENTS

3

5

AMERICA: WALLET S, BULLET S AND ROSES

By: **N S ABDOU**

ALSO CHECK: **THE BARBED –FENCE ROSE**

E-mail: **abdounagueh@yahoo.com**

TWEETER: **Nagueh Abdou**

FB: **Nagueh Abdou**

IN THE BLAZE OF YOUR HATE

9/ 11, 2002

It is the first anniversary of the destruction of the Twin Towers where 3000 precious lives have vanished forever. I cannot help but to share the sorrows of my fellow Americans. But why can't nations coexist peacefully?! What's wrong with peace, after all?! You may accuse me of being a dreamer, someone who lives on the edge of reality. Well, I ask all the promoters of violence: What kind of reality are you living in? Aren't you perpetuating death?! Osama, What could you tell a baby who had lost his mother or father? Whose breasts will s/he suck, and whose shoulder will s/he lean on? I know your fallacious, twisted, and wicked logic: We are reclaiming our freedom the West had robbed us of for centuries. And I said unto you, a true freedom cannot be born under the auspices of violence, rather through the painful flow of evolution in man's head and heart. Yes, the ultimate attainable freedom is a gift man can give to himself and to others through genuine communication with his God and consequently with his fellowman. Osama, I sincerely believe that you are consumed by hatred for those who don't share your religious beliefs. But hatred doesn't advance freedom, rather kills it. Unfortunately, institutionalized religions have propagated the fallacious notion that there is a God for Jews, a second for Christians and a third for Muslims. In fact, there is only one God; call Him Yahweh, Messiah or Allah, all are beautiful names given to an awesome God. Let's stop deforming His face by appropriating Him to a particular religion. Only when man worships God in sincerity, can he recover his long lost true freedom. The dangerous freedom given to him through hate is like a gun given to a child that will eventually shoot himself in the heart.

Today, on the ashes of the three thousand dead and the tears of the hundreds of thousands who mourn their death, we must dream to build the monument of a true freedom for all, a monument so solid that will extinguish the fire of hate. This divine monument will be a sanctuary where men of the West and East gather to worship the same one God; and all religions will become pillars in the holy sanctuary of His.

AMERICA WILL WEEP AGAIN

9/ 12, 2002

The event of the last three days has created great havoc for my race in America. Three American- born Arab medical students had been heard in a public place, saying: "On the thirteenth America will weep again." Immediately a waitress in the Shoney's restaurant, where they were taking breakfast, alerted the FBI; and the three musketeers have become subjects of manhunt in twenty-two states. Crossing the Everglades of Florida, they were caught. They pleaded total innocence, attributing their arrest to a prejudiced America toward Muslims. Gentlemen, could it be that you are prejudicing America?! Well, I am in no position or disposition to take sides. But I can say the following: no man comes to this life without drinking from the poisonous cup of prejudice. I, too, had often approached it unto my lips. Thankfully, I quickly rejected it; convinced by the knowledge that he who drinks poison dies by poison. Therefore, here is my advice to all prejudiced people: In the day of your thirst for condemning, seek the limpid fountain of understanding. Yes, you need to reconcile with your brothers, so you may be reconciled to yourselves, and consequently to God. Do not dance in fire, rather around it; warming is fire but it also burns; seek warmth and not burn.

If facts dismiss prejudice, meaning: that you had uttered such a hateful statement- wishing America to shed abundance of tears- you must examine your conscience; your love for America is required under all circumstances. She is the mother whose breasts have nourished you with love and not hate. When you were born, it had opened its arms to receive you with the rights and dignity granted to all Americans. Therefore, as a gesture of gratitude, you must sing: "God Bless America…" However, if your hearts can't bless her, you have the choice to leave with the same dignity she had received your parents when they landed on its soil. In betraying one's own country, one betrays oneself and betrayal turns the milk one would have sucked from the motherly breasts into poison that will run through one's veins. Finally, may I remind you of our good Arabic adage: "Don't cast stones into the well from which you draw your water?"

A BROKEN RIDDLE AND A BOUQUET OF ROSES

9/ 19, 2002

I had a rendezvous breakfast with my friend Edward Azar. As he stepped out of his condo at the Imperial Cove, I was saddened to notice that he was running out of breath; his ailing heart was acting up, and apparently modern medicine had failed to fully control its irregularities. I held Edward's left hand, his right one was holding unto a cane with a crystal head. The cane and I cooperated to walk him to my car.

"How do you feel now, Edward?" I asked soon as I seated him.

"Well, dear Nagueh, the years don't pass in vain," he said with deep sadness. I knew what he was regretting: "La Jeunesse, mon cher ami, c'est le don le plus précieux que Dieu pourrait donner aux hommes-Youth, my dear friend, is the most precious gift God could give to men," often said he, sighing.

"Friend, we are beggars, whatever we receive is never ours, that's why the ultimate gift a man can give to himself is not what he saves on earth, rather what he stores in heaven."

"Nagueh, I never thought of the day you would abdicate the earthly pleasures. Have women lately been treating you badly?"

"Nothing is new; it's always the mutual lust that binds us." I, too, sounded very depressed; I was dying from within. Was Marla's love unable to keep me alive? Worse, have I become incapable of loving?

The brief time I spent with Edward in the Paradise Restaurant was for us an opportunity to reflect on the vanity of life; unlike previous times when we used to reminiscent, most often, about our lives in Egypt, a county we so much loved.

Soon as we finished eating, Edward asked me to take him to a flowers shop. It was Edith's forty- fourth birthday and he wanted to send her a bouquet at work. I took him to the colonial florist, located one block away on the opposite side of the restaurant in the main street of Safety Harbor. There, Edward sat on a comfortable sofa. With aging eyes he started to turn the pages of the catalog that contained a variety of arrangements. Finally he made up his mind: "I want this bouquet." It was an arrangement made of red roses and blue violets.

"This will cost you $52.99," said young Joseph, the shop's owner.

"Wow! Women are costly," Edward commented. I considered that tone of astonishment an instinctive response rather than a discovered reality. Being a man of age, he must have known this long ago. Slowly he pulled the visa card out of his pocket, and before handling it to Joseph, he asked: "Nagueh, to whom am I sending these flowers?"

"To Edith, your girlfriend, the daughter of an Arabic father and a Jewish mother, the one who is separated from her Danish husband," I reminded Edward. This response forced the young florist into a mixed smile. I stared at Joseph, and said: "Well, young lad, we old men have nothing better to do than ridiculing one another."

"He is quite an interesting character," mumbled Joseph.

"He is just a man, a delusional creature," I said.

Joseph asked, "Why do you think man is a delusional creature?"

I responded with a wicked smile. Edward was then patting his female poodle. Immediately Felicidad slightly bit his hand. Was she telling him, do not touch me; you need to invest all your affection on a female of your own species?!

"Young lad, you must pray for our salvation. Indeed, we men of old age are crazy; the only difference between Edward and I is: he doesn't remember, I do."

Suddenly Edward began reciting "Roses are red..." he couldn't finish the classic riddle. Failing memory, and that's where our happiness lays.

Thank God, the arrival of a tall young man with pierced ears and nostrils halted my unhappy remembrances. He was carrying between his arms a male poodle called Castro. Soon as he put Castro down, Felicidad ran to greet her fellow pet with genuine gesture of affection. Castro did not respond with the same warmth.

"Sorry, Castro has only one girl on mind. He loves Catarina so much that he did not want to calm down until I brought him here; he wanted to send flowers on her tenth birthday. He had been doing this for the last three years," thus the pet's owner informed us.

My great admiration goes to Castro, I never sent flowers twice to the same woman- I could not hold onto a long- term relationship after the death of my wife of ten years. Suddenly I remembered how my Chilean girlfriend of five years had betrayed me. Yes, women always betray their men: The good ones by dying, and the evil ones by throwing themselves into the arms of strangers. After concluding the deal, I bade a farewell to all the creatures in the shop to drive Edward back to his Clearwater condominium.

"Nagueh, Did I smell the flowers?" he suddenly asked.

"Yes, Edward and you said they were fresh."

"By the way, to whom I sent those flowers?"

"To Edith..." I smiled lightly, and suddenly a big tear escaped my eyes; I became certain that my best friend's end was nearing.

THE POISON OF THE CONSERVATIVE MEDIA

9/ 22, 2002

I choose to ignore the today's events to reflect upon the poison of the conservative media and the Bush Administration they serve faithfully. Manipulated by wicked politicians, its broadcasters and talk show hosts have been constantly reminding us of the 9/11 heinous crime the Arabs had committed against our country; and thus spreading the fear that more of a similar crime yet to be carried against the innocents. O masters of big lies and prophets of small predictions, your daily depressing news make me vomit my entrails. You and your politicians are united by a single goal: to confuse us, and you do a very good job thanks to the naivety of the many of us. From you we seek truth, only to poison our minds with your deceitful language. You might have a point though; the hardened small minds of the populace must be destroyed; truth does not grow on rocks rather in sponges. You keep echoing George W. Bush's voice constantly reciting the litany of Saddam's dangerous arsenal of chemical weapons and germ warfare. Well, I have more frightening news for you: It is easier to control weapons of Mass- Destruction than to control lies. Your insanity is spinning out of control to the point you wanted us to believe that Saddam had struck us with the West Nile Virus that have lately plagued our country. Some of your experts have even suggested that he will be using the claws of birds to destroy our civilization, the greatest of all times. I have sad news for those who are kept in darkness: Our civilization is on the verge of being destroyed by your lies, arrogance and manipulations.

 Mr. President, I humbly break away from the populace, and refuse to enlist in your army against Saddam, although I despise the monster as much as you do. I shall join your crusade only when you submit to me a convincing proof of his nuclear weapons that are capable of blowing up our valleys and mountains. Sir, I despise your efforts to sell us the notion of a preemptive war as the only way to get rid of the tyrant. Please allow me to get your attention to this simple reality: all tyrants are cowards; they abuse only the weak and fear the strong. If you do agree to this premise, why are you constantly firing at us with your deadly rhetoric? I must accuse you of the same crime; you and Saddam are equal in tyranny. He preys on the powerless; you prey on the meek. We have become a confused nation thanks to your lies.

 America, you have nothing to fear but fear itself. You have developed a technology beyond fear and hunger. Having accepted this evidence, allow me to put your finger on the real problem: Darling, you are today a victim of an administration that hungers for power and personal gains. Mr. President, you have already sent our children to the caves of Afghanistan under the cover called: "Operation Enduring Freedom." And very soon you will be sending dozens of thousands of them to the swamps of Iraq to save, in your fallacious logic, the civilized world from sinking into the darkness of tyranny. Mr. President, we must ascend to the high mountain of peace. There the Prince of peace will speak to us; and then we will sing and dance around His forever- burning flames of a true freedom for all. Freedom is divine; it rejects the shades of prejudice; despises the forms of manipulation, and feasts not with the belligerents or hypocrites. I humbly say this: until man becomes as wise as the Serpent of Eden, and as gentle as the dove of peace, God's greatest gift, freedom, can he not deliver to himself or to others.

THIE KINGDOM'S CLOWNS

9/29, 2002

The president succeeded rallying his loyal patrons the leaders of the far- religious right to go to war against Iraq. Indeed, the best way to get to the sheep is to court the shepherds.

Mr. President, you have started your journey unto the presidency under the umbrella of "my Idol is Jesus Christ." Indeed, you have served them the biggest dosage ever.

 What a blasphemy to confuse the dark gold, oil, with the precious blood of the Prince of peace and light! Misled and misleading, those so- called godly men had already given you their blessing and promised their fervent prayers for a sweeping military victory.

Woe to you preachers when you claim that you are the guardians of the Lord's Kingdom. Indeed, you are working hard, not only for the destruction of this kingdom but also to hasten your doom's day. You have always bombarded our ears by verses from the Holy Scriptures. You wanted us to be virtuous as our heavenly Father is. How about you? Are you truly virtuous and virtuous enough to lead us to the One who said, "I am the Way, the Truth and the Life?" You are never short of answers. To every question we ask, you give us ten answers. Why is this abundance? Is that because you are so knowledgeable? No, you are far away from knowing the Truth (God), and unfaithful to the little you know about Him. Your answers always depend on your conservative political affiliation; you, too, have a destructive agenda for a world you want to save, so you claim. Hypocritical and unfaithful, you can't mislead me by preaching that your mission is to create heaven on earth. The truth is: you succeeded defaming heaven and earth. Nietzsche, the most prominent brain Surgeon of all times, pronounced: "God is dead." Not because he had killed Him but because you had already buried Him. O you gravediggers for the dead gods, how could you invite us to a banquet of cadavers? Love, ah that source of light and power of grace; it has never visited your wicked hearts. You walk amongst

13

us wrapped in garments of righteousness, and I wonder: what deadly weapons are you hiding beneath those holy garments? Your faces are washed in the blood of the heavenly Lamb, you claim. If so, why then have you been in such a hurry to slaughter God, through your choice of war; just to smear your dry faces with His blood? Alas! You are but clowns of heaven. Why don't you kneel down in humbleness at the foot of the cross to inhale the mist of the true holiness that will transform your rocky faces into sponges? Yes, this humbling rite will help you to absorb God's grace that will fill your hearts with compassion toward others.

You have often spoken to us about redemption. Why then have you abandoned His mighty redemptive grace of self- sacrifice to linger under the heavy darkness of greed, condemnation, violence and war? Like all thugs of the world, you are searching only the earthly commodities at all costs; including that of the Lord's precious blood. Indeed, your sanctuaries do not emit scent of adoration, rather they are constantly shooting suffocating smoke of hate and prejudice against those whom you call: "the others." Did He or did He not die for all? If He has died for all; why then you call "the others" those for whom He has died?! Worse, you are so anxious to annihilate them from the face of earth. In so behaving, you're loudly claiming that the Nazarene has died in vain. Indeed, His blood runs dry on your lips. Poor son of Joseph, have you missed the golden opportunity to hold onto the better rewarding job of a carpenter, putting pieces of wood together to make doors and windows; instead of tearing up to pieces your own body? Pardon me, I am missing the essential: You have come to this world to do your Father's will. What a great son you are!

Now, hypocritical preachers, please bring down the volume of your shouting. Rather, like confident children, cry aloud: Abba! Abba! Save us from ourselves. What a morbid pleasure man finds in preaching! Away from me all preachers of death, just let me struggle with God, like Jacob did; I am jealous of the man. I even want to grind up the heart of God with my teeth; I dream to be one with Him. O preachers of division, you divide because you are unable to fuse- unite.

THE BIRDS ARE SINGING ON MY TREES

10/ 1, 2002

Autumn is pushing forwards and behold my fruits are ripening steadfast. Lately it had been abundantly raining here in the Tampa Bay and the fruits of my garden are constantly breaking open; so are those of my heart. Away from me, O parasites, you cannot harvest what you haven't sowed. Today I squeeze my soul drop by drop for those who have lost a limb while ascending the luminous mountain to meet God. And like a happy snake, I linger in the jungle, shedding my old skin and releasing my venom into the veins of the lazy ones.

As my autumn moves steadfast towards my winter, I dream to enter the cold season with warm blood; I cannot count on my leaky chimney. Today as I was lying in bed for my daily nap, delightfully listening to the chirpings of birds perching on my trees, I said a prayer for the falling leaves. I also prayed for those birds that have labored hard building their nests to hide from the heavy rain; may praise be to the sweating wings. And when I saw their wings outspread in the warm sun, I thought of my own flight to eternity. Like a spider I patiently weave my web; I dream to catch God. And like a butterfly, my wings beat against the icy winds. I do not travel downwards in search of precious stones. Rather, I dream to ascend to carry God on my wings and bring Him down to earth. My soul, weep not, you are not dying, rather ripening and the gods are ready to share your earthly banquet. Let's invite the caterpillars; they, too, need to metamorphose under His auspices. Until all rest in God's heart; our lives are but phantoms of a missed evolution. So friends, I ask you today: whence lay the delights of your hearts? Do you dream to become butterflies or piles of dust? Butterflies must you dream to become; all earthly possessions are heritage of the wind. All will vanish, only butterflies will endure and their happy flapping will bring the dead alive again. Fly, fly O my soul; the bird that does not leave its nest will never discover the delightful secrets of the sky.

JESUS AND THE RED DRAGON

10/ 9, 2002

The Red Dragon film made the top list this weekend. Poor Jesus, you have wasted your saliva preaching on high seas, mountains and rocky sterile terrains. Yes, you have missed the great opportunity to become an actor in Hollywood. Had you taken this route, at least you would not have been hanged on the cross, a price paid for your crazy love of humanity.

--What's more on today's menu, besides the electrocution of el Señor Sanchez who had killed six of his coworkers? Even the plea of Cardinals and bishops has failed to spare his life.

-- And Aileen, that highway hooker, she, too, was fried, a price she has paid for having had killed seven of her clientele. Not all was bad news though, Sanchez was granted his last wish: a plate of rice mixed with black beans; a half roasted chicken; a piece of pumpkin pie and a big mug of Colombian coffee. Having deposited all those delights into his body; his soul cried out: "I love you all."

 Aileen was arrogant though; she refused her last meal and shouted: "I shall be back with Jesus."

-- Hail to our Chief! In a matter of hours, he will obtain the congress' approval to attack Iraq. Yes, the Middle East is a vast land inhibited by thugs who scorn our democracy. They will come to our opulent table when we

15

serve them our bombs, thus preached the Chief.

O Jesus, how could you have forgotten your brethrens? Does breaking bread with someone mean a thing to you or the America dollar has seduced you so badly to betray your Semitic race?! Aren't you the son of Joseph the carpenter, the one who had made our doors and windows?! Still I pledge allegiance to you, despite all the evil forces are smothering me.

On Sundays, in our diverse sanctuaries of worship, we join hands to pray for the world's peace as well for the safety of our sons and daughters who will be soon rolling to the heart of Baghdad.

-- How could we have overlooked praying for those three teenagers- the minor was ten and the oldest was eighteen? They had beaten to death a homeless man. It was a price paid for having had punched one of them, they claimed. Yes, he did, he was provoked; the teenager had sent a raw egg onto his face. Having dealt with him once and forever, those young criminals went to eat Kentucky fried chicken in the midst of laughter as they recalled their great achievement.

Let's not forget to congratulate the father of the ten- year -old boy.

"Why your son participated in beating to death that man?" asked the news reporter.

"Well, kids will always be kids," replied the wise man.

--And let's not dwell either on the minor fraction of that man, who filled his truck tank and drove away without paying. Arrested and questioned by the police, he replied: "Jesus told me that the gas was free."
It was a bit of a surprise to me though; I never thought that Jesus was a consultant in the petroleum industry.

--We may have failed all the Ten Commandments; still we take great pride in our scientific achievements. In a few days our spaceship will be zooming through atmospheres in a voyage to heavens, where God might be found at the reach of our Astronauts' hands. Thank you, Lord, for our scientific ingenuity. However, would you please help us to refine our character so we can save this endangered earth?

KNOCKS AT MY DOOR

10/ 10, 2002

I heard repeated knocks at my door. It was Gary, my drunkard neighbor and a close friend of mine. As usual, he needed my attention.

"How the world is treating you, Gary?" Just to say something.

"I expect nothing from this world, I create my own."

"This is the best world one could have," I said to please him.

"This is the only world one must have," he challenged me.

"Well, you're a man born with an instinct for clarity, and I'm a man known by his passion for confusion."

"Man, do you know why you are so confused?" He did not wait for my answer. "Because you let women run your life."

"Speaking of the damages women bring into my life; I must get ready; Javier has to be at Safety Harbor elementary school at 7 p.m.; he is in the chorus, rehearsing for Christmas carols."

"Since when do monkeys sing?" I displayed a neutral smile. "Yes, he is not a canary; he's a little Latin monkey, give him a panama, a kick in the ass and send him back to the Jungles of Colombia."

"Gary, I do share your dislike for the kid. However, for the sake of his mother, I've to show some interest in his life."

"How about yours, do you have one?"

"I never had a life of my own; I've always lived caring for others."

"That's your greatest crime, my friend… to hell the others. If it does not please me, I will not do it. The world exists only for me and I exist to enjoy it; anything wrong with this philosophy?"

"It is impossible to live this way."

"Man, the world is like a whore, you screw a whore for your own pleasure and not for hers; just get over your priestly upbringing."

"Enough, Gary, I've learned my lesson for today."

"You never learn your lesson until you start getting a life for yourself. Go hear the little monkey sing and let me know later what enchantment he has brought into your damn life."

I smiled and slowly raised my arm to wave a farewell to Gary. Energetically he pulled it down and said:

"Well, I journey to the land of booze and you go wandering in the jungle of duty, that self-inflicting torture. Yes, duty is man's greatest aggressive act against himself. The ultimate greatness of a man is measured by his Nays and not by his Yeas… only one must say: yes to hell the world of duty."

"Well spoken, Gary, let's part as friends."

"No. We're just acquaintances who have agreed to disagree."

"That's fair," I said, pressing his beer belly with two fingers. We shook hands, a way to say we are true friends. I then dashed in to tell Marla and Javier to hurry up; it was already quarter off seven. We arrived five minutes ahead of time. As we entered the school, hand-drawn arrows guided us to the auditorium. We sat in the third row of the front section and soon we were advised to seek other seats; the whole section was reserved to the parents of the next year's prospective students. At seven o'clock, exactly, the angelic voices of the fourth and fifth graders sang: "America, America, God shed his grace on thee …"

A few tears escaped involuntarily my eyes; I recalled the image of that America I had dreamed of when I was a young lad, thirty –three years ago. Ah! That lost paradise where people of all nations have bathed in pure honey and milk. In today's America I have found honey and milk tampered with the poison of greed and arrogance, I murmured into myself. Quickly and respectfully I recollected my attention to listen to the singing angels with sentiments of reverence, love and hope for today's America; despite poison had tampered its honey and milk. And that is everyone's ultimate duty to a country that nourishes one's belly and dreams.

A THUG AND A SAINT

10/ 16, 2002

I heard the applauses of the wicked in the White House; Bush was preaching death to Saddam. The streets of Baghdad did not inspire me less disgust. I saw the populace dancing as they were voting to routinely re-elect the angel of death. "Saddam, you're the blood that runs in our veins; we can't live without you, you are our sun and rain", chanted the frightened masses.

 To the pleasing puppets of the White House and to the oppressed in the streets of Baghdad, I advise: cut off the umbilical cord, get yourselves a life of nobility and independence; Parasites live but not for too long. Like desperate mourners, for so long you have danced in circles around your dead in the hope to resurrect them. Instead, soon you have found yourselves lying dead next to them. Blessed are those who dance in their own shadows, they will never lose sight of themselves; nor will they die rather will fade away. Those who have eyes may see, if not let the blind bang their heads against the hard walls of the others' tyranny.

 I would like to digress; I want to write about some past events of which I was not aware at the time they occurred.

--On October 8, Pope John Paul II has elevated to sainthood the founder of "Opus Dei – God's work", Monsignor Jose Maria Escriva de Balaguer. As a Catholic of a different breed, I will not rush to lay a bouquet of roses before the icon of that elitist. On the contrary, I have genuine reverence for Mother Theresa. I have enough modesty to kneel before her icon and kiss her bony feet; she is my heroine in heaven as had been on earth.

-- Early October, Bush had signed legislation recognizing Jerusalem as the capital of Israel, thus aggravating quite a controversial problem. Mr. President, let Jerusalem be a holy ground for Jews, Christians and Muslims. Let all feet stand on the holy ground to offer praise to the One God we all are proud to declare as

18

our unique Lord. Ah! When will come that day Jesus had spoken of?! Like Him, I have a dream. Yes, I dream of that holy day when man will worship the Lord, not only on the hills of Jerusalem or on his mountains but in the holiest of the hollies, in the sacred temple of his own heart, the true Jerusalem. Holy mother, Jews and Arabs dream to lay on your chest their tired heads at the end of their long and weary days. Have mercy on your confused and tired children. Accept and protect them all. Like desperate hungry jackals, they are in chase to tear off one another's skin. May you remind them that on your big chest there is a place for all? Call on them and say: come and lean your tired heads and hearts. Holy City, peace unto you and your children!

THIS IS YOUR WEDDING GIFT

10/ 17, 2002

A bomb exploded in a nightclub in the resort island of Bali, Indonesia. Amongst the 180 persons killed was a newly wedded British couple, and three hundred were wounded. It was the work of al- Qaeda, our greatest enemy, reported the American media. How about the exploding bombs in Australia and Finland? Are they, too, the work of that organization of terror? I will be foolish to agree or disagree; like Halloween children, the sources of evil are masked. Since one cannot identify one's own child on Halloween's night, I still would like to stand on the firm ground and preach peace to all. No single man dies by hope, many die by despair. Yes, we must hope for peace, even as we breathe the deadly smoke of bombs. Hope is the most solid foundation of our survival.

I AM JUST A SPECK IN THIS VAST UNIVERSE

10/ 21, 2002

In the evening, I called my children who are in Diaspora. I spoke first to Nafré (an ancient Egyptian name meaning: nice). She lived in Barbados with her Barbadian husband.

"Life is good. Takaya is doing quite well in his school; besides, he is taking martial art classes," she informed me. Why not, the poor kid has to be ready to wrestle with any shark he might encounter in the infested waters of Barbados. Nafré was managing a yoga studio, besides preparing for her entrance exams for graduate studies. Her husband Adrian worked as art teacher in a high school during weekdays and in weekends he worked as a newscaster in a local radio station. Their struggle was nourished by the hope that in one year they will return to the U.S.A. to start their graduate studies.

Tameri, Nailah and Babafemi lived in Los Angeles, California. I had the chance to talk to Tameri (a

Pharaonic name meaning: motherland), and Nailah (a Pharaonic name meaning: successful). They had just arrived from their hot yoga class- the traditional yoga practiced at 110 degree; People need to dispose of their poisoning worries through the process of sweating. That day, Tameri, The Associate Planner for the City had delivered a lecture before 300 citizens. It was designed to enlighten her audience about a ten year plan to beautify the deteriorating Western side of the city.

Nailah, too, had her own task. Teaching an undergraduate psychology classes at the UC LA, she lectured her students on how the interaction of different cultures has made America's soul optimistic.

Having finished talking to the young ladies, I spoke to Babafemi, a Pharaonic name meaning: loved by his father. The environmentalist and microbes' killer, was, somewhere, in one of the California's deserts. For a couple of years now, it has become a sacred ritual for him to spend a week alone in that vast territory he called "God's virgin land."

"At night when I look at the stars I feel how tiny and big I am: tiny because I am just a speck in this vast universe." He even informed me that he didn't want to leave the mountain because of what he called, "man's uncontrollable appetite to destroy this planet."

I could not figure out though whether the next spiritual step would lead my son to a Far East monastery, or would he take a dive into the cult of a Western form of solipsism. Although I was not sure where to he would be heading, I remained confident that he will honor the family in whatever road he might undertake; so conscious he is of the family's name. I remained quite consoled to know that our family tree is solidly rooted and it will not be eradicated by the strongest of winds, by God's grace.

THE DEATH OF A DEAR FRIEND

10/ 24, 2002

It was very sad news for me. Around six a. m., I received the surprise call from Edith; Edward had died at five o'clock that morning. "He had a heart attack," she reported, weeping. Instantly I became engulfed in a sea of guilt, it was just yesterday I had planned to take Edward out for breakfast at Denny's, a restaurant we had frequented for years. What a shame, I did not listen to my inner voice.

"The wake vigil will start tomorrow morning at nine and the burial will be at two p. m.," Edith informed me while still sobbing. I, too, was on the verge of breaking down. However, I have managed to contain my emotions; she needed to be comforted.

"My deepest sympathy; have you called Perla, Edward's sister in Tel Aviv, and his cousin Nessim in Los

Angeles?" I knew Edith was overtaken by grief and I was willing to undertake this tough task -I had the phone numbers of both.

"Yes, I did. Also I will call a few of his many friends. I thought to call you first; for years you had been a dear friend of Edward."

Indeed, we had a long and genuine friendship. For the last fifteen years we've met twice a week, and spoke by phone four to five times. I cut the conversation short; afraid no longer I would be able to sustain the strength of a consoler. Instead of breaking in tears, I found myself feeling numb and gazing at the white ceiling for a while. Suddenly the bedroom closed door opened. Marla dashed in and flipped the light switch on; she had spent the night next to her son, who had been suffering high fever. I didn't acknowledge her presence.

"Hello, stranger," she said, a bit disappointed.

"Edward died," I told her, sobbing.

"I'm sorry; I know it hurts so much to lose a good friend." She sat to squeeze me with the might of motherly warmth. For a few minutes she caressed my back, while I was lying on my stomach and head buried into a pillow. The back caressing was her customary way to relieve me from a rising stress. I asked her to turn off the light, under the pretext I wanted to sleep. Indeed, I needed time to be in touch with my feelings; darkness is the only light that guides us to our innermost. Observing silence, Marla laid next to me; arm was wrapped around me. I dove into the gentle world of my friendship with Edward. I felt sad and happy. I was sad for having had lost my best friend, but happy for having had known him and his many warm ways. Suddenly I started shaking; in my hallucination I was trying to escape a fat snake. Struggling with somnolence and a hallucinatory state, I felt that snake was biting my ankle. Fully awake, I thought that attacking poisonous reptile was no other than death whose venom no living entity can escape.

I went to the Sylvan Abbey funeral home around nine a. m. to see my dearest friend. The coffin was sealed. Ah, how I wished to see Edward's face shining and joyfully shouting his most favorite expression: "Bonjour mon cher Nagueh - good day my dear Nagueh." Every time I heard it; my heart pounced of joy. I buried my face against the coffin for a minute or two to say a brief prayer for the repose of Edward's soul. While slowly detaching my face away, I heard myself murmuring: "Old friend, let's go for breakfast at Denny's." Once again, I felt guilty of negligence; I knew from our last meeting, less than a week ago, Edward was not feeling well and sadly I sensed that his end was nearing. It was too late; Edward was dead and the time of his funeral was now counted by hours. At noon I went to Dunedin High School to pick up Marla; she wanted to say her final farewell to Edward. She, too, has cherished his friendship, in spite the brief period she knew him. How could she forget that shining light in his eyes as he spoke perfect Sephardic Spanish and the many compliments he had showered her with?! Indeed, Edward was a great ladies' flatterer. Well, here, regretfully, I was dressed in black suit and Marla in black outfit, on our way to the Ahvat Shalom Cemetery. By the way, Edward, what does the word Ahvat mean? I wished you were alive to explain it to me; you had always given the most elaborate answers to the simplest questions. Arriving there, I hugged Edith, her son Shawn and daughter Gwen, while mumbling words of sympathy. The children, too, had very much loved Edward. Once more Edith threw her head on my shoulder to moan:

"Nagueh, I can't believe Edward is gone."

"He will be watching on you from above," I said, hoping to console her. Releasing my hand from hers, after having tightly squeezed it, I proceeded to silently greet the mourners who were there for the last goodbye. Many of them were Edward's close friends. I was bound to them; we all were connected through Edward's goodwill. His philosophy was: my friend is the friend of all my friends. And his death was celebration of this philosophy. As the coffin rested on the edge of the grave, the mourners shock hands and mumbled words of praise for a dear friend. Then came the moment when Rabbi Weisman commanded silence to begin the burial rites. After reciting the burial prayers, came the eulogy that was brief and reflective. The young rabbi recalled with admiration Edward's talent for languages, and how he used his seven tongues to spread the notion of brotherhood of all races.

"What a great God's given gift! I could use it in my job as a rabbi."

He ended his eulogy with, "we are dust and to dust we shall return."

Before lowering the casket, we recited in one voice "the Kiddush, Holy…" -In the Jewish tradition this prayer is celebrated with wine to transform man from his wearying weekdays to the day of rest.

The casket was lowered, and the rabbi instructed us to throw some dirt onto it, a Jewish symbol of participating in the great charitable act of burying the dead. Half of my shovel's load fell on the casket, and the other half fell over the grave's outer edge, as if it were my unconscious attempt to hold onto Edward and not let him disappear six foot under. Only after the casket rested at the grave's bottom, I fully realized Edward has truly died. My eyes began engrossing with tears. Noticing all the mourners have found a reason to celebrate Edward's life, I blocked from my mind the idea of death to participate in the celebration of that beautiful life of my friend. Edward dear, how could I forget that morning when you had made me aware of the presence of that sixteen- year old? Slim and dressed in black, she dashed into the Olga's restaurant like a mighty arrow. Her beauty has forced your bony finger to flip into the air like a spear. You were not timid to whisper, "Look, Nagueh, what a beautiful young lady!"

Rest in peace, big flirter and keep up the good gift of your charm. And if, by chance, our kind father Abraham would seat you next to a woman, don't forget to use one of your cute lines. Your power of attracting women was even a reason of an occasional envy on my part. Finally, let me recall another reason of a more selfish nature: Certainly I will miss you paying for my breakfast; for the last year you had unfailingly done that. "Nagueh, let me pay; too many women in your life and they are quite costly," was your kind friendly joke. After the burial we drove to condominium 30D at the Imperial Cove to eat and drink in a continual celebration of your life. In great affection we recalled our memories with you and finally dispersed hoping to meet again in happier occasions. As I was leaving, Edith hugged me and said: "Although Edward is gone, our friendship will endure."

"Certainly it will," I replied, eyes engrossed with tears. For the first time I've realized the power of friendship.

In the evening, while lying in my bed, I felt all my mundane worries have become lighter. I even thought of the vanity of the carnal pleasures, my most tyrannical vice. Having thought of Edward's death, I came to this conclusion: life is a weathering flower; soon the wind of time will carry it away. Edward's death was eye-opening to this truth. I said a brief prayer for Edward and for myself. Having realized my mortality, I began investing again in God's world. As a good start, I reconciled with my wife Marla, after a week of tense relationship. That night we surrendered our fleshes, souls and hearts to God. Happy are those who sleep under the Lord's watch.

Although Edward's death has left a hole in my heart; his memory continued to give me warmth as I recreated his presence whenever attacked by loneliness. Friendship is that flower whose aroma never fades away despite the destructibility of its source.

DEMOCRACY IS A MYTH

11/ 5, 2002

It is the midterm election in the United State. For quite a while we had been bombarded by the candidates' expensive and, oftentimes, deceptive ads. Indeed, it is democracy working at its highest capacity of treachery. Most of us, Americans, believed that we are better off than the Iraqi people. After all, Saddam has been running the country as he pleases for the last twenty- seven years without the dare of anyone to question his policies. On the contrary, our government is based on the principle of checks and balances of powers dictated by the Constitution. Moreover, it commands the change of the guard, the President, every four years, unless s/he is reelected for a second- term. All is good on papers, though. Frankly speaking, it is erroneous

23

conviction of superiority. Both forms of government oppress their constituents. The- so- called democracy often oppresses its constituents through the power of money, and the tyrannical regime oppresses its subjects through the power of gunpoint. The earlier is assault to the human intelligence and the latter is freight to the flesh. At the end of the day, both systems are guilty of a killing. After all, the mind and the body form an inseparable entity. And I wonder if the day will ever come when we call democracy by its right name, i.e., a clever but brutal deceit. That's why I have never voted, except for Mr. Clinton. I was overtaken by the man's intelligence, added to it his unique charm. After the Clinton's era, the Democrats have lost the power of the majority in the Senate as well as in the House of Representatives; they were in great disarray. Yes, fallacious and destructive is the notion of a baked cake for all. Am I then converting to a republican, or at least becoming a sympathizer of? Far away from me, they're but arrogant brutes. Am I still a happy butcher in the slaughterhouse of the Democrats? I refuse to slaughter others to satisfy my own hunger. Am I then ultimately an independent? I wonder of what? So, who am I exactly? I am the scourge that dreams to lead the herd to the icy fountains installed on mountaintops. Since man is ultimately a holy thirst and hunger, I abstain to lead my flock to the green pastures that nourish only the lazy and satisfied. Rather, I shall keep it on top of the rocky mountain; it needs to create its own food from rocks. Ultimately, man must choose between the rocky mountain and the muddy abyss. A reminder: the stars can be clearly seen only from the mountaintop. Tedious but exalting is the ascent.

AMERICA, MAY GOD SHINE HIS LIGHT UPON THEE

11/ 7, 2002

Today is the beginning of Ramadan, the month when Muslims fast seeking atonement for their sins. President Bush invited the ambassadors of the Islamic world to a rich banquet. Before their breaking a long day of fast, he opened his brief speech with these words: "America has no hard feelings toward Islam." He even preached them what they wanted to hear most, i.e., Islam is a religion of peace. Such statements spread balsam over their wounded hearts and made saliva run through their dry throats. After hearing this brief, but well- calculated political speech, they broke bread and rose cups of soft drinks. Certainly the Prophet will not be pleased if his followers indulge in wine, a drink reserved for them in the world beyond, after a long and tedious journey of righteousness.

For a moment I savored the taste of delusion. Suddenly reality hit me hard; there was no genuine peace.

Frankly speaking, it was war in disguise of peace. Could it be that peace is a protocol of trickery for most of the today's politicians? Yes, their hearts and minds are the graves for the human sincerity and peace. However, if their job is to lie to us; ours is to detect and reject their lies. Politics is a melodramatic theater one needs to enter it with more than one handkerchief.

That night the world slept wrapped in the thin blanket of peace to wake up on the shrilling sounds of menace of war.

"Saddam must disarm or he will be forced to," thus shouted 'the great Pharaoh', barrowing Osama Ben Laden's words- talking about Bush.

America, may God shine His light upon you, you are not evil, you are just this adolescent; who cannot see clearly all the complex and dark realities of the world. Unfortunately, in the midst of your confusion, you want to offer clarity to all. Moreover, you dream to be accepted by the whole world; you are starving for love. Although you deserve it, I must remind you that even love can be a weapon of mass destruction.

--You are trying hard to present an amicable image to my people. On March, you had launched your radio emission SAWA, together, a mixture of your pop music and news of and about the Arabic World. Your hope, America, is but your disguised despair. Wise up and your hopes will become realities. The Arab world fears your -free- spirited culture. You are paying a high price for your ignorance of the cultures of others, a shortcoming that causes your fatal confusion and often renders your foreign policies a failure.

-- Just yesterday evening I watched one of your daughters led to the altar by her dog. The pet was a substitute for the father she never knew. Now tell me, America, what are your credentials for your pretense to lead the world and to where?

A LONG RUN WITH THE WOLVES

11/ 10, 2002

It is my sixty- second birthday. The sun was timid, and I felt a bit lonely. Have we grown weary of one another? If not, where then the passion has gone?

No. I have not lost my zest for life, nor has life has lost hers for me; we have just come to a greater understanding for our bents. During my sixty- two years of wandering on this fragile planet, I have practiced all the dances of the world; run with the wolves of many deserts and have climbed many perilous mountains. Farewell, high seas, icy mountains and vast deserts. Now I need to have an answer for the –ever- persisting question: who am I and to where I going? Hurray, I have found the ultimate answer to the first part of the question: I am the one who must become, creates himself from nothingness. As for the answer to the second part of the question: I am going nowhere else but to myself. I am the alpha and the omega of my existence. May praise be to the evolutionists and to hell all the creationists!

To redeem such a mortal seriousness, let me report to you some indicators of my life's fragilities: today, early morning, Marla presented me with an unimpressive card, whose words were chosen by the Hallmark Inc. On the contrary, her son has challenged my emotions, as he wrote on a crumpled yellow paper: "Old charmer, have a happy birthday."

Javier Cervantes.

I knew there was persisting rivalry between us to win his mother's affection; but heck the kid deserved my admiration; he had spitted out his hate. Yes, he was not celebrating my life, rather the rapidly folding end of it. By calling me "old charmer" he might have thought of me as someone whose eyes had grown dimmer and consequently was unable to see the pretty women. Still I thanked him for having involuntarily shared with me one of them, his beautiful mother and now my wife. I took refuge though into the sincerely expressed sentiments of my five children. I thought then if the blood of life would stop running through my veins today, I will depart as a happy man; so long they would take charge of my funeral cost, of course.

Life is a war; we win it only through fierce fights. So tell me of your struggle; I tell you of your victory, bearing on mind that decay is our ultimate reality.

I expressed special thanks to my youngest child Amon (a pharaonic name, meaning: the hidden one). From his hard -earned money he has spent $30 to celebrate my birthday. And to my good friends Jim and Barbara, who, for the last three years had been inviting me on this occasion. Certainly I thank you for the delicious supper. I especially liked the big piece of your homemade chocolate cake. I also thank you for your sense of compassion. Despite you are born again Christians, you have always abstained to give me even a small dosage of religion; you knew that my stomach didn't digest well that heavy heavenly food. I'm a worshiper of this earth and no other nourishment has a better taste on my tongue. Ah, if man could stare at the stars with the eyes of the heart. He will ultimately become under the protection of the true God; instead of the false one he forges for himself through poisonous indifference, false piety and sterile prejudices.

TURKEYS ARE HAVING AN UNGRATEFUL DAY

11/ 28, 2002

Today millions of turkeys are thrown into the oven to commemorate the pilgrims' satisfied hunger. I wondered who were those pilgrims and to what destination they were journeying. I have no pressing desire to put them in the negative light of being heartless invaders, nor I am anxious to paint them as religious freedom seekers; they were just men and women who wanted change.

I had been a noble humanist until I entered the kitchen. So soon I have realized I was that wolf in sheep's clothing. Yes, one of those victimized birds was destined to land tonight on my own table.

--The turkeys' slaughtering should not make me overlook the electrocution of that prostitute on her wedding anniversary in the state of Texas, courtesy of the laws our religious President Bush had established while being its governor.

--As I was distributing left and right my sympathy to God's creatures, suddenly the phone rang. On the other end was another humanist.

"Greetings, great father of mine," echoed Babafemi's voice.

"Happy Turkey Day, son," I responded with the same warmth.

"Today many things compel me to give thanks to God, but having you as a father is the most compelling reason."

"I am, too, proud to have you as a son."

"Father, have I not spoken, the stones would."

"Thanks a lot, son. What are you doing?"

"I'm painting."

"I thought you might be working on your building."

"No, father, I'm painting my thoughts and feelings. Life is a canvas on which we must record our innermost feelings and thoughts, if we genuinely believe in evolution… Speaking of evolution, let me just say a few words…" He stopped. I knew he was for a long rambling.

".. Father, the beauty of evolution is to unite; oneness is the ultimate step in the ladder of a true evolution."

"It sounds as an improvement on Darwin's theory."

"It's a great improvement. Darwin had spoken of the survival of the fittest, a self- defeating theory because eventually the fittest will destroy one another until reduced to a lonely one who, at his turn, will destroy himself. I believe that the universe is an- all- embracing energy. In evolution nothing will be left behind; everything will be elevated and moved forwards… To put it in mundane words: as we eat our turkeys today, we're not eliminating, rather elevating them. That is why we must honor our ancestors. We are their evolved energy, improved but not better, bigger, but not greater…. If we can rid of raging racism and nationalism, we can deliver the ultimate reality of evolution."

"That's a very noble theory, son."

"Well, father, in this life we're like a sailing ship to the shores of eternity, we must all arrive, or we all perish. We..."

I finally decided to put the break on Babafemi's thoughts; they were getting heavier as he was just warming up.

"Where are Tameri and Nailah?" The patriarch wanted to let his son know that love is the binding force between all. I had already contacted Nafré and grandson Taka. Amon had called from his mother's house to wish me a happy Turkey Day. What a nice son, he offered his company to a lonely divorced mother. Marla, Javier and I spent a great portion of the day beautifying the house and making sure there will be plenty of food on the table for our new extended family. Photos will be taken and this will serve, according to the laws of immigration, as a proof that we were truly married and that the granted marriage license was not a faked document just to earn Marla the legal status of residence.

Finally, toward seven p.m. the victim appeared on the dining table. Its brown color, mixing with the bright evening lights, was an unusual sight. The three of us took turns giving thanks for the most distinct blessings we had received throughout the year. Engorged, we went to sleep; dreaming of more victimized turkeys in the years to come. What a long nightmare the turkeys' life is, and what a brutal consumer man can be.

THOSE BULLS NEED A HEADBUTTING BOUT

12/5, 2002

The blood sweat in the Garden of Gethsemane and the Golgotha were the culminating harvest of the Nazarene, after thirty- three years of loving labor that produced many doors, windows and miracles. Indeed, He had loved so much the world to the degree of madness. And what have we given Him in return? Unfortunately, not much, if anything at all; just turns on your TV and you will realize what I meant. Yes, Bush is unhappy; the United Nations inspectors have not yet found Weapons of Mass- destruction in Saddam's land. "We know he has them," still affirmed the Texan Cowboy. This bull might need a tour of head butting with Saddam. How cruel is the diplomatic protocol! Why can't we let them exercise this sport, it is the call of their nature and let's enjoy whatever outcome may be. Indeed, arrogance is poisoning the only big boy left on the block. And the small ones have no other choice but to be slapped around. Some of them are even grateful to receive the mistreatment. I've been slapped by the giant, bragged those mediocre. Today the butcher of Baghdad is the false martyr, and George Bush is the loose tyrant. Whom should we despise more?

Both must be equally despised. Since the military service had ceased to be a patriotic duty, we were left with a professional army, whose present- Chief thirsts for blood. What a menacing force to world's peace.

DECK THE HALLS AND BE JOLLY

12/19 -23, 2002

Christmas is fast approaching, and the inhabitants of the Del Oro Groves Estates have begun their annual competition: Who would have the best and most expenses decoration of their homes. Even my pagan house has displayed the Christmas spirit this year; Marla liked to celebrate seasons. Why not, women give taste and color to life and Christmas season is a nice tradition, if one could strip from it the human vanity.

The erection of the Christmas tree next to the fireplace, and the display of the modest lights in front of our house brought me the joys of the Holy Season. My new small family delighted itself listening to the Christmas carols: *"DIG THE HALLS…*IT IS THE SEASON TO BE JOLLY ….

JOY TO THE WORLD….

I WILL BE HOME FOR CHRISTMAS…. - a Russian Jew immigrant to America composed the nostalgic song. It is the soldier's dream song.

Those songs echoed even in the streets of Baghdad, so reported the news media. Certainly the Iraqi dictator wanted to convince the world that he was a peace loving leader. Besides, he might have dreamt to convince the Iraqi Christians that he was worthy of their lives.

The joyous songs filled the hearts of our small family, certainly for various reasons: It was nostalgia for Marla and me and expectation for Javier.

"I can't wait to open my Christmas gifts," the child fantasized. "Nagueh, aren't you going to buy me one?" he inquired, several times with apparent anxiety.

"Yes, Javier, I will."

"But when will it be?"

"Don't worry, you will find it under the tree on Christmas Eve."

"Wow! I can't wait," he bewildered, eyes wide open. For days Javier kept wandering in great excitement; Marla and were quite calm; we knew what he wanted. Happy those who know, but even Happier are those who live in hope.

NOT THE SENDER'S FAULT

12/ 24-25, 2002

It's Christmas' Eve. At 6:30 p.m., I turned on my favorite TV local channel 28 affiliated with the ABC net news. It was His Holiness Pope John Paul II reminding the world of the main message of the incarnated God. Yes, Peace. Truly, the infamous thief called man has stolen peace even from the eyes of the child God.

The beautiful Miss. Paragas read the international news. What else? Destruction after destruction, cunning after cunning! I wondered has God wasted His time on man; or has He just become a natural rot in man's storage of time? Poisoned by the evening news, I planted myself into my recliner to watch the flashing lights of our Christmas tree. Marla played some Christmas carols. O Lord of mercy, in the days of my distress, let me hold onto your mighty hand; I thirst to drink from your well of joy. Like a thirsty beast of burden, allow me to drink from this limpid fountain. Briefly I drank from that limpid fountain of the divine tenderness, as I started thinking of my children. Three of them were in Barbados; visiting sister Nafé and her son Takaya. I said a brief prayer for everyone; certainly not forgetting Amon, who was fighting the cruel attacks of his teens.

The midnight mass was majestic as the middle-aged pastor Clark Schneider of the Espiritu Santo Catholic Church surrounded himself with two assistant pastors, four deacons and half a dozen seminarians. We returned home with reddened cheeks to find out that the turkey had gained the same color. It had been metamorphosed by the oven's heat, and we were tainted by the coldness of the winter. We engorged on elaborated meal. Finally Javier got his long- awaited Christmas gift: a bicycle with a helmet. He wrapped his arms around us, shouting: "Thank you, thank you; it was all what I wanted." Tears of joy dripped off his cheeks as he was hugging both; kindness obliges. We went to sleep, our stomachs serving as a burial site to this misfortunate young turkey, whose mother might have been so much missing it, in case it had not been itself slaughtered. Ouch! Thanksgiving Day and Christmas are two days of nightmare in the life of turkeys; truly they are days of genocide in their history book.

On Christmas Day, early morning, Javier put his helmet on and took off to the street to ride his brand new bike while singing: "*Joy to the world…*" He has gotten his Christmas gift; mine is yet to arrive. It was not the fault of the sender rather the receiver; I had not been living in hope.

FACTORS OF OUR MORTALITY

12/ 26, 2002

I called nephew Harby to wish him and his immediate family a merry Christmas, and afterwards I asked:

"How is the family across the Ocean?"

"Everybody is doing fine. Mother went to visit my sister Matilda in Upper Egypt… By the way, our uncle Shaker died a week ago."

I was not surprised, rather saddened, uncle had been very sick for the last three years. His death has closed a long chapter in my life. Yes, although Mother had died over fifteen years ago, she continued living through her brother; he was a solid emotional bridge connecting me with her.

"Death served him well though; asthma had lately impaired his life," Harby commented.

"May God rest his soul," I said, resigned. The news hit me hard after I finished the brief conversation with my nephew. Many memories have then submerged. I recalled those happy Wednesdays of summer vacations when uncle had unfailingly invited his nephews: Mayez (presently Fr. Paulos) and me for dinner and a sleepover. We were then young seminarians. Ah how delicious was the goat meat and the sweetness of watermelon! And how could I forget those steaming buffed raghieves, (a raghief is a flat mass of barley dough) baked by the aging hands of our grandmother. The beauty of the memory was the warmth that emanated from all, including the family's pets and domestic birds. In sum, the whole memory of that customary visitation was a delight, if one would exclude from it the aspect of uncle inviting us to join him in his evening prayers. Yes, the Baptist service drove me out of my mind as uncle and a handful of his male followers pounced up and down like slaughtered roosters. Even the mud- built mandarah- a vast reception hall- remembered them: leaving holes on its walls, as they banged their heads. They were mostly asking forgiveness for their futile sins: such as ignoring a wife, overworking or overloading a beast of burden, or squeezing milk from a domestic animal for their own needs, thus depriving its newborn cubs from the maternal gift.

During our ritual visits, uncle often tested our biblical knowledge. At times, he even tried to convince us that the key to heaven was not in the hands of the predecessor of Saint Peter, the Pope, rather in the modest hands of a Baptist country preacher. In fact, uncle wanted both nephews to become Baptist country preachers just like him. What a heretic was he then for me! Yes, I do remember how much I scorned his religious ideas. I have even felt sorry for him; his religion was giving him nothing but bruises on his forehead and many holes to the frailly- built mandarah.

But how could I forget that day when I walked through the creeping water of the recently flooding Nile to bid a heartfelt farewell to uncle and his family. I had to leave Egypt to study at the St. Joseph Jesuit University in Beirut, Lebanon. Many things I used to love about the controversial uncle. For instance, he had no regard for time and space. To sum it up, and in the words of my cousin Lahzy: "If our uncle tells us that he will be coming from the East, let's wait on him in the West. If he says he will be at noon, let's hope he will arrive at 3 p.m., the earliest."

 The disregard for time and space made me miss uncle so much. He was incarnation of the Egyptian old culture, and that tickles me today with great nostalgia. Yes, I had grown up in this culture that scorned time and space. It was then the gentle life, similar to that of Adam and Eve in the Garden of Eden before the fall; it was a time of innocence. It was the pure immortality; time and space apply only to the mortals. Therefore, in disagreement with Harby, I state: it wasn't asthma that had killed our uncle, rather his hunger for wealth. Twenty- years ago he had left the peaceful gentle Upper Egypt village to dwell in Cairo; city even angels might get lost in. There, through his vending of sugar cane juice, he had accumulated great wealth that has elevated him to become a very successful real estate developer. It was in that period he became conscious of time and space, sure factors and signs of mortality.

JEALOUS OF THE WIND

12/ 28, 2002

As the aging year agonized in its deathbed, thick clouds appeared constantly in the tormented December sky. The joy of Christmas has slowly begun to escape my heart, as if happiness and peace were but passing winds. That day joy and peace were absent from my heart as I breathed in deep the fear of war. To ease the pain, I took refuge in reading Camus' *"l'homme révolté- the rebel."* In fact, we do not need to read about revolt; it is presented to us on a big platter throughout every moment of our daily lives, courtesy of our materialistic society. Suddenly a series of peeps vibrated throughout the telephone wires.

--"Hello," finally I answered, running out of breath.

"May I speak to Mr. Abdou, please," said a very feminine voice.

"It is he."

"It's my pleasure to have the opportunity to speak to you, Mr. Abdou."

"Regarding what?" I asked dryly, thus refusing to exchange a cheap courtesy with the suspected to be a salesperson.

"Well, Mr. Abdou, as you know we grow older with every ticking off the clock…"

"And so…?" I interrupted the angel of death.

"To get to the point, Sir, we are *a U.S.A. Seniors Home Health Care*; we have a good plan for your latter days when you won't be able to care for yourself. We…"

"Stop, stop your nonsense speech. I shall always be able to take care of myself. Yes, I'm determined to remain the master of my own body, heart and soul till the last breath."

"That's very romantic, Sir, but we must remember reality and romance are quite two different things."

"Well, whenever I lose passion for life, I'll end it on my own terms."

"That's not the best plan, Mr. Abdou."

"Lady, why are you complicating the matter?" I know there is life and death, and the absence of the one claims the presence of the other. Would you object to this logic? If you would, then suffer the consequences of your ignorance and let me enjoy mine."

"Sorry, Sir, talking to you has convinced me that you need immediate mental care." The woman's voice has changed from feminine to monstrous because of a deal that was not going a bit in her direction.

Having vented out my rebellion, I felt very satisfied. After all, if the wind, a simple element of nature, has its own course, why modern man should be forced to change his? Aren't we in God's eyes as precious as the wind?! Or is He ultimately the only wind and we are but dry leaves to be blown in His mysterious course? If so, tyranny is the heritage the gods have left to their heirs and we must make the best investment of it through rebellion.

KEEP ON SCRUBBING

1/17, 2003

Today I heard the good news diffused by two Arab ambassadors in Bahrain. Yes, Saddam was willing to go to exile in an Arabic country, under these conditions:

1. He will not be arrested and tried before the International Court.

2. All sanctions against Iraq must be lifted.

3. American troops must withdraw from all Arabic soils.

How uplifting! Finally the wolf cared about the sheep. Or was it another ruse from the king of deception? The major question remained: would our belligerent King George accept such conditions, especially he had been constantly affirming that the thug of Iraq has Weapons of Mass- Destruction, in spite of the contradicting latest findings of the U.N. inspectors?

How could we stop that ferocious belligerent? One of his admirals had already stood before 7000 marines telling them, as they were being mobilized to the region of the Persian Gulf, "You're going to make history." I wondered though what kind of history they would be making, other than flooding the streets of Baghdad with the blood of the innocents. If this history; then man is still an inhabitant of the jungle.

In an immediate response to this menace, the trapped rat of Baghdad made a lengthy speech defying, what he called: "The great Satan- America- and commanding his people to fiercely fight"the today's Mongols" whenever they will appear at the gates of their capital.

Lord, every day I become more confused than the day prior. What news should I believe and what others should I dismiss? It does not matter any longer; I just want peace. Could I have a piece of peace? Please, Lord, relieve me; I am quite troubled.

--Although I was disappointed at the state of politics throughout the world, I remained greatly disillusioned with America; many of its children were going wild. Yes, I was thinking of Lacy Peterson. The eight months pregnant woman, reported missing a week ago, was found dead and her husband was the prime suspect. Rumor has spread that he has a lover, and was securing the collection of a large sum from his wife's life insurance. Those two known reasons, according to the mass media, have pushed him to commit the heinous crime. Lord, have mercy on our sick souls.

-- Have I forgotten to talk to you about that greedy preacher, who is one among the many?

I paraphrase: You're wasting your money buying shoes, clothes, cars and many other expensive destructible worldly possessions. Wise up; give this money to the man who knows how to invest it for God's Kingdom... I take any money, drug money included, to promote His Kingdom; money is neutral, thus spoke the canny, and all the Philistines applauded, nodding their dizzy heads with a loud Amen.

Angrily I shut the TV off; I could not bear to witness the heavenly robbery. Consoled by the thought that no one can mislead you, Lord, I sat on my old sofa. Closing my eyes, I imagined this conversation:

Lord, you know everything.

Don't dare to ever doubt my omniscience.

Well, then, how much did the suit of that preacher cost?

He paid five thousand dollars and one cent.

Damn me, I should have become a preacher, I murmured.

Don't you wish it, his suit has millions of invisible holes; they're all a reminder of what he had robbed from people in my name.

Energetically I stood up and walked into the kitchen to scrap the pots and pans I had burned last night while preparing our dinner; Marla was then at the Scientology Org. of Tampa for her weekly audition.

Bravo, son! Keep on scrubbing; better to scrap pots and pans than preaching long sermons to rob others in my name.

Thank you, Lord, for the good advice, I abide.

VOYAGES IN NAKEDNESS

1/ 18, 2003

Dear children, how could I tell it without offending your filial love for the mother whose breasts had generously and lovingly sprouted milk into your mouths? Do not ever think for a moment that I hate your native country; it had adopted me, too. I criticize America because I wanted her to be as blameless as humanly possible.

--Two days ago, I heard the news that one of the airline companies had flown 175 nude Passengers from Miami, Florida, to Cancun, Mexico. Naked ones, please gently fasten your belts, quite sensitive is the human skin. Now that you are up in the air, i.e., closer to God; please don't forget to ask forgiveness from the Creator. As a punishment of the original sin we are struggling today to observe the Ten Commandments; could we bear the yoke of adding another? This is not a condemnation rather a lament. I, too, have undertaken many voyages in nakedness.

--Hail to you Lady Jane Shaheen (I hope I got your name right), your confinement in a wheelchair, topped by old age, didn't stop you from joining the crowd to protest an impending war with Iraq. Forgive me, brothers and sisters; demonstration in the streets is not my style; I protest through running my pen. I salute though your devotion to peace; war is man's fascination with savagery. And to all of you warmongers and agitators of the masses, I say: you may win all your fought wars but ultimately you're still big losers; you have failed to tame aggression, a strong instinct of the arrogant. Yes, I'm specifically talking to you, Mr. George W. Bush. You are the biggest whale in the ocean; you make other whales and all the other fishes of the sea dream to be in the circles of your mighty ripples. You have called the Continent of Africa, the "nation of Africa." It's just a reminder of your gross ignorance about the world's geography, to speak not of its diplomatic matters. No offense. After all, you are a former Yale graduate, thanks to your father's monetary contributions.

--On the domestic front you warned to file a suit on behalf of the white students, who demanded a reverse discrimination in admission to the institutions of higher learning. You wanted to champion what you called "justice for all Americans."

35

Mr. President, I must remind you of centuries of slavery- a long period during which the blood of others was for White America cheaper than water. You have said, "We are through with the past." I respectfully disagree; the past may not be yet through with us. Yes, Mr. President, black people need the same amount of time, if not longer, to heal the deep wounds of the most brutal past. Societies can abrogate, create or modify. However, laws and political changes alone can never bring justice to all; change of hearts can.

INTERVIEING THE IRAQI DEPUTY MINISTER

1/ 20, 2003

Today is the beginning of a whole week during which Peter Jennings will be reporting from Baghdad. I personally like the man; he asks rational questions, unlike the many news broadcasters whose main goal is to entertain the populace's low intelligentsia. The infamous broadcaster has interviewed Tarik Aziz, the Iraqi deputy minister of foreign Affairs. Although the man was dressed in a military uniform, he looked more resigned than militant. I paraphrase:

You know that you're on President George W. Bush's list of war criminals, stated Mr. Jennings.

The Deputy Minister: I know I am not a friend of your President.

Have you ever thought of leaving Iraq?

No. This is my country; I shall stay in it until I die.

Some in the Bush Administration believe that Iraqis will meet American soldiers with flowers.

This is the delusion of the American leadership. If Americans come to the mainland, our people will meet them with bullets.

Those questions and answers forced me to reflect upon the President's latest menace: Saddam is running out of time and war is becoming inevitable. Only his exile can prevent a devastating war for the Iraqi people and will guarantee them freedom. What a sad decision. The saddest of all, at least according to the latest poll, 59 percent of Americans supported that decision, and will increase as the drums of war become louder.

The anti-war protesters have accused their government of wanting to control Iraq's oil, rather than seeking freedom for its people. My son Babafemi went this weekend to San Francisco to join the thousands of protesters. We Arab Americans must be thankful as we enjoy dissent, a right we are deprived of in our native lands. In fact, it is a sad joke to call any Arabic country democratic, with the exception of Lebanon that enjoy some freedom. Arab leaders are Kings, who have decided not to crown themselves publicly, just to appear democratic to the outside world.

--Enough of the depressing thoughts on democracy. I must report the national news: Today in Saint Petersburg, Florida, a man has shot to death his roommate, who had refused to evacuate the premise.

-- Somewhere in Oklahoma, a sexual predator entered an apartment, where a woman laid naked. He assaulted her, and the violated did not resist. Rather, she has chosen to pray while enjoying the ungodly act. What a submissive religious animal man is in spite of his belligerent nature.

HOLLOWNESS IN THE STATE OF THE UNION

1/ 28, 2003

Mr. Bush ceremoniously walked on the red carpet in the midst of the applauses of the official corps of his government, the foreign dignitaries and a few privileged citizens, who were invited for political reasons. In the midst of this frenzy excitement, he smiled, shook hands and finally reached the Presidential podium. Behind him stood erect two opulent men in size and honor, the Vice President and the majority Speaker of the House.

"My fellow citizens, I have the distinct honor to present to you the President of the United States of America," shouted the House Leader. This brief presentation earned for the most infamous clown of the circus a deafening applause, prolonged screams and whistling, which might have left some of them with thrilled throats.

The President opened his- one –hour- long speech with the protocol of acknowledging his Vice President; the majority Speaker of the House; the Armed Forces; the foreign dignitaries and finally the invited and the watchers fellow citizens.

After the dust of political protocol settled down, he began the State of the Union. These are its major points-speak not about the truthfulness and sincerity of its content. I paraphrase:

1. Decisive days lie ahead of us. We will work for the prosperity of America and we will meet any challenges that menace the well-being and security of our great nation. Prolonged ovation, or better said ovulation were released.

Mr. President, when you spoke of Saddam and terrorism, this foxy face of yours lit up, and your fake smile became more disgusting. With power and decisiveness, you have communicated to us that war against terrorism must go on, and we are winning it by killing one terrorist at a time.

Yes, by now those devils must have understood how tough America is. Do you hear, O the greatest Satan, Osama Ben Laden?

2. We will not pass to the next President our problems that will burden the future generations, as did the previous administration.

This swift and immediate attack of your predecessor pleased the fellow Republicans, leaving the Democrats in a fighting mood.

Then the President went on to enumerate his midterm's accomplishments and his vision for the remaining period; all for the hope to secure his reelection.

3. We have established the home security department to protect our people.

4. We did and will hold the cooperate executives accountable.

Let me interrupt, Mr. President, what accountability are you talking about? The thugs had already bankrupted the country. Worse, they continue to enjoy drinking from the same golden cup of robbery as you speak. Many senior citizens had already delayed their retirement because of this -all- sweeping robbery. To make it up for their losses, many of them have even started scavenging the aisles of dog food, they wanted to recover a long sustained, but now lost, dream of financial security against the hardships that await their latter years. By the way, Mr. President, I am not one of them, I haven't invested one penny-I had no money to invest, anyway. Rather, like a tiny bird constantly flying in the vast sky of faith, I depend on the mercy of the crumbs of God's abundant generosity.

5. We will create hydrogen powered cars to eliminate the pollution in our cities and to make our nation a lot less dependent on the OPEC (Organization of Petroleum Exporting Countries).

6. We Americans are generous people. To energize this spirit of generosity we have launched "the -Faith-Based Community Initiatives."

Congratulations, Mr. President, you have opened a wide door for a holy robbery. Just a reminder: religious institutions are no less greedy than the secular ones. If they do rob God, they will have no moral scruples to rob His children, just ask Tammy and Jim Baker: how they had acquired the golden doorknobs of their mansion. "Hallelujah, praise the Lord!"

7. We have created "the Freedom- Corps," where good- willed Americans can serve as mentors to the children who hug their parents through bars.

Mr. President, do you have any plan to rehabilitate those prisoners?

8. We are winning the fight against drugs.

How victorious are you in this fight? Just ask your niece, poor little Noelle, daughter of your brother Jeb, Governor of my Florida State.

9. No human life should start or end for the sake of experiment, and let's ban cloning.

Indeed, Mr. President, preserving the life of the unborn is a noble cause and at the core of morality of any civilized society. However, my admiration comes with a warning: in banning cloning, you seem to be overlooking the greed of our capitalistic society. Yes, selling human parts is a very lucrative enterprise. As the human body ages, we need to replace its parts. We do have *Auto Zone*, and we must have access to Man Zone, cry the greedy.

Well, nothing is wrong with cloning. We will classify them as sub-humans. They will be used for cheaper labor.

As the President progressed in his speech, the populace of the world might have discovered his hidden virtue of compassion. Really! In my opinion, The Republicans and compassion make a dangerous mixture that can explode with disastrous consequences. Anyway, let's hear more; it is the day of the great circus, after all.

10. Today the aids virus plagues 30 percent of the population in the continent of Africa. Only 50,000 of them receive treatment. To fight this mortal disease, I pledge ten billion dollars.

Wow! I applaud you more, Mr. President, you have made great progress, not only in the field of compassion; but also in that of your geographical knowledge. You haven't called the Dark Continent "the Nation of Africa," as you did before. As for your promise to fight the killer virus, widely spread amongst its population, I hope you are speaking as a humanitarian and not as politician. Indeed, words of compassion escape your mouth as economically as the tears of the Weeping Madonna of Syracuse.

11. You called for "project Bio-Shield Act" to protect our people against the unpredictable evil of terrorism. You even have been an exemplary leader, receiving this vaccination to silence those skeptical critics of yours, who see this program as a health hazard.

12. You proudly reminded us of the fall of the empire of evil, communism.

In my humble opinion that fall has created a great vacuum of Power Balance. Yes, America is the today's drunken arrogant giant. Indeed, power corrupts individuals as well as nations.

You have elevated this drunkenness to a new height by chanting the mighty will of America. Once again, you have reiterated your determination to insure the security of our people and the hopes of humanity, and we must accept this responsibility. To inflame the sick egos amongst us, you have emphasized your often repeated and dangerous slogan: "The course of our nation doesn't depend on the decisions of others."

May I ask, Mr. President, who those others are? Are you not dismissing the relevance of the United Nations that was born to clean up the mess created by some tyrants of the past? Are you then working to resurrect that past, by disregarding this World's Organization? Hail to you, new tyrant.

With big smile you turned your face 180 degrees toward the Joint Chiefs of Staff of the Armed Forces and said: "you believe in America and America believes in you. The dictator of Iraq is not disarming; he is deceiving the world and he must be disarmed."

And the subordinates nodded with a silent, submissive and prolonged Amen.

You have not failed to remind the oppressed people of Iraq that, although our army is surrounding your country, your real enemy is the one who is ruling it. "We will force him out."

You played well that music to their ears.

Great liberator of the oppressed, have you yet consulted with the history of other tyrants. Ah, the mighty drifting Toxic River of tyranny! Just a reminder, Mr. President: no man can liberate another; a true liberation comes from within. Yes, freedom is a tedious and long process. A rabbi once said: "The first step toward freedom is to miss it. The second is to seek it, and the third is to find it." In other words, Freedom is man's awakening to himself. Mr. President, Aren't you just playing the game of dangerous politics?

I had the chance to scan today's St. Pete Times. I was struck by Mr. Niko D. Kristof's article titled: *Arrogance comes home to roost.*

In this article, the writer asked the question: which country poses the greatest danger to world peace, 2003? With 318,000 votes cast, so far, the responses were: North Korea 7 percent, Iraq 8 percent, and the United States 84 percent.

The author concluded his article recalling John Le Carr's words: "America has entered one of its periods of historic madness."

LIVING WITH MICHEAL

2/8, 2003

Tonight I watched the televised program entitled: "*living with Michael Jackson*". It was a lengthy interview by the English journalist, Martin Bashir with the Pop Star. I paraphrase:

Martin: Why you call your residence the Nederland?

Michael: Because I want to live forever.

Martin: But, Michael, you're mortal, just like any other human being.

Michael: No. I'm Peter Pan, the child who never grows up...that's why I like to climb trees; it's the most fulfilling hobby of mine.

Martin: Even more fulfilling than your musical talent?

Michael: Yes, climbing a tree is more appealing to me than my music.

I: Well said, Mike, indeed, climbing trees is the universal nostalgia of humans; we all like to follow the steps of our ancestors, the apes.

Martin: Besides climbing trees, what other hobbies do you have?

Michael: I like balloon fights.

Martin: What about singing?

Michael: Singing is a gift.

Martin: Who helped you to discover this gift?

Michael: My father, but he was a cruel man, though. He used his belt to bring forth this God- given gift within me.

Martin: Did he really hit you?

Michael: Very badly. He was a heartless trainer. He used to tell me: 'Don't call me daddy, call me Mr. Jackson.'

Martin: What do you like about Las Vegas?

Michael: The entertainment and shopping.

Martin: Did you have many girlfriends in Las Vegas?

Michael: Only one, she used to call me and tell me how badly she wanted me.

Martin: Did you like those erotica?

Michael: No. I was scared.

Martin: Why scared?

Michael: I wasn't ready for it, sex frightens me.

I: Mike, Mike, you just didn't want to become a man, you wanted (and still do) to remain a Peter Pan, the eternal child. How unrealistic.

Martin: How much are you worth now?

Michael: A billion.

Martin: Is your face natural, Michael? If not, how much in it is natural?

Michael: 100 percent.

Martin: Not even one surgical operation?

Michael: Not even one surgical operation, except the one in my nose.

Martin: Let's talk about your children.

Michael: I love them very much.

Martin: Why then are you depriving them from knowing their mothers; they need the motherly love?

Michael: I give them all the love… Besides, there are a lot of women who attend to their needs.

Martin: Do you home schooling them?

Michael: Yes, I do.

Martin: Why is that?

Michael: Because the outside world is very dangerous; I want to protect my children. I want to be a better father to them than my father had been to me.

Martin: But the public might not share your claim after the incident in Berlin.

Michael: so the world wants to accuse me of endangering the life of my baby? Having dangled him out of the window was just a gesture of love for my fans.

I: Mike, Mike, It was a desperate gesture of love for yourself. You knew very well that you were not connecting with the audience in general, and especially the young, so you have decided to use this angel in the hope to revive, at least momentarily, your fading glory. You're guilty of endangering the life of your child in exchange of the vain brief attention of the public-assuming you are still worth one billion.

Martin: Let's talk about your relationship with children in general. You know you had been accused of child molestation, ten years ago. Still you continue to bring children to your Neverland Ranch. Not only that, they also sleep in your bed. This kind of behavior is unacceptable to the public.

Michael: I don't sleep with them; I leave my bed for my guests. I sleep on the floor in the same room though.

Martin: Nothing happens sexually?

Michael: Nothing…I love children, I see God in their faces.

I: After hearing you, Mike, one would think that Saint Francis of Assisi has resurrected. Yes, the saint saw God even in the faces of birds, donkeys, monkeys and other animals. Now you want us to believe that you are the modern saint Francis, don't you? Mike, you need the children's company because you are still a child living within a 44 year old body. May God bless you, Peter Pan…but please do realize that we live under the scourge of legality, and prudence must prevail over any other virtue… Or you would lose a big chunk of your imaginary billion dollars to the vultures of money hungry, and too many of them are out there. Well, Mike, just remember: hell houses the unwise virgins.

AS YOU OPEN THIS DOOR….

2/ 14, 2003

It is Valentine, a day of resuscitating the chocked relationships; may God have mercy on the mortals, all are crying for a sign of love.

I took Marla and little Javier for a treat in the Oriental Supper Buffet, our favorite Chinese restaurant. Afterwards, we decided to visit the Moccasin Lake Nature Park. We drove the three miles distance under a clouded sky. It was my first visit, although I have been living in its vicinity for the last eighteen years. I had always presumed it was a natural habitat for snakes, and I don't like snakes, or any word that reminds me of, such as sneaky. To my surprise, I discovered that it was a center for environmental education. We climbed the thirty feet tower to observe the aquatic life. We heard snouts and saw sneaky eyes; an alligator was gliding silently across the tiny lake. Having surveyed the small park and its vicinity, we descended to visit the wounded birds that were there for rehabilitation. That eagle impressed me the most. Carefully examining it, I noticed heavy sadness in its eyes. That invited me to investigate its life's story. It was a sad one. They've brought it into the center, a year ago, after had been shot down while flying low. From reading the sign, I learned that its mate had passed away on the 12th of December. In total sympathy I bowed before the lonely survivor, and recited a brief prayer for the deceased. We then went to a wooden building. At its entrance hang a sign that read: As you open this door you will see the most ferocious animal." We opened the door and instantly saw our own faces in a mirror. We laughed and I thought: How true! We then proceeded to the antechamber where we saw skeletons of several killed animals and birds. When a man kills an animal or a bird, we call him a skillful hunter. When an animal kills a man, we call it ferocious. What a twisted logic! Man's logic oppresses the logic of all other creatures, small and big. My sympathy goes to you, Mr. Skillful hunter; you are shooting yourself in the heart, thanks to your lack of sense of justice.

THIS IS NOT A JOKE

2/ 26, 2003

Dan Rather sat sternly this late morning with Hussein, the master manipulator of the mass media. I paraphrase:

Dan: Mr. President, are you willing to go to exile, the latest demand of George Bush?

Hussein: Iraq is my country. There I was born and there I will die.

Dan: Aren't you afraid to be captured?

Hussein: We're all in God's hands; nothing is going to change God's will.

Dan: Do you intend to destroy al Somoud missiles to comply with the UN?

Hussein: We have committed ourselves to respect all the U.N. Security Council Resolutions and we fully reject the allegation that we have violated any of them.

Dan: The United States believes that you have Weapons of Mass- Destruction, are you willing to get rid of them to save your country from imminent destruction?

Hussein: Our position is clear, we don't sacrifice our dignity. Twelve years ago, they thought to push Iraq to the prehistoric ages. Here we are still a prosperous modern nation. We hope to avoid war; but if it comes; we will defend ourselves. Our country will not be finished; it has a history of 4000 years of survival.

Dan: America is concerned about anyone who has connection with al- Qaeda. Are you connected with this organization, in one way or another?

Hussein: We have no connection whatsoever with Osama Ben Laden; we believe in humanity.

I: What is humanity to you, Mr. Hussein? Could it be equated with humans? If so, what have you done with a million and a half of your own people? Have you not fried them, just to make the story short? May God fry you in hell!

Dan: Aren't you annoyed to see Ben Laden the champion of the man in the streets of the Arabic world, and no longer yourself?

Hussein: Jealousy is for women…I must leave you now, Mr. Rather, to fulfill my religious duty. The master manipulator left to recite the noon prayer; certainly he wanted to convince the Islamic world that he was a model Muslim. Fifteen-minutes later, he reappeared looking pious. Indeed, you are, Mr. Hussein, if one could overlook the bombs you had lavishly rained on your own people. Besides, it was just twelve years ago when you had invaded your neighboring Kuwait. There you have killed tens of thousands of your Muslim brothers and sisters. How pious of a Muslim are you, unless piety for you equals carnage?

Dan: What is the most important message you want to communicate to the American people?

Hussein: The Iraqi people are not enemies of the American people. I am ready to conduct a satellite debate with Mr. Bush in front of the whole world. The world will then decide who is right and who is wrong. Why should we hide from the truth?

Dan: This is not a joke?

Hussein: I call for this debate because war is not a joke.

Dan: Would you be prepared to come to the United Nations headquarters in New York?

Hussein: the debate can be conducted through satellites. We then will have the opportunity to explain our position to the whole world.

Dan: Mr. Bush sees this proposal as another ruse added to Saddam's list of deceptions.

Interpreter: "Bush…"

Hussein: "Ya walad- boy- Mr. Bush; we must have respect for authority."

I: please stop the dirty game calling for respect for authority. Just that same day the Baath newspaper, controlled by your son Oudeh, has called Mr. Bush "the son of a snake." Don't worry; the world understands your hate for the Bush family. Twelve years ago, his father had kicked your... out of Kuwait.

Dan: You seem to understand English, Mr. President, say something in English.

Hussein: I don't speak it but I understand it; our language is Arabic.

Dan: In case of invasion, would you set your oil fields afire?

Hussein: Iraq will not destroy its oil fields; it will protect them.

I: Just let's hope that your explosives, already wired around them, will not go off as you speak. You are a fox who rather sees the tree of the unreachable grapes turn into ashes.

Dan: Some elements in our government believe if Americans invade Iraq, they will be greeted with flowers.

Hussein: All Americans are welcomed as friends but not as invaders...just think of the warm welcome you're receiving.

Dan: In 1991 you had faced the father, now you're facing the son, who is equipped with a greater military force; shouldn't this make you reconsider your decision not to leave your country?

Hussein: It's we who decide and not the American Administration. We will not surrender to the law of the jungle.

I: only the law of the jungle dominates the world. It is a fact, and all the other laws are but mere façades. You are a great patron of this law. Tyrant, don't worry, soon the sun of God's justice will shine and then the solidity of your elusive power will melt.

THIS IS AN ULTIMATUM

3/ 17, 2003

It is the day of the ultimatum. How idiotic of some humans to menace others; overlooking the fact that only God can decide the fate of man. Well, the arrogant George W. Bush has given himself this power. The twenties century was a blessed era; we had only one supper aggressive Hitler in its first third. In the nascent twenty- first century we are a more cursed generation, we have already two internationally active Hitlers. Yes, Saddam and Bush had already decided to stain the face of that infant with the blood of the multitude. Ah, the awakening of the evil giant that exists within tyrants. It easily snaps out of its slumber; it is the display of the untamed nature of the beast.

45

My fellow citizens, the truce of 1991 has required that Saddam dismantle his Weapons of Mass- Destruction. He has not acted in good faith. Over the years the regime of this tyrant has been mocking the U. N. Council resolutions. Yet, some governments (alluding to: France, Russia, and China) have decided not to enforce the demands of the free world, thus discoursed our President.

Are you for real, Mr. President? How arrogant of you to condense the whole world into your inflated personality. You are not a lone wolf, you have already three puppets: The long- gone- British Empire, Australia, the land of leaping kangaroos, and the Kingdom of Spain, land of wading flamingoes. It is the sick conviction of those nations' leaders that to become big, one must walk in the shadow of the giant. It is a belief history yet to confirm. I have observed many rats walking along lions in the twilights, yet the magnified shadows of those little rodents still depicted no others than the originals.

Mr. President, for the last four and a half months, you have recited a litany of accusations against your enemy. Nobody believed you, except those insanes like yourself. This is not an accusation, rather an observation.

I have mistakenly turned on an evangelical radio station. The host asked: Do you believe that America is a blessed nation to have a born again Christian President? All the callers agreed that America is very blessed to have you Mr. President; and that the impending war will be another blessing in disguise for America- apparently they were all from the far- religious right.

Wow! Holy men what did you do with Jesus, the prince of peace? Forgive me; peace is only one of your jargon vocabularies during the nativity. Now that we are in the season of crucifixion, let's hang Him on the cross of your false propaganda. Why not? Throughout history the so- called godly people, like yourselves, have killed God and blamed it on the Nietzsches of this world, like myself and my fellowmen who depict your insanity. So you had decided to go to war against the will of the majority of the world?! Yes, righteous ones, diplomacy is dead; vive la guerre!

"Let those who rush to war be responsible before God, their conscious and history,' thus spoke the aging lion, the advocator of peace, Pope Jean Paul 11.

Mr. President, you have given forty- eight hours for Saddam and his two sons to leave their country. I have no quarrel with the ultimatum, except it is incomplete. For its completeness; how about an exchange: you will be exiled in Iraq, and the tyrant and his sons will be offered home in America. Here, they will learn about the so- called American democracy and there, in Iraq, you will learn at firsthand about the evil of tyranny. At the end, both will be truly liberated; you are equally slaves of the evil instinct of tyranny. No, no, there is yet a better way to solve this most complex conflict. Mr. President: how about a duel between you and Saddam in the stormy desert of Kuwait? The winner will rule the two countries. Although I find this solution quite original, I credit it to my alcoholic friend Gary. Honesty obliges the honorable and the dishonorable despises honesty.

GOD, I AM MAD AT YOU

3/ 20, 2003

Good God, could I have a word or two with you in private. Yes, I am mad at you for a thousand- and- one reasons. I know you are busy; you have 6.3 billion whiners like me to listen to.

Well, today I woke up a bit late, exactly at 8:20 a.m. Turning the TV on I was shocked to hear these three words: "War with Iraq." After a brief reaction of sadness, I resigned myself to the- long -expected tragedy. Lord, I began to invoke your name in fervor. I asked for your mercy on behalf of the helpless people of Iraq. Scarcely had I finished my invocation, I realized that I did not have to remind you that they are your children, and I had no business telling you how you should care for them. Suddenly I have found myself angry at you again. I even held you directly responsible for what had happened to me personally this morning. Why cannot you, or the telephone company, where I have an unlisted number, protect me from the marketing firms? My phone had already rung four times in the first thirty minutes since I woke up. Two calls were from the Scientologists, a third from Capital One and the fourth was from Window Protection Inc. would you please protect me from the evil of this world? I do not need the Scientologists to cross the bridges of life; nor do I hunger for the material comfort offered by any of the two other marketing companies. All what I need is peace. Have mercy on me, I am, too, at war with myself. I am not another Saddam though. I have no Weapons of Mass Destruction, nor have I ever harmed any of your children, at least intentionally. I'm just a Bedouin, who is happy to pitch his tent in the hot desert and his only dream is to dig deep enough four holes so the wind wouldn't blow it away; I need to shelter my harem and my children. Oh well, I, too, might be selfish and self-centered, complaining so bitterly about those unsolicited phone calls. After all, the sound of the phone ringing cannot be compared to the sound of bombs falling today on Baghdad. I thought of its children and elders. While our children here in America are giggling with laughter at homes, schools and in amusement parks, Iraqi children are killed in Baghdad. While our elders are sitting in restaurants, sipping on their hot coffee and eating scrambled eggs with the choice of bacon strips or finger sausages, the bones of their peers in Iraq are cracking in a blaze of fire. I blamed it on Saddam and Bush. Let me ask those tyrants the simple question: Why have you chosen the devastating path of war? Beware; eventually your doomsday soon will come.

Saddam, how foolish can you be calling on your people to fight the invaders- certainly not for their sake but for yours. For years you have abused them, and today is your payday. Tyranny you have cultivated, and abandonment you are harvesting today. Even your defecting former mistress Parsoula is rejoicing for your immanent end.

"Dude, where's My Country?" This is not my question; I am just using the title of Michael Moore, Bush's avid critic. Yes, Mr. President, where is that beautiful face of our country? It has been smeared with shame thanks to your foreign policies plagued with arrogance and ignorance. We liberals will continue to criticize you for your suicidal adventure in Iraq, even at the price of being called un- Americans. We are not traitors; we are just dissidents. Your administration continues to sing we needed the invasion to fight terrorism. We differ by saying: the true terror is within the White House. After all, who have the most powerful Weapons of Mass- Destruction? Mr. President, we know of your love for the rich. Yes, you want to draw for them all the oil of the Mesopotamia, if not the whole Middle East. How generous of you, although at the cost of the blood of our children who continue to die daily in foreign lands.

 Here at home, your economical, or rather comical policies, have added three more million citizens to the rank of poverty in the first two years of your reign. If, by misfortune, you would be reelected; then this great country of ours will be eligible for financial aid from Afghanistan; Iraq; Pakistan; and possibly from Bangladesh. And what do you say, Mr. President, about the more than fifty million uninsured? Sir, do not worry, it's only one sixth of the country's population. It is even useless to mention the uncounted such as my wife, her son, I and the hundreds of thousands like us; we are from the underground. If diseased, we will run to one of the Indian Reservations to solicit old remedies from their medicine sages. In case they are unable to cure our diseases, we will not be chagrined; we are mortal and it doesn't matter how all must come to an end. Nor should you worry about our moral scandals; we are a society without moral scruples, anyway. But if you would continue being so arrogant, just save us the eagle, symbol of our lost freedom.

Enough talking to and about you, rather let me make a statement about war and peace: War is the sword the savages use to settle their disputes, and Peace is the creative art of the civilized. Humanity has two choices: to subjugate itself to the law of the jungle or to elevate itself to the thrones of the gods. The choice(s) we make decide who we are and will become. Now, good luck to all, especially to the tyrants of the world. Lord, help us to raise the flag of permanent freedom on the Iraqi soil, and not just a showdown of force.

ARMS DON'T DELIVER A LASTING VICTORY

3/ 24, 2003

It is the 34th birthday of my oldest daughter Tameri. Darling, today I thought a lot about you, your mother, myself and my own mother and father; birth is the incarnation of love that matures between two lovers. How I wished today telling your mother these same words I had told her, thirty- four years ago: "Congratulations, honey, now we're a complete family."

- As war on Iraq continues with its ravaging effects, I took a moment to think of the millions of the inflicted families, here in the USA and Iraq. I also thought of the madness of the world's tyrants. They are the kind of people who have a narrow vision of history. History for them is now and here; it is a static reality. The truth is: history is a dynamic reality that speaks only to the visionaries. A dictator is a blind force, whose impact on the march of humanity is more disastrous than that of an atomic bomb. However, at the final account, all tyrants die without memory, and history will live forever in the memory of the wise and humble. Mistakenly we identify history with heroes and villains. The truth is: history is the making of all. For that reason I bow before humanity and disdain the arrogance of individuals and nations. As I was watching the today's news of war, I saw American soldiers commanding, at gunpoint, the surrendering Iraqi soldiers to lay flat, to stand up and to bend forwards and backwards. They wanted to make sure that their enemies were totally disarmed, so they justified their commands. How could man dare, even at the risk of his own life, to humiliate so badly his fellowmen? Why can't he be satisfied to see the enemy's hands up, an unquestionable sign of surrender? Ah the drunkenness of the victor! "Vanity, all is vanity under the sun."

There is no true victory born out of arms; the authentic victory is when man finds a place in his heart for the suffering of his fellowman. What we need is not a humiliated bow from the other, rather a sincere dialogue that will insure the meeting of minds and hearts through compromises although our differences might remain. Like microbes, differences can make us stronger or cause our death.

WOW! TWO FULL HANDS: A WIFE AND A BIBLE

3/ 30, 2003

Mr. Bush entered the church holding a fat Holy Bible in one hand and with the other he took a jealous grip of his wife's. The pastor of the Methodist church opened his prayer, thanking God for a sure victory against the enemy.

49

Certainly, Mr. President, soon the military victory will be yours; your troops had already killed tens of thousands of the innocent Iraqis; many among them were children, elders and women. I call that a lamented defeat.

I turned another channel on. It was another church, another pastor and another audience. That church was in an isolated town, somewhere in Oklahoma. In this town there is a factory that produces more bombs than any other chemical factory in the world. In fact, it had produced the bombs that have fallen on Germany in World War II; Grenada; Somalia; Afghanistan and now on Iraq. And they will create the same havoc on any other countries that will dare to challenge America, militarily or even politically.

The Baptist pastor of the Latter Saints Church, who worked in that factory, began his service with these mortal words: We must be proud of our town; it produces all the bombs we're dropping today in Iraq. He has based his sermon on Solomon's wisdom: "there is a time for peace and there is a time for war…"

Ignorant, religion is one thing and its interpretation is another. The so- called guardians of their religions are greedy merchants, they price God's message according to the law of supply and demand. Pastor, your life could be summarized in these words: fire the bombs and pass the plates. How holy could you be! Well, allow me to ask you: wouldn't you be better off, spiritually speaking, to work in a chocolate or toys factory? Please, do not give me the evasive answer: I'm doing what the Lord has asked me to do. The truth is: you are under the command of the tyrant of all tyrants, the mighty dollar. How pretentious! The Lord is always speaking to you, O merchants of religion. Is it not your easy way to prey on people and kill God? Well, I do not feel sorry for God; He is mighty able to defend Himself. However, a deep sorrow weighs heavily on my heart for the meek and weak, your followers.

-- I also heard the story of the shooting in a church in Michigan. One might wonder: where and who would be the next victim? Certainly not God, although we all have aimed at His heart; we have simply brought damnation upon ourselves.

ANGER WILL FILL UP THEIR HEARTS

3/31, 2003

At eight p.m., I watched Peter Jennings reporting about the Allies' progress in the war against Iraq. They had already encircled Saddam's elite guards. Still they would have to fight against the will- be- scattered pockets of the Iraqi army and certainly the proud national elements of insurgents. O conquerors, may you have pity on the holy cities of Karbala and Najaf. Mr. President, today your army has reduced into ashes a truck loaded with women and children. You aren't the only ravaging force in the land of Babylonia. Also your counter barbarians, Saddam's army, are killing the Iraqi people by using them as human shields.

--I heard Tarik Aziz praising the fedayeen coming from all over the Islamic world to fight the invading forces, a reminder of the Crusaders. It is man's madness to repeat the mistakes of a tragic past. What a definitive proof to call him the dumbest animal ever existed!

A few doubt that the power of arms is the ultimate guarantor of victory; I am one of those. In my humble opinion, this administration is shortsighted and has superficial knowledge of history; topped with a dim understanding of the human nature. Yes, as the American Forces and their allies ravage Iraq, they are building giant factories of hate throughout the Arabic World. Anger will fill the hearts of Arabs, and this is more devastating than the power of bombs. An advice to you, Mr. President and to all your political advisors: Do not count heavily on the distribution of your packed food and distilled water to erase the anger of the conquered. What goes into the stomach is disposable; everlasting is what enters the heart. In simple words: Do not kill the parents and expect the friendship of their children through packaged meals and medicines; children are the extension of their parents and that is the natural law. We brag too much for bestowing generosity upon strangers. However, most of the third world countries believe that we are unfair in our wheeling and dealing: we demand an Arabian horse for a frozen chicken.

Mr. President, your administration has cunningly sold us the idea that war is the only means to bring freedom to the oppressed people of Iraq. You and your aides have failed to comprehend, or have intentionally overlooked, that freedom is God's gift given directly to man without the intersession of another. It is God's voice echoing not against the mountain of man's vain ambitions, rather through the fibers of his soul, heart and flesh. The Holy Scriptures presented God talking to Moses through the bushes. Could it be that those bushes were the multi-layers of Moses' soul?! As God was speaking to Moses, Moses, too, was speaking to God, and both were gradually introducing themselves to each other through genuine willingness to communicate. Mr. President, Perilous is the lack of genuine communication with the enemy. God spoke to Moses without losing His divinity. The humble is strong and weak is the arrogant.

PORTRAITS OF WAR

4/ 4, 2003

At three a.m. I was awakened by the Phantoms of yesterday's evening breaking news headline: *Portraits of War*-presented by Peter Jennings. There were many scenes of great devastations. A close look at Baghdad gives one a clear picture about that state of doom. One of those portraits was that of a mother beating her chest while screaming of dolor, her son was severely wounded. A second portrait was that of a teenager digging a ditch to bury his grandfather, who was killed as he was running to shield him from flying bullets. The third portrait presented an American soldier rushing toward a hill. He did not even bother to give a second look at the Iraqi soldier whom he had just shot; the soldier's eyes were concentrating on the next kill. Wow! Certainly war has the power to bring out the worst in man.

-- In Palestine -a farms town in West Virginia- the entire population of 900 people have gathered in a small church to give thanks to God for the rescue of Private Jessica Lynch, a nineteen year old soldier. A year ago, she was drafted; dreaming of visiting exotic lands, and building a bright future for herself.

"Hallelujah! Hallelujah! For sure God is still in the business of miracles," thus the Pastor of the Baptist church opened his service of thanksgiving. And I asked myself:

Are there two Gods: the God of the West and that of the East? Well, whatever masks we may choose to put on His holy face, He is certainly the same God, and it is up to us to discover Him under the many disguises. I don't question God's love for all. What I do question is man's humanity toward man. Thomas Hobbes couldn't be more right when he wrote: "homo homini lupus-one man is a wolf for the other (man)."

If this is the ultimate explanation, how could a good God have manufactured such a rotten product? This kind of absurdity had forced Nietzsche to throw stones to dethrone God. Dear Lord, stones I do not dare to throw at you, rather I choose to come out of my dark cave; I dream to have a personal encounter with you. Now that I see you in the light, do hold my hand and lead me to the peak of your holy mountain. There speak to me in its holy silence; no longer can I hear your voice in the dark caves, nor in the agitated valleys; quite deafening are the roars of the wild and the sounds of wars.

THE CULMINATION OF THE HUMAN TRAGEDIES

4/ 5, 2003

Today I have seen the culmination of the human tragedies. The dramatic scene presented the Iraqi teens soldiers. There were 8000 of them waiting to fight the invading enemy. "Saddam's Ashbal-cub lions" had been drafted from poor families for the reward of a bigger food ration. Death was a sure fate for parents who would have refused the deal. First I didn't believe what I saw. Then the reporter went on to say, "75 percent of fighting nations use children as soldiers." He even became more specific, indicating that 10 percent of their fighting forces are children. I began to doubt the merit of the Darwinian theory of evolution. Yes, ape should have been the final by-product of the biological process. I do not know of any animal that sacrifices its cubs to save its own skin. Man is the only animal that does commit this act of supreme brutality, and yet he dares to call it a war tactic. I call it a work of sick intelligence and wicked heart. Lord, give me the ferocity of a lion when I meet my matured enemy; but elevate me to the docility of a lamb when I encounter his child in the battlefield. Often we are exceptionally sensitive to the religious sites of the enemy and that is admirable. But why can't we be as sensitive to his living sanctuaries, his children? Lord, help us to extend this sensitivity to the fighting children of our enemy; they are the holiest sanctuaries of humanity. We all know, Lord, they have been brain- washed; forcefully elevated to a false adulthood. Lord, help us to preserve their innocence, your most precious gift to man-kind. Lord, their angelic wings become broken as soon as we put guns into their hands. Please, Lord, protect the innocence of the children. It is in their innocence that we dream to purify ourselves from the stains of war. If we kill the children, what dreams left for us when war ends?! Vain and temporal are the dreams of war; the most exalting dream is when we're held into the arms of our spouses while listening to the enchanting boiling of the family's teapot and the joyous giggles of our children.

HUMILIATED

4/ 6, 2003

Lord, the portraits of war are constantly occupying my mind. How could I forget the scene of the Allied Forces breaking the door of that Iraqi family? All its members came out, hands folded over heads. The father came first and then the mother, followed by their three teenagers. Scarves covering their heads; they looked very frightened. Tears were running over their paled cheeks; they thought that the end of their lives was inevitable. The American soldiers interrogated the father. The rest of the family was ordered to kneel down on the concrete, always hands up. Lord, may this sight be a fervent prayer for the safety of the father and peace in Iraq. Thank God, the father's safe return made the family's member felt a certain security, although they knew quite well that he can't protect them.

I also saw the American tanks demolishing the cedar doors of two of Saddam's palaces in Baghdad. As the soldiers got in, they knocked down the tyrant's photos hanging on the marble walls.

"I have the key, I own this palace," shouted one soldier. A few soldiers of the third battalion have decided to loot the palace, pulling a doorknob, a toilet seat, picking a vase, a sword and an ashtray, all made of gold. Ah, the spoils of war!

I was more than relieved to see the Allied Forces knocking Saddam's statue that stood like a lion in front of

53

the palace main iron -gate; tyrants must not keep reminding us of their tyranny days and nights. Death to them and may freedom come to their peoples! Yes, let the bells of freedom toll today in Baghdad, tomorrow in Tunisia, Cairo, Tehran, Damascus, Sana'a, Tripoli; Amman and in Riyadh. Let the Middle East become a large monument to freedom. I dream of this day for my race, regardless of their creeds. Still I raise my opposition to the idea of war. America is powerful enough; it has a thousand and one different ways to get rid of Saddam. Therefore, I seriously question the motive of the Bush Administration taken the destructive path. Now that we are at war, Lord, help us to finish it, causing the least trauma on the most vulnerable.

The question to be asked: once that Saddam's regime has come to an end, would we still be able to raise the statue of Liberty in a country that for almost three decades had seen no statue other than that of the tyrant? What a silly question, let freedom march; it has the capacity to navigate through the dark and serpentine paths. A true liberty will never lose sight of itself.

THE WEST AND MORAL RESPONSIBILITIES

4/7, 2003

--**Today** George W. Bush went to Ireland to meet his British counterpart Tony Blair in a castle located somewhere in the Irish countryside. They were to draw the face of the post- Saddam's Iraq. In fact, the President had already drawn the portrait; he just wanted Mr. Blair to put his signature as a seal of approval for a- save- face policy. Lord, help them to understand that man's hunger for personal, or even national, gains must not hinder other man's survival.

 --Marla received a letter from the desk of a certain Lauri Webster. It read:

Dear Scientologist,

As a veteran scientologist, I know that you have a very great responsibility on the urgent need to handle rapidly this planet before any further decline occurs.

Leonard. Ronald Hubbard stated: "Some time ago, I realized the resolution of this scene would require a powerful tech, tailored to check this downward spiral at each step of the way and get it reverting upwards. I set about to study and research and develop processes that could accomplish this. The result of that work is super power. Super power is the answer to a sick, a dying and dead society. With it we literally revive the dead. With it we have the means to put Scientologists into a new realm of ability enabling them to create a new world."

It is vital that we work hard as a team to release "Super Power" as it is this planet's solution. The active and participating individuals like you have a greater understanding on what it means to clear the planet. Therefore, I am asking you for your help now.

With a contribution of $100, $250 or more, you will be giving man-kind a gift of freedom like no other.

Thank you for what you do to expand "Scientology" and thank you in advance for what you will do to help clear the planet with Super Power.

Much Love,

Lauri Webster, Executive Officer.

A Super Power Expansion Project!

Here you have it, Lord; every institution in the Western World is pretentiously seeking the clearing of this planet. The question to all is: Who has gotten us in this mess in the first place? Certainly it wasn't the work of the apes in Africa or the donkeys of the Middle East and South America. O Westerners, you are constantly seeking to dominate others. You take no moral responsibility in speeding up the destruction of this planet. Lord, have mercy on its misguided inhabitants. Scientology is declaring to have the power of freeing all nations. George W. Bush and his aides are more modest; they just wanted to bring freedom to the tiny country of Iraq and, perhaps, the entire region of the Middle East.

 A senior Scientology official, during his long speech, has made this remark: "How wasteful Washington is. If Scientology is given 1percent of the eighty billion dollars thought to be spent to bring freedom to Iraq, we will clear the whole planet." His audience broke into frenzy applause. Ah, the greed of the Western World! If Jesus would return to earth, He will lose His garment to the highest bidder. The Western man is so devoted to the Kingdom of money to the point he is ready to sacrifice his own soul. This is not exaggeration or insult, just watch the so- called evangelical healers, how sickening is their hunger for money. Every one of those sorcerers delivers in one minute more miracles, curing the sick and giving sight to the blind, than Jesus had performed in His thirty-three years on earth. Poor Jesus, He wasn't blessed enough to have had the today's fast technique. Just to open the eyes of a blind, He had to kneel down for hours, begging, in sweat, for his Father's assistance. He had sweated blood to raise Lazar from the dead.

Having learned so much from the fast food industry, those modern healers, with heads high, knock down their victims and instantly s/he is cured. The well- paid sick subject shakes his/her body for a moment, after being raised by the muscled employees of the circus, to scream: "I'm cured! I am cured!"

 "Alleluia! Alleluia, praise the Lord!" shout the philistines.

Those circus' owners and their employees are on constant tours all around the world. What a way to bleed the resources of earth in the name of Jeeesuss. Why am I so incredulous? Why can I not give them the benefit of the doubt? Yes, Lord, one day I will carry a rock into one of those circuses. I then will ask its master sorcerer to transform this rock into bread; I need to satisfy my hunger for a solid faith. If he succeeds, then I will shout: Halleluiah, Halleluiah, it's a miracle. After all, what a miracle is other than changing the substance of things?

Lord, we need your genuine miracle to transfer those deceivers into authentic stewards of your kingdom; or else send your consuming fire.

BLOOD DRIPPING FROM THE ANGEL'S LIMBS

4/ 9, 2003

The portraits of war, ah the portraits of war! They haunt me all the time. In my sleep, they are more vivid than in my awakening. Today, Peter Jennings presented these portraits:

First, a magnified portrait of Saddam was in flames. For that I rejoiced and for a moment, I even saw a positive side of the war. Then, I saw the blood of the innocents spilled vehemently on a street in Baghdad. It dripped from a truck; an American soldier had killed the oldest of the three brothers, who were fleeing the city in flames. While one soldier attended the second, who was severely injured, another was consoling the youngest, whose life has been miraculously left unharmed.

"Why? Why?" moaned the injured, in great pain. The wounded legs were closing on his stomach as if he wanted to go back to the safety of the maternal womb.

-- Even the motherly womb is not a safe place in time of war. Another portrait presented a mother shot in the stomach. The husband, a young man in his early thirties, was crying inconsolably; he might have been suffering the guilt of having had caused the death of his wife and their -soon- to- be born infant. They were on their way to a secure hospital in the Iraqi countryside, where she could have delivered the pre- massacred Messiah.

--On the American side, war presented a different portrait. A tearful soldier smelled the perfumed handwritten letter his wife had sent; so much they must had been missing each other. Lord, have mercy on the bleeding legs and the scented letters; they all testify to the human sufferings. As for the dead, may they rest in your everlasting peace!

LONG LIVE THE PEOPLE

4/ 10, 2003

This morning I shaved my beard. For the last three weeks it has been growing like a wild bush, the war had taken its toll on me. However, I was consoled to watch the toppling of Saddam's statue erected in the center of Baghdad. Yes, any decent human being must rejoice for the falling symbol of a dictator. As the American soldiers were bringing it down, it hung for a few moments on the pedestal; it was the rattle of the snake's spirit. The statue of the false god came down in the midst of the shouting of a jubilating crowd. Stones and shoes have flown into the face of that thug.

"À bas le roi, vive le people-Down the king, long live the people," was the final cry of a nation that had been oppressed for almost three decades (so had been the ultimate cry of the oppressed throughout history). Children, women and men, young and old, were dancing; the light of freedom has finally shone on their nation. Several youngsters were dragging the head of Saddam's statue while a few others sat on it.

"Please touch me and tell me that Saddam is gone," shouted middle- aged Iraqi as he wrapped his arms around a young American soldier. Man has always sought assurance of another whom he considered more powerful than himself. However, in parts of the liberated city, the scattered groups of the dictator's soldiers were fighting in his name; the tyrant's ghost was still haunting them. They feared the dictator as small children fear strangers, genies and ghosts. Those cowards are well aware of everyone else's power, except of their own, and that is the great obstacle for them to have an authentic life.

While the Iraqis were celebrating their ambiguous freedom, the conquerors began falling in acute worry. Now that the ghost has been cast out of the prairie, whose cows will graze on its rich pasture?

Well, for every conflict there are two camps of defenders: those who claim to be on the right side of law, and those who claim not to be wrong, meaning: they, too, are on the right side of the law. The Bush-Blair's camp will say to the rest of the Allies: we've run the frightening evil ghost out the opulent pasture. To evict it, once and forever, we will catch it and slaughter it. Once the opulent prairie is secured in our hands, our cows will have the exclusive right to graze on it. However, we will be willing to give you the pleasure of watching them getting fat. We might even give you a taste of those fat cows, once slaughtered.

We have helped you in casting out the evil spirit that haunted the prairie for so long. Like you, we have shed the precious blood of our sons and daughters. Like you, we have asked our holy men to help casting that evil ghost by their ardent prayers. Therefore, our cows, too, are entitled to graze on the green prairie, thus will plead the opposing camp. Personally, I am afraid that the spirit of the chased evil ghost will continue to haunt the prairie, and thus will make it unattractive to all the cows that dreamt grazing in it. True, the Western technology is so powerful that it can even slaughter the ghost. However, I predict the slaughtered is so evilly powerful that it will cause the slaughtering of some of its slaughterers before disappearing forever from the memory of the prairie. Only time will reveal to us the perils of the dreamed spoils of war.

Since I have formed a camp of defense of my own, I would like to wrap my plea: poisoning are the stolen fields and cursed is the freedom that sucks the blood of the innocent. True freedom will rise at its own timing through the struggle of those who had been deprived of it. A final word to all dictators: You were a tragedy for humanity in your birth, and you will end in shameful death. Yes, all dictators share the same fate. Good luck, false gods; join the ghosts of the below.

TODAY THE SUN SHINED A BIT MORE BRIGHTLY

4/ 14, 2003

Today the sun shined a bit more brightly than yesterday. I turned on the local channel eight to hear the noon news. I then saw the Messiah of the latter days. He was a redeemer, and not a judging one, as many of the Bible's foretellers had predicted. Could it be he has come to finish up the incomplete redemption undertaken by the Son of Joseph, the docile lamb of the cross?! I have no time or desire to debate the mercenaries of God, the theologians. The twelve- year- old Iraqi boy, the Messiah of the age of war and destruction, was lying on a stretcher. He was ready to be transported to a hospital in Kuwait. He smiled in tears and waved with the remaining limp of his right arm to familiars and strangers. Through the mist of his tears, I saw the most touching smile I had ever seen on a human face. A white blanket covered the two- thirds of his burned body and his arms were lost forever; a bomb had fallen last night on the home of his sleeping family thus killing all its members, including the unborn brother / sister. Yes, they all had been burned beyond recognition, to say not to ashes.

"I was the only lucky one, al hamdou lellah - thank be to God, I love you all," he responded to a journalist who had asked him: "How do you feel?"

 Sir, you could have asked him a more humane question such as: What do you think the world must do to alleviate the children's sufferings? Instead, you have chosen to remain impersonal and cold, like a surgeon cutting through the human flesh. I apologize to all surgeons of the world; they do feel their patients' pains. That is why they anesthetize them and prepare ahead of time remedies to alleviate their pains. Yes, through cutting, surgeons remain humane. In contrast, some journalists, like you, approach and leave humans as if

58

they were phantoms that appear and disappear instantly. May God have mercy on you, Mr. cruel!

I know how I do feel. But who cares!

Pardon me; I have keen eyes for the dark side of the human condition, unlike the majority that is scared to face the truth.

Mr. George W. Bush and Saddam Hussein, your redemption, if possible, will come from the smile of that innocent bleeding young lad. May the train of waste depart soon; it has your rotten ambitions.

THE ROAD OF DEATH PAINTED WITH COLOR OF HOPE

4/ 15, 2003

Today I saw the ugly faces of war with little, if any, sentiment of compassion for the world of adults. This mad world forces one to wish for war, rather than peace. Yes, death to all the monsters who live in the dark caves of amorality. Amoral is the right word describing those three thieves of Baghdad. American soldiers have subdued them to the ground after being caught stealing from the International Bank of Baghdad a pile of cash that amounted to four million dollars. Follow the leader, Saddam had already robbed the oil- rich country by billions.

-- I also saw his so-called loyal guards abandoning their weapons. Dressed in civil clothes, many of them were running barefooted in different directions; they lacked patriotism, only a true leader can inspire. Run cowards, run, you were mercenaries in one man's country, and since when a country owned by one, can be defended by mercenaries? You are all robbers, only the legitimate sons and daughters can defend the honor of their country.

Dan Rather continued to report under the title: *the Road of Death.*

It was the same road he had traveled, a bit over a month ago, to interview Saddam. Jammed with destroyed military armors, it looked like a junkyard. Most disturbing of all was the smell of the many corpses of Iraqis. That scene testified to the destructive power of the wicked human heart.

-- Death did not confine itself in Iraq; it also has shown its face on the victor's backyard. Yes, a drug dealer in Saint Petersburg, Florida, shot to death the FBI agent, who had paid him an unexpected visit.

--And the comical scene of that husband who went to meet his released wife from prison. It was a pompous reception as he arrived at the jail's gate in a stolen car. He even has brought her a bouquet of flowers. He was arrested on the spot, upon a tip from the local police. Let's hope that his released wife would pick him up from prison in a properly owned car, once he is released. And please, sweetheart, don't forget to bring flowers; he did it for you; it is fair that you will do the same for him.

--All those ugly faces were challenged by the beautiful faces appearing on the screen of a Latin TV. The dozen of nude Mexicans were hugging and kissing while chanting: *"hacemos el amor y no la guerra* – let's make love and not war."

--Finally the uplifting faces of the competing Colombian young women appeared. It was the night of "Señorita Colombia." All the contestants looked beautiful and spoke with juvenile hope for a bright future, not only for their country but also for the whole world. A young male singer has chosen the most appropriate song for that occasion, *"El color de esperanza*-the color of hope." And hope has all the colors without exclusion.

"Plantemos el don de la Corazon-let's plant the gift of the heart," enthusiastically sang the crowd.

Yes, Mr. Bush, the future of this planet does not depend on your military power, rather on the aspirations of the human heart. Only a hoping heart, and not vain ambitions, can give life to our dying planet.

CRUCIFIED TILL THE END OF TIME

4/ 18, 2003

It is Good Friday, the commemoration of your hanging on the cross. Lord, many of your so- called followers have been rushing to the land of Mesopotamia bringing all kinds of materialistic aid. They went to hospitals and brought medicine to strengthen the lungs of those babies, who were forced to a pre-mature birth because of the shrilling echoes of the Mohawk Bombs. They've caused the burning of eighty percent of the bodies of thousands of children to have the sick self- gratification of providing the medications to heal those burns. The greatest farce of all, they continue to pride themselves of being the messengers of your love. It is noble to care for the wounded, feed the hungry, console the widows and repair shattered habitats. However, they've forgotten they were the ones who had shouted war against the poor people of Iraq, thus causing the destruction of their country's infrastructure and thousands of deaths. Lord, have you known of greater hypocrisy?

Today 75 percent of American's population approves this war. This high percentage is mainly made of the self- appointed bearers of your love. The true humanists, the discarded voices, had vehemently opposed the war, and continue to do so even at the price of being called un-patriotic, traitors, ignorant, coward and appeasers of tyrants.

The greatest farce of all, those self- righteous hypocrites continue claiming to be the messengers of your love.

Ah their poisonous piety! Brutes, stop beating the hell out of others, then you won't need buying handkerchiefs to wipe away their tears after having caused them unbearable sufferings. Lord, I believe a true love causes no harm.

RESURRECTED TO ETERNITY

4/ 20, 2003

Many of us have rushed to our churches in new clothes and old weary hearts to welcome a risen Christ back to our world. How divisive of space and time the human mind is, Jesus has never ceased a moment to exist everywhere. Lord, are you rising for all, including those religious fanatics who had arrived on Holy Friday with hammers in their hands to reinforce your nailing on the cross? You have us all in your big heart; just help us to nail our doubts. Lord, at the foot of your altar today there were many bouquets of flowers your daughter nature had abundantly supplied to welcome your resurrection. We read the great story of your rising and chanted the rituals of your victory over death. The joyful celebration of your victory made my heartbeats pouncing like a drunkard behind the wheel on a highway. However, how quickly have I, too, betrayed you! Yes, that beautiful young lady has diverted my eyes that were fixed on your image rising like a phoenix. Defeated, they landed on her hefty and untimely covered chest. There, for a moment, I drank from the cup of lust. Marla's glaucoma's high pressure has prevented her to catch me. But you have seen me, Lord. Well, forgive me for another sharp new nail I have drawn into your flesh and soul. Was my lust the right rose to offer you after three days of confinement in the tomb to redeem my sins?! My restless heart, Lord, today and forever, I offer to you as is. It is quite savage; still it has the capacity to compose hymns of praise to your divine ears.

You are a tough God with a gentle forgiving heart. You know very well how rocky is the road to man's heart. Still, you have chosen no road other than that of the cross to reach him; so much you have loved us. Are you really a mad God?! Well, you are who you are, and that is why you have loved us for what we are not. O divine mad lover, shine your bright light on our hearts; heavy is the darkness weighing on them.

You have risen, not through the chanting of the Gregorian mass at the Saint Peter Basilica in Rome, nor through the preaching of the eloquent; rather through the sorrows of that archeologist English woman. A few days ago, she was beating her heart for the looted artifacts from the museum of Baghdad; she wanted to preserve the heritage of man-kind.

"They had stolen the treasures of humanity," she moaned .She truly cared.

61

Lord, Mother Theresa, who was as tiny as an earthworm, has known the deepest secrets of your Sacred Heart. She needed not to convert others to you; she was quite sure of your presence in every one of them. Indeed, in your Kingdom reside Jews, Christians, Muslims, Buddhists and Pagans; they are all dwellers of your paternal heart. Man has always known you, even in the pre-historic times; and you have never been absent to him, not even while being hanged on the cross. As gazelles run to the fountains, as the sun shines in the sky, as birds chirp on the trees, and flutes produce enchanting melodies on the mountaintops, so man's heart is naturally driven to you, O God of songs. Indeed, Jesus has died and has risen for all. Preachers of religions, God can't be owned. He owns all and none owns Him. And if you still do insist to claim an exclusive ownership over Him, it is because arrogance has vanquished your hearts. Mortals, it is modesty at play. Are you really more than dust? If not, how then can dust claim ownership of God's heart? Only when you stop appropriating God to yourselves, will you find yourselves, along with others, in God's heart.

LITTLE TIME AND MUCH YET TO BE DONE

4/ 27, 2003

Tonight I called Babafemi to wish him a belated happy birthday; five days ago, he turned twenty- six.

"Father, It is never late, your good wishes are always welcomed," joyfully echoed his voice.

"Son, are you feeling now the weight of time?"

"Well, Father, time never works against man. In fact, it's man's most precious treasure."

"You sound to be quite satisfied with life."

"I'm, Father. I have been lately writing with great flow, without neglecting my painting. Life is beautiful; even my boring job is inspiring me three major inventions." He went on to give me a brief description of each. They were of environmental use "to increase man's respect for nature," so he claimed. Although listening attentively, my mind was not capable of grasping all what he was talking about; still I enjoyed listening to him.

"...Yes, Father, there is so much to do on this earth and one needs at least 5000 years to accomplish some of one's pressing dreams. Our great ancestors, the Pharaohs must have been quite conscious of this truth and that's why they've built their enduring dwellings."

"Indeed, Son, man has always carved immortality through his dreams."

"Well, Father, he is immortal as long as he doesn't lose the playful child within. In fact, he can capture all the joys of life only through his playfulness; serious people die with great regret. They haven't played enough;

they didn't discover the child within. That's why I have lately acquired for myself a hula hoop."

I laughed.

"It's true, Father. Modern man has lost his freedom on all frontiers. The only freedom left for him is within, and even this private territory of his is now being invaded."He breathed heavily for a moment to add: "He must not give up his playfulness to sit on the table of the life's banquet toasting the cup of poison to his fellowmen."

"What else, besides the hula hoops, must he apply to safeguard his small territory?" I asked, a bit sarcastic.

"Well, Father, the two ideologies of capitalism and communism fiercely applied in the twenty century have squeezed him like ham between two rotten slices of bread. In fact, in neither did he find his true freedom; both systems have served him as a concentration camp."

"What is the alternative?"

"He must question his traditional values. It is ultimately a downwards venture; it is the diving into one's deepest self. So far man has worked hard to promote only his sick and sickening ego."

"Who is there other than oneself?" I asked just to incite his imagination. I knew from past experiences, once his imagination is stimulated, it erupts like a volcano.

"Well, Father, how about sharing himself and his dreams with others; we are only strong as we embrace others; exclusion leads ultimately to destruction… Here we have it, too many diverged voices in the air," he commented as his cellular phone suddenly became jammed with statics.

"Anyway, a happy birthday, Son, and don't forget to include into your life even the people and forces that work hard to exclude you."

"I will. And you, too, my good father, do the same, and that can be achieved only by reviving the playful child that exists within." His emphasis on the importance of the notion of the playful child has convinced me that he was so much missing his deceased mother. Lord, have mercy on all your children as they leave the warmth of the maternal womb to be thrown into the icy arms of the world.

TILLING MY GARDEN

4/ 30, 2003

Today Gary and I had tilled a portion of my garden to plant cucumbers, tomatoes, watermelons, melons, eggplants, zucchini and pepper. What a great joy to communicate with mother earth! While pressing downwards the shovel with the whole weight of my body, the phantom of my father visited me. I began hearing his words: gently, Son, it is God's heart that you are opening up. Finally, the sun sat smiling at our hard labor, and before leaving the premise, I bowed to kiss the mud.

"Akhmed (the name Gary has lately given me), is this the terrorists' sunset prayer?" commented the silly one in giggles. I ignored him; the deep reverence I had felt for the mud has obliged me to overlook the cruelty of politics.

"Well, Gary, they are those who believe that their sweat is good enough to produce a fat harvest, and those who tint this sweat with a prayer. Yes, we must kneel down in mud for the blessing, not only for the harvest but also for those who had labored labor in hope," I said, smiling.

"I don't give a damn to the philosophy of a Bedouin; just drive me to Hess gas station, a quart of icehouse beer will close my day in good terms with all the Arab terrorists." He laughed hard and I smiled without saying a word, I was hoping to shut him up.

"You people of the Middle East pray a lot, is that why you have achieved so little? At least talk back to me; I did most of the work."

"Fools, your achievements are but dark smoke, just think of that smoke that has been clothing Baghdad with thick clouds for days now."

"I' m proud of the smoke of our mighty destructive weapons," Gary challenged me. Silently I drove him to the Hess gas station to get his favorite beer. I knew his cruelty was the rough façade he puts on, at times, to hide the cold reception he had received at birth (mother had given him for adoption because of her serious illness).

We parted reconciled and I considered that was the day's greatest achievement.

RIPPLS AND A WEDDING

5/ 19, 2003

I went to Clearwater Beach to walk on the gentle fine white sand. How good it felt! Suddenly I noticed a half dozen of old people were trying to challenge time as they rippled through the calm morning waves. I watched them for a while and blessed their struggle. I then move on, walking northward. And behold, my eyes caught, just right off the shore, a dozen of people forming a circle; a new marriage was in the making. The bride and groom were of pure Caucasian blood. A young black woman attended the wedding. And I thought it might have been her hope that the offspring of that couple would be kind to hers, certainly she was challenging history. A young woman played a piece of music that was unknown to me. I remained glued to watch the ceremony until its closing.

"By the authority bestowed upon me by the State of Florida, I pronounce you husband and wife," solemnly said the middle- aged female civil officiator. There were loud applauses and shrilled whistling from the invited, and bewilderment emanated from the uninvited few. After three broken marriages and a shaky fourth one, marriage for me has become a sad farce. Having surveyed the other watchers, I could only theorize: For some it might have been a happy remembrance, and a ravaging one for the others, like me. One conviction we all shared though: marriage is a fleeing moment of happiness that is worth capturing. The lenses of various photographic apparels were mainly focused on the newlyweds to capture that illusive moment. The music gal played happy tunes that enchanted all, including the sea and the wounded seagull that limped in search of the leftovers from the healthy agile ones. For all our dreams and nightmares, may the mercy of the Lord be upon us!

Relatives and friends smilingly surrounded the couple in the hope to steal a fleeing fragrance of their elusive happiness. A young man and a middle-aged woman walked toward the sea to throw a bouquet of white roses. "What is the meaning behind the throwing of roses?" I dared to ask.

"For the newlyweds and the invited to make a wish," warmly explained the tall blond young man named John. "Where are you from?" He asked

"Egypt."

With extraordinary warmth, he immediately said, "Egyptians are the gentlest people I've ever encountered." A decade ago, while working in Central Africa, he has visited Egypt several times. His kind comment relieved me greatly. After all, I belonged to a race that has been lately viewed by the Western majority as terrorists. John's kind statement has even left me with a feeling of pride to be Egyptian. It was the overpowering voice of the great Nikos Kazantzakis. Last night I was reading *"The Rock Garden"*. In his reflection about race, the illustrious Greek author wrote: "…you are a leaf on the great tree of your race. Feel the earth mounting from dark roots and spreading out into the branches leaf, or flower or fruit, so that within you the entire tree may move and breathe and be renewed."

Now that I was left alone, a sentiment of innocence dominated my heart for a moment when I saw the young bride kissing the two veiled girls handling her bouquets of white roses. Yes, it was my hope and prayer that the two little ones will keep up alive that purity symbolized by the white veils they wore and roses they offered. I murmured a good luck wish for the newlyweds, and then plunged into the sea; I, too, needed a certain ritual of purification.

The sun's heat became unbearable and I decided to return home. Later, I prepared dinner and patiently waited on Marla, who was working in the office of a fellow Scientologist. I, too, wanted to share with my wife a few moments of that evasive sweetness found in the marital union. After all, love is fragments of small acts of care, and that's marriage in its purest wedding gown.

EVIL DOES NOT PUT OUT EVIL –LEO TOLSTOY

5/ 23, 2003

I sadly thought how the month of plentiful flowers was fast vanishing, when we needed them more than ever before. Just two days ago, terrorists had attacked the foreigner's quarter in Riyadh, Saudi Arabia. This brutal attack has left 35 dead, 25 of them were Americans, and the remaining 10 causalities were from the terrorists and the Saudi guards while exchanging fire.

--Today, terrorists struck again. This time it was in Casa Blanca, Morocco. They were mainly aiming at Jews. The attack has killed over forty people. In that very same day a young Palestine woman has released the explosives strapped around her waist, killing two Israelis and wounding a dozen. It was a response to a series of bloody raids the Israelis had executed in the occupied territories, said the Palestinians. In retaliation for this latter attack, the Israelis killed 10 Palestinians and wounded 2 dozens.

How cruel humans are! Lord, all religions have failed to tame man, so help him to awaken to his true self; his moral confusion holds him down. He must take a leap of faith, enter into himself. There he will find a solid ground to build his character.

"As fire does not put fire out, so evil does not put out evil. Only the good meeting the evil, and not becoming contaminated by it, vanquishes the evil," wrote Leo Tolstoy.

Forgive me, Lord, for not having mentioned directly your command to turn the other cheek; the thought of how deep is your ocean of forgiveness makes me tremble. Please, help us to understand that if hatred is transformed into a positive energy, it can build fortresses of brotherly love. We all have our reasons for anger and frustration, but I know that even oppression, depressing as it may be, must not give us a license to kill our oppressors. It is my deep conviction: If we smile at them, their hardened hearts will soften up.

PREMEDITATED GENOCIDE

5/ 25, 2003

Today the UN has agreed to lift the embargo against Iraq. People of Iraq, rejoice, soon you will have food to fill in your empty stomachs and medicine to cure your many wounds caused by war. Forgive us; we have failed you because we had put our fear against your sacred survival. A special curse goes to you, Saddam, i.e., if you are still alive. You have caused the misery of millions of your people, just to satisfy the hungry tyrant within you. I also raise my complaint against those who had imposed the embargo. After all, to isolate a nation from the rest of the world is a pre-meditated genocide. Who causes the starvation of millions and still can claim to be close to God, the- all- embracing?!

-- Not only have the Iraqi children been victimized by isolation, but also those two American young girls kidnapped by their Saudi father. I have learned about their story through the fox news network. For over twenty years, their American mother had worked hard, but unsuccessful, for their return.

"Many times I've become so close to bring them out of Saudi Arabia, but I've failed because of the politics of oil," said the mother while weeping out of despair. Are we so immoral to think that man is saleable as any other commodity?! If so, how dare we claim that we are the only animals governed by ethics.

INVITED TO BE A MEMBER OF *THE BATS SOCIETY*

5/ 27, 2003

The first thing I did was to call Babafemi.

"Hello, dear Father," he answered after two peeps.

"How are you, Son, it has been a while since we last spoke; I didn't want to distract you from the demands of your hectic daily life."

"Not anymore, Father, I have lately become convinced that man has a single urgency."

"And what is this urgency?"

"Fighting for the honor of his race..."

"Oh no, please, Son, we have enough madness in this world."

"Dear father of mine, I would never call on man to take arms against his fellowmen. Rather, I am calling on him to fight against himself. We can prosper on all domains when we conquer our egoism. I believe in the infinite power man has to transcend his self- interest to serve his own race."

"In this case we're in full agreement," I commented, relieved.

"Father, there are so many negative emotions that paralyze us to meet our human challenges. One can live righteously only when one is himself, complete. To be a whole, man has to have a defined body, a defined soul and a defined space he can call self. It's a total self-annihilation to let others invade our space."

67

"Son, I know what is troubling you, war is a terrible thing; let's hope that at the end it will serve the good of the Iraqi people; at least they are now free, no more Saddam to kill them."

"I despise those criminals, Saddam and Ben Laden; no man has the right to take away the life of another." He went on telling me about his latest retreat in one of the California's deserts. "…As I was staring at the bright stars, I saw that bat whose wings were engulfed in fire. It flew over me, entered my brain and instantly I felt metamorphosed. "You're the creature that yields the night into the day," I heard myself shouting out of joy. It is the light within that helps us to conquer all forms of darkness. I truly own this great awakening to that nocturnal bird…As a gesture of gratitude, I am seriously thinking to form a society to revere all bats and you are more than welcome to be a member of this society. "

I remained silent; he knew well that I am not fond of organizations or any other forms of affiliation. Finally he has realized that and went light on me, at least so he thought.

"…In the morning as the sun plunged right into the rocks, I saw hundreds of bats coming out of their dark crevices to welcome the mother of light. So man must behave. Yes, Father, bats are spiritual mammals; they have warmth. They are the only mammals capable of a sustained flight, and that makes them more appealing to us than any other mammals. . Besides, they perform vital ecological roles of pollinating flowers and in eating insect pests they reduce the needs for pesticides, all which make them more appealing to us than any other mammals. I also love birds. In fact, I always wanted to be a bird and not a reptile; reptiles are less spiritual creatures…" Babafemi wanted to go on, perhaps, explaining how reptiles are creatures of a lesser spirituality. Thank God, he has finally realized that I was overwhelmed by his rattling.

"Father, have you ever felt a connection with any bird, and if so, of which species?" he asked

"Doves…"

"I have great admiration for doves; they teach us how to be gentle."

"Speaking of gentleness how is life with the lovely Miss. Ghazala?"

"Leila is the perfect woman. Through her I see the beauty and the intelligence of the Arabic woman."

"If so, why don't you get married? You will form an excellent family." So much I've desired to hold my grandchildren.

"Father, I'm taking time to know myself. Only when we enter into ourselves can we reach to others .In so behaving, we immortalize our fathers. Immortality I owe you, dear Father, but I must be prepared for it; only the holy ones can enter that temple. I am working on my holiness, pray for me; I want to be worthy of you and of our race."

"You're already, Son, just continue listening to that fiery bat that entered your brain," I joked.

"I wouldn't let it fly alone to heaven; I will be the companion of its flight. All things in the universe are bind together through the collective consciousness that redeems and eliminates our individual scrupulous and crippling conscience that seeks survival at all cost."

Suddenly we realized that we must bid farewell to each other, promising to talk again soon. And I remained hoping that one day the fiery bat would leave my son's brain.

BRUCE ALMIGHTY

5/ 29, 2003

For many hours Gary and I were quite visible to the neighborhood. He was painting the awning above the main entrance of my house, and I was caring for the vegetables and plants in my garden. Ah, the evening sweet aroma of those two gardenias planted in the narrow strip along the eastern wall of the white house. And the bloody blossoms of those two small pomegranate trees that out branched the borderline between my property and that of Mr. Cliff, the psychologist, who had died six months ago. Indeed, they delighted my eyes. Poor old Cliff did not harvest the fruits of his papaya tree of which he was so fond. I hoped it will not be my fate and that I'll be there to harvest my pomegranates and suck delightfully their bloody nectar.

"? Amor, podemos irnos al cine para ver está comedia – love, Could we go to the cinema to see that comedy?" suddenly erupted Marla's voice. I was then lovingly irrigating my pomegranate trees.

"Con placer, querida – with pleasure, dear."

Quickly I stopped and went to shower so we could arrive on time to watch *Bruce Almighty.*

The film was played at the America Movies Com. theatres of Largo.

 We arrived at eight and that was fine; we only missed the preview.

The movie opened up on a scene of the biggest cookie man has ever made. An old couple in Buffalo, New York, has baked it after the health department had shut down their restaurant for violation of health regulations. The unusual seize was a way to bring their customers back to a business where they had invested thirty prime years of their lives. In the course of the movie, Bruce, the news reporter, has become subjugated to many dooms of life. Unable to cope, he rebelled against God. Well, God, too, had His own complaints against him. To settle their grievances against each other, God made a deal with the protagonist that he could not refuse. Now Bruce is God on a trial basis. Let's see how the new god will behave. It was disastrous in spite of the good solid advices from an older friend! Some of them were:

First: do not show yourself often to humans; you will not be able to handle the fame of being God.

69

Second: respect their free will.

"That's easy," replied the mortal and he immediately took charge. Soon a perfect chaos has befallen unto the world. Reasons: the new god has made himself more visible to man than he should; to serve no purpose other than to satisfy his hunger for self-promoting.

Second violation: Bruce had no regards whatsoever for man's free will. He began dropping thousands of winning lottery tickets to please the Buffalonians. Still that generosity didn't stop them to raise millions of grievances against him.

Bruce regretted the deal and wanted to become again himself, just a simple man; playing the role of God is not an easy job. To recover his status of a human, he knelt down in the middle of a highway, praying to God that His will be done. As he was praying, a car hit him. He began complaining again. Suddenly God appeared to remind him how important to do the right thing. Yes, he needed to pray but he must have had chosen a safe place.

Distorted are the desires of the human heart. What was the ultimate desire of Bruce's heart?

Answer: to love and to be loved by Grace. Yes, he needed the earthly Grace, that young woman he loved so much. Still he shouldn't have had forgotten his need of the heavenly grace as well.

It takes a divine grace to fill up the chest of man with tough love. Lord, today I thank you for being you and me being me. Stay in your heavens but don't forget to look upon me with mercy and grace; so that when my earthly dreams crumble I still will have you to hold me together in one piece. To you, O good Lord, I offer my dark earth, I dream of no less than you fill my heart with your light and loving care. You're as good when you say no as when you say yes.

Theaters of Largo, thanks for the senior citizen discounted ticket; in a harsh economy every penny counts.

AWARDED: A KICK AND A LIFE- LESSON

5/ 30, 2003

At twilight I walked alone along the breezy shores of Clearwater Beach, Marla had left for audition at the Tampa Organization of Scientology. According to her, the first audition was quite beneficial and humans innately ask for more of whatever raises their hopes. Upon her return she reported that Mr. Hubbard's E-meter has indicated she was born on the fourth of July,1776, and that at her twenties birthday she delivered a son whom she named Joseph. The child died at birth and his death caused her so much grief that she became victim of her present glaucoma. To get rid of this impediment, she must undergo several sessions of audition; so they advised her. Those auditions will help her to get rid of her reactive mind; bad memories are the source of all our problems. I let out a sarcastic smile to which she responded by citing Mr. Hubbard's words: "The E-meter is never wrong. It sees all; it knows all. It tells everything."

Lord, I rest my case and put it all under your care; I am truly overwhelmed: My son Babafemi believes that he has found his spiritual freedom through a bat that entered his brain while he was sleeping. He even has invited me to become a member of his recently founded "Society of Bat worshippers".

And my wife has found hers through the magical power of Mr. Hubbard's E- meter. Worse! Both expected me to believe them unquestionably. Lord, who they thought I was, a pail of sorceries? But why am I such a skeptical! I should be proud to have a wife who is as old as our beloved mother America. I also blame my stubbornness for not joining my son's new found religion; bats have a divine light and light must be revered. Oh well, Lord, help me to accept all the inflections this crazy world throws at me. Or is it just the ongoing war within?!

While enjoying my lonely walk at the beach, I became a bit agitated. How could I ignore that funny bohemian who paced side by side along? He was a young man with tattoos all over his body. The bright purple color of his hair matched poorly his yellow shirt. He was wearing gray shorts, an old pair of black shoes and a funny brownish straw hat. Around his bony neck hang a faded leather cord that balanced an old rectangular radio. His left hand held tightly a reddish microphone. At one point, he shouted: "I am Frank Sinatra." A moment later, and in a more vehement and prolonged intonation of syllables, he shouted again: "Ladies and gentleman, I give you the man." And the man started to sing: *"I did it my way... "* a famous song of the original Sinatra. Politely I applauded him as the song ended. I smiled and started a conversation with him, hoping to find out the reason(s) behind his weirdness. He gave me a well- deserved kick, and I had no other choice but to move away. I then remembered the comic film: *Bruce Almighty.* Its message is: if God respects man's space; you too must do the same.

Indeed, for a safety reason, no man has the right to stick his nose in the affairs of another. I have failed the test by annoying my fellowman. I began watching from a distance that baby seagull. Slowly and carefully it hopped amongst rocks in desperate search for food, it was dinner time. In the sea, a mighty pelican glided to pick up fishes with precision rivaled only by the United States Air Force. The baby seagull noticed the banquet and flew to stand on top of the self- engorging Pelican. Well positioned, the feeble managed to receive whatever that kind and mighty pelican tossed as it wiggled upwards its long neck. Praise the Lord for the goodness of sharing amongst His small creatures. That's a valuable lesson on authentic living. After all, when was the last time we've heard that the Pope or Bill Graham had shared their dinners with the meek of their own species?!

Lord, for the kindness of the mighty pelican toward the baby seagull, I accept Hubbard's E- meter that gave me a -227- years old wife, who still wiggles her hips and apply mascara. As for my son's fiery bat, that source of divine light, I wish it were a dove; doves are universal symbol of peace. But since things are what they are, help me, dear Lord, to believe more so than to question; just for my own sanity.

THE DECEIVER AND THE DECEIVED

6/ 3, 2003

Today Marla and I went to the Natural Botanical Store. Behind the counter stood a middle- aged blonde, who greeted us with serene smile.

"We're here to buy a small container of estrogen," said Marla in broken English.

"I remember you," the shopkeeper replied. "Are you, too, becoming menopausal?" Putting her hand over Marla's, she said, "yes, you're and estrogen is a savior. Personally without it I could have become a widow or, at the best scenario, a divorced woman by now."

Certainly she was exercising her selling ability. I smiled.

"…Oh yes, dear, because of this womanly curse I became so neurotic that I once attempted to murder my husband. Thanks to this miraculous herbal lotion I am now standing before you as a wife of a happy man," she elaborated with a sustained sneaky smile.

"Ladies, Apparently we men are no longer safe being around you. Since this is the case, we must encourage the space program, just to have a place to escape to whenever madness takes over you, certainly due to a lack of estrogen I must add."

"By the way, my name is Sandra, what is yours, Sir?"

"Shaky." I was not joking; deep inside I was seriously frightened. She broke into a victorious laughter.

"We're not that violent; just too moody," said Sandra in defense of her species. She then began asking Marla if she goes through mood swings, outbursts and even, at times, acute depression. All that can awaken in a woman the violent desire of killing herself or her partner, explained Sandra.

"Yes, I go throw all that," affirmed Marla with grim.

"Give us then two large jars," I requested. It was worth it; my life might have been in jeopardy.

"Since my last period on April 10th, I feel my stomach heavier than ever before… Thank God, I'm not pregnant," Marla reported.

"You're not the only one who is frightened to have kids, my husband and I hate kids; I had four abortions," proudly commented Sandra. I sadly thought of the one million and a quarter aborted babies this year in the USA. Besides being a Catholic; I am also an ex-seminarian, after all. Sinful as I may be, I still believed aborting a child is just like aborting God. And if God is gone from the human heart, it becomes a crevice for evil bats, unlike the good one, I would hope, that has entered my son's brain. Sandra opened a sampling jar, dipped a finger and applied some estrogen on Marla's left arm.

"How do you feel now?"She asked with the usual sly smile of a merchant.

"I feel very relaxed," replied the duped customer."

"Then give us four bottles of estrogen," promptly requested the frightened husband, hoping to save his own life. Sure life is precious, and man must give up all his earthly possessions to preserve it. After all, what good is to possess the world if one loses his life?!

Child of the Carpenter and man of nails; you, too, might have had your own reservations about the Magdalene's intentions.

THEIR LACK OF SINCERITY AND EXISTENTIAL NEGATION

6/ 4, 2003

The Quartet invited the Israelis and Palestinians to make progress on the Oslo Accords.

Citing, the following points of conflict, outlined by the Bush Administration, were at the table:

1. Palestinians must renounce violence.

2. If phase one is achieved, they will be rewarded with a State that will enjoy a "Provisional status," conditional to a new Palestinian constitution and democratic elections.

3. Once the Palestine territory is governed by a democratic election; the International community will provide economical assistance to the provisional State that will become a "de facto State" on the year of 2005, with the borders of the pre-1967 war.

4. All Arab nations must restore diplomatic relations with Israel.

The negotiators shook hands, lit one another's cigarette and sipped hot coffee. Prayers of people of goodwill from both sides flew ardently to heaven in the hope that their politicians will finally reach the -long- awaited peace for the sake of all.

Having anointed their faces with the oil of justice, and bowing to their own logic; the delegates started negotiating the sensitive issues of borders, Jerusalem, Palestinian refugees and Jewish settlements. A lack of clarity prevailed with respect to some of the details. From what has filtered out via media, the following picture emerged:

A- Israel didn't want to dismantle all the roughly 100 settlements and their military outposts built in the West Bank and East Jerusalem, because of the Palestinian continual violence, so it claimed. However, the Jewish State was willing to put freeze on new settlements when a crackdown on Palestinian militants is fully achieved.

Palestinians responded that the isolated instances of violence were reactions to Israel's continual building on their territories. Therefore, all settlements must go and stop; they restrict the area available to the future Palestine State.

B- Israel agreed that refugees will have the right to return to their homeland, meaning to the future Palestinian State. Also, Israel was willing to absorb within its border limited numbers of returning refugees over a number of years, based on "the Family Reunification scheme."

For the confiscated properties, the Jewish State has accepted to be a major contributor to the refugees' compensations that will be sponsored and mainly funded by the international community.

According to the Palestinian negotiators, the Israeli delegation has focused on the human aspects of the refugees; their social welfare, and not on the political aspect, meaning: their full right of return.

For Israel, a full return can destroy its Jewish character, due to the foreseen accelerating birthrate amongst Arabs. Consequently, violence will inevitably show its ugly face in the remote future.

Palestinian negotiators insisted that Israel must accept the legal and moral responsibilities of the refugees' problem and that can be met only by accepting, in principle, their "Right of Return,"

Meaning: they must have the right to live where they want and the right to fully reclaim their confiscated properties by the Jewish State.

As for the fate of Jerusalem, under the international pressure, apparently the two sides were contemplating a shared city, meaning: The Israelis and Palestinians can establish their own capital in their part of that city.

Without condemning any of the two conflicting parties, I would like to voice the following opinion: Acts of violence initiated by one side, and responses to those acts from the other, must be condemned as equal parts of cycle of violence. Violence and peace can't coexist.

Despite the Political merits of the performance, based on the roadmap launched by President Bush on April 30, 2003, the negotiators have made a zero progress. Reason: Both sides had put much emphasis on the calculation of the mind and undermined the grace of the heart, meaning: their lack of sincerity. The effects of such a virtue are so powerful that they can put to shame even the mathematical precisions upon which the great pyramids were built. Without genuine sincerity, from both sides, I see in that historical roadmap to peace nothing but the face of an aborted infant. Peace has been sucked in by the policy of the devious ping pong game, each side tossing the ball into the other's court in the hope of exposing his weakness, if not wickedness.

It must be emphasized that peace is not a game, rather a serious commitment that requires the deepest of the human sincerity, faith and trust. I wonder how any of the two sides could dare to impose unilateral conditions without being guilty of the crime of aborting the peace process, the dream- child they both have claimed to impatiently await his/ her birth. Conditions imposed upon the other will remain insurmountable obstacles; so long we continue to hold onto the erroneous belief that we are always right and the other side is always wrong. This arrogant logic to settle any dispute is not only illogical but criminal; it robs the contract of its content.

Once, my- then- thirteen year old son posted on his bedroom door this sign:

Rule No.1: Babafemi is always right.

Rule No.2: If you disagree, please go back to rule No 1.

In the words of an American Secretary of State: "I am sure there is agreement if one side is given all what it wants."

Such arrogant and greedy attitude is a flat existential negation of the other. Concretely speaking:

Palestinians must accept Jews as a historical human reality rather than looking at them as aliens, who had conquered their land in a misfortunate period of history. Jews must abide to the same. Both parties are entitled to inhabit the land through the legal, historical and moral microscopes. This realistic approach of accepting one another is not only the right path to coexistence; it also serves as an energizing force to achieve a true, lasting and peaceful coexistence. Arabs will cease to look at the Israelis as a cancer in their body to be eradicated. Such an attitude will help the Israelis to overcome the fear of their impending destruction. In summary: both sides must concurrently and unconditionally accept one another as solid ground of their own survival.

Some political thinkers see the Israeli- Palestinian conflict can be settled through the approach of one- state solution. Others see the two-state solution is the best way out of this long labyrinth of conflict. I see no serious merits to any of the two approaches; both are wasp nests.

Israelis and Arabs, you must realize that only from within you can create peace for yourselves. The so- called defenders of your cause(s) are using you as scapegoats to foster their own political interests and flatter their sick religious beliefs. You are peoples of suffering and you must work hard to alleviate this suffering for yourselves and for the others. By subjugating yourselves to the tyranny of violence, a legitimate daughter of exclusion, you're simultaneously committing acts of genocide and suicide.

Empathy is not the child of fantasy; rather it is rooted in our biological make- up. It's our natural capacity to connect emotionally with others to feel how they feel. In his book: *Whose Freedom?* George Layoff, professor of Cognitive Science and Linguistics at the University of California at Berkeley, wrote: "When you see another person's face and body registering the physiological correlates of emotions, your own mirror neurons are activated, and via connections to emotions region, you can feel what someone else appears to be feeling."

Empathy as an innate altruistic capacity is the most effective force to solve the impasses of the egocentric capacity of the mind. It is founded in the human nature deeper than reason. Hence, to be empathetic is of a greater importance than to be right. The notions of right and wrong are flaws; they can be rightfully and indefinitely challenged under all circumstances and from all angles. Ultimately, empathy is naturally a divine and compelling force.

If you do think this a futile romantic approach to a problem that requires the power of outstanding minds, I invite you to think of Einstein's words: "One can't solve a problem with the same logic that has created it".

EPHEMERALS

6/ 5, 2003

Members of the Capitol Hill are discussing the two major questions:

First: where Saddam's Weapons of Mass- Destruction might be.

Second: how to provide drugs for the sick elders, and assure $400 tax deduction for the poor.

As of what concerns Saddam's Weapons of Mass- Destruction the following warning is imperative: Please do not follow the wicked logic or false propaganda. Let me get your attention to Hitler's rise to power; thanks to the German Right Wing. If you believe that Hitler has achieved anything other than destruction, meet him in hell; maybe he will reveal to you some of his achievements the world might have been so ungrateful to acknowledge.

Yes, apparently history is repeating itself. Recently the American far religious right has brought into power that so- called godly man, who has adopted the most hypocritical mode of political course. King George W. Bush Often recites the Holy Book, old and new just to flatter their sick ego. Let me briefly address the most urgent question, and history will be the judge. Our so- called godly President had sold the war to the nation under the disguise of Saddam's ephemeral chemical and biological Weapons of Mass- Destruction. One often sees in others the demon that lives within oneself.

Mr. President and monstrous Saddam, both you have contributed to the misery of the Iraqi people and brought great shame to the civility of man. Saddam has become a ghost; you are still a visible reality, traveling the globe, preaching peace and harmony. I would hope that our legal system will impeach you and send you into Saddam's world of ghosts. Once united with him, both will be capable to build an empire of ghosts. However, humanity will continue to struggle in suffering until it will find the Truth, the true liberator.

As for the one -time $400 tax cut to alleviate the suffering of the poor, please keep it, your government needs it to kill more of your imaginary enemies. Sir, don't worry, I have equipped myself and my children to arrive to the safest shores, to ourselves. And if we would fail to build the ship of wealth, we will navigate the high seas of life in our own canoes; a voyage undertaken in a canoe maneuvered by humbled vigilance is safer than sailing in the Titanic led under the dooms of an arrogant captain. Unto those who oppose the Bill, I say: your cruel logic that the poor is not entitled to that small benefit, because he doesn't pay taxes, is just the kind of logic that can be elaborated only in naïve minds and wicked hearts. Yes, although the poor does not pay taxes, you must not ignore the work of his hand; little rewarded by your cruel greed. He needs that modest recognition, just to preserve his right to the human dignity. However, if you keep up denying it to us, good luck to you in hell. It is not the anger of class- envy, rather a legitimate call to the human justice. It is a fact that throughout history the few rich, under the diabolical disguises of personal merits, have mercilessly robbed the wealth of their nations. You might say that you are the brain of the national economy. I agree, however, the brain needs the hands, the feet and the other body parts to execute its commands. But if you would call on the robots' help, soon your own creation will dismiss you, too. It had happened to the most powerful Creator. Voltaire once said: "God has created man to become god, and man gave Him back his own image."

Are you wiser than God?!

SPIRITUALLY SPEAKING

6/ 12, 2003

Man was a microbe that grew through billions of years to become who he is today. It's tragic though that his biological evolution is far ahead of his spiritual one; he is still a cannibal, spiritually speaking. The only difference between today's man and the caveman, the latter ate meat to survive; modern man creates carnages to feed his ever- increasing appetite for destruction. How savage and wasteful can he be!

Today I watched with minor bewilderment a massacre in Jerusalem. An Arab disguised as an ultra-orthodox Jew, has killed sixteen and injured over one hundred Israelis. As I listened to the CNN channel news, I learned that the brutal attack was a response to the Israeli bombardment of the Gaza Strip. Mission was accomplished, killing ten ordinary Palestinians and a Hamas leader. And the newscaster continued reporting that the Israeli raid was a response to an attack the Hamas movement had launched a day prior against the Israeli settlers in the occupied territory. And so the vicious circle of violence continues to go round and round. How tragic! It seemed as if both sides are competing who would drive the last nail into the coffin of the roadmap for peace. Since the mind has its deadly sins, let me remind both parties, over and over again, of the grace of a pure heart. It is a garden of flowers, only divine hands can care for. Today we need purity of the heart more than we need the sophistication of weapons; weapons kill, the heart cures. Lord, have mercy on Jerusalem; breathe your spirit unto her; so may peace grow in the hearts of her children. Israelis and Palestinians, you dream of greater skills of war for the sake of your children. Why cannot you deliver them the greatest weapon of all, love? I am not a preacher. In fact, I disdain those charlatans. However, I am confident that one cannot love oneself, if one hates the other; the other is but oneself photographed from a different angle. Yes, in the beginning there were no Jews, Arabs, Americans, Africans, Europeans, Asians, Spaniards, Latinos or Eskimos. We all were microbes that evolved. Let's keep up the wheels of evolution running. We shall arrive to the peaceful shores so long we have the heart as our motor. Yes, true power is granted only to and through the heart. However, great warriors, if you do insist to exercise your muscles, let me lead you to the jungles of Africa. There the hungry lions are waiting to wrestle you.

Lord, please put me into deep sleep, harsh are the realities of modern man. But if you do insist to wake me, please do plant me in the great Sahara. There I shall live in peace with its beasts; ferocious are the inhabitants of the valley. Today I dream to become once more a microbe. However, this time I wish to take a different course, I want to revolve around myself rather than to revolve around the stars, and that's the true security we all must seek.

IN THE JUNGLE OF RELIGION

6/ 18, 2003

I woke up quite depressed, the woman I have wedded, exactly thirty- five years ago, was not by my side. And I thought how cruel time is! For a relief, I walked toward the small forest that surrounded the Countryside

Christian Center.

"Young man, have you taken your breakfast?"

Turning around, I replied: "Not yet."

"Well, you're in the right path. Let me lead you to the banquet that will feed your flesh and eventually your soul." I let out an ironical smile, without saying a word. We walked toward each other.

"I'm Saint James, one of the deacons here at the Countryside Christian Center." He was a well- groomed man, who seemed to be in his early sixties. Still I observed a stony silence.

"And your name is?"

"Beast, a child of the jungle," I finally spoke. I was repulsed by his name: Saint James, how pretentious!

"Brother, this whole universe is the Lord's dominion, even beasts are His subjects, come along to His holy house and become one of us."

"Why not," I said.

He felt victorious and I was hungry. After a short walk, I found myself in a long zigzagged and dimly lit hallway. He stopped to push a button, and the elevator took us to the second floor, where the source of temptation has originated. As we got off, my eyes were struck by the largeness of the hall, where a gourmet breakfast was being served. A whole crowd was there. They all were devouring their food in silence. I wanted to sit down at the first seat available but Saint James prevailed, parading me throughout the big salon. Perhaps he wanted all to see that savage sinner he had hunted in the early morning from the jungle for God's Kingdom. My feet followed him, in spite of the resistance of my heart. Finally he led me to a table where a plastic basket full of candies was standing tall. He grabbed a handful and shoved it into my right hand.

"Here, brother, have a taste of our sweetness," he said smilingly. I took a piece out of its buffed golden wrapper and nervously shoved it into my dry throat.

"Hmm, too sweet, is it not, brother?" he asked, noticing that I was avidly sucking on it.

"Yeah," I replied unenthusiastically.

"Oh well, more sweetness yet to come." He led me to a bald man, who seemed to be in his early fifties. He was John Lloyd, the pastor; or in secular terms the CEO of the prosperous Countryside Christian Center.

"My name is Mouftada," I introduced myself, using a fake birth name.

"And what does that mean?"

"It simply means saved in Arabic, my native language. I thought to immediately alert him of my race as a token of having nothing to hide. I was afraid he might think of me as a terrorist, a stigma of which we Arabs have been suffering after 9/11.

"Well, brother, we can claim salvation only through the precious blood of our savior Jesus Christ. It does not matter where you come from. However, it greatly matters where you are heading to," he said, releasing a sneaky smile. I was relieved but not so happy by his preaching. I, too, smiled. I knew why though. Whenever you are in the jungle of religion, one must be as sly as any of its foxes. After that brief exchange of faked smiles, which had no common denominator other than our mutual mistrust, the pastor presented me with a white guest card. Trapped, I filled it in. Soon as I gave the useful information, I was permitted to eat. The breakfast was delicious but quite costly. Yes, I have become an obliged clientele, a potential contributor for the finances of the Countryside Christian Center. Why some Christians can't follow the example of our greatest leader ever? After all, Jesus never attempted to solicit money from those whom He had fed. Yes, the meal of fish and bread was free; He did not even question their religious or political affiliation. He even knew quite well that many among them did not give a crap about His Kingdom; they were hungry and wanted just a fill in. The greatest fisherman fished without a net. His only net was His sheer benevolence and goodwill toward all. Ah, goodness is the greatest net ever cast into the sea of ingratitude. I then realized what a bad dealer man is. He has learned the art of bad commerce from Eve and Adam, our first parents who had exchanged paradise for an unripe apple. As a result of that sour deal made with the devil, apple sauce has become the primordial source of nourishment for the Western babies. Being a descendant of maladroit merchants, I, too, have exchanged my paradise, my spiritual liberty, for a hot tasty breakfast. That day I have left behind a part of my liberty at the Countryside Christian Center. But I was consoled by the knowledge that every new day God rides His chariot to distribute the light into the darkened heart of man, despite the long nights of religions.

MARTHA STEWART'S PILLOWS AND COOKIES

6/ 20, 2003

God has promised man that he will inherit the earth because of his intelligence. Well, his intelligence did not deliver him the earth, nor has it introduced him to himself, at least not yet. I don't desire to write exclusively about the events of the day. Rather, like a butterfly, waking up late to a spring morning, I want to spread wide my wings in various directions.

--The queen of home improvement, and the founder of Martha Stewart Living Omni-media, was incriminated on nine counts. Still she held unto the innocent smile of a high school girl. Obviously, she was determined to continue selling more cookies and pillows to America. For years, America slept with a stomach full of the sweetness of Martha's cookies, and rested its tired heads on her fabricated soft pillows. Unfortunately, today America woke up to a nightmare, realizing that those cookies were tampered with the poison of greed and those soft pillows were stuffed with powdered stones. In fact, Martha had eaten all the sweet cookies, and kept for herself all the soft feather pillows. My only hope that justice will be served as the legal system had promised. Martha, I still fear your diabolic manipulation. Yes, America's laws have become lollipops on your tongue of a viper. Goodbye, Martha, I hope this is the last time I hear from your cunning world.

-- For entertainment I clicked to another channel. It was then Wayne Brady's show. He joked about those naked travelers. The merit of this form of traveling was to eliminate the smuggling of drugs and weapons. But if anyone was capable to get away with them in the state of nakedness, s/he deserves to own the plane, joked the host.

--But America always manages to find a redeeming grace for all its sins and crimes.

One of Wayne's guests (Sorry, Sir, I haven't retained your name) has made a DVD to help locating some of the 2000 missing American children daily. God bless you, caring man.

--After Wayne, the black entertainer appeared the white Reverend James. Kennedy. He was to deliver his Sunday Sermon.

"Enough is enough, we're going to take America back," shouted the evangelical voice. Reverend, only the apocalypse can halt the chaos of modern America. Now that we've lost hope in man's civility; let's join hands and ask for a second divine breath; the old clay had hardened.

PEACE, THAT FRAGILE CHILD

6/ 29, 2003

Welcome the ceasefire between the Palestinians and Israelis. I hope that fragile child would grow to be á pillar of peace. However, let all be reminded: if birth is painful, growth is even more so. Since nothing is dearer to my heart than peace amongst men, I raised my hands to heaven. Thus I prayed: Please, Lord, plant the seed of peace and help man to tend it. However, let him not be discouraged nor be overconfident, only you can transform the seed into a plant and the plant into the generosity of shading and feeding the needy. In reverence to the solemnity of this rebirth of peace, I refrain to discourse; just I would like to send to the conflicting parties this brief message: a true peace is found in a heart that has room for others.

AARON SPEAKS FOR THE STUTTERED BORTHER

7/ 17, 2003

The eloquent Aaron spoke once again for the stuttered brother Moses. Yes, the uncharismatic George W. Bush has called upon Tony Blair's eloquence to remind the American Congress of the good reasons behind attacking Iraq. Although both Hawks of war could not substantiate their decision, still they insisted to replay the same old litany: "We've gotten rid of the tyrant Saddam and brought democracy to the Iraqi people," Blair reminded his audience with a large smile covering his foxy face.

True, Saddam has vanished and eventually will be caught, and that is good. Still this heavy cloud hovers over Iraq: How to bridge the impending great division between the Iraqi ethnic factions? Brothers will kill brothers, and chaos will spread throughout the country for years to come. Getting ready of the tyrant is only one step on the long tedious road to freedom. In the end, only the Iraqis can bestow upon themselves dignity or mercilessly strip themselves from it.

They must nourish and cherish their newly- born freedom, or it will die and its death will be the death of their own souls. Can a body or a nation advance without a soul? To all freedom seekers: tame the beast within and then you will truly recover your stolen freedom.

NELSON MANDELA IS SOUTH AFRICA'S GANDHI

7/ 18, 2003

Today the nation of South Africa celebrated the eighty- fifth birthday of Nelson Mandela. The Statesman looked frail. Still his serene smile defied the weight of his age; he was reconciled with himself, knowing that he will leave behind a better world than the one he had come to. A mission well accomplished, Nelson. Really! Nelson is not your birth's name, rather your colonial name. True, they'd changed your name but couldn't leave the mark of the beast on your heart. You have refused to bow before their tyranny. In spite of twenty- seven years of imprisonment, you have lived as a free man, and freedom you have poured into your people's soul. You could have fallen victim of anger and hate, but your wisdom was a greater force. Rather, you have preached peace and your race has received it well. Even some of those barbarians, the colonialists, have responded to your noble message.

--While South Africa celebrated today a birth, the Great Brittany witnesses the death of Dr. David Kelly, a

biochemical scientist, who was a former inspector of the so -called "Iraq's Weapons of Mass- Destruction."
He had revealed to the news media the fabricated lies of his government to go to war against Saddam, and the
Blair's government rendered his life unbearable. No one yet knows, for sure, the true cause of his death. It
could have been the outcome of a government ploy or an act of suicide, having realized the evil of science he
had been promoting. If his death was a case of suicide, no one should blame him; rather we all must sign a
petition against the world's armaments in honor of his name.

Well, one may say, the destructive weapons, or any other invention, are the inevitable evolution of man's
quest for knowledge.

True, however, one can't help but to become nostalgic. Yes, humanity was better off when man and animals
roamed the jungle side by side. Human life was shorter, but equally true, it was happier. With modern
technology we're left with deceit; tyranny; fear; anger; vengeance and destruction. Could the inevitable
evolution of the human intelligence be the greatest curse of man-kind?! Truly, it is the original sin.

--Nowadays we live in such anger that our fists are less than one inch far from one another's nose. If you do
think this is the creation of my imagination, check today's debates in the Congress of the United States. The
Republican Chairman of the House and Means Committee has called upon the police to restrain a Democrat
representative. According to the young Republican representative, the elder Democrat colleague was on the
verge of punching him in the nose. For fact, they did not fail to exchange insults. Supporters of both
representatives from the news media have disagreed about who was culpable. Where there is a lie there is a
murdered truth; only a pure heart can deliver the truth. But purity of the heart is the lost dream of modern
man. Reason: he has prostituted himself to the material comforts and to the transient worldly pleasures. We
must bow to Henry Bergson's wisdom that stated: "The saint is today's greatest hero."

THE- ALL- AMERICAN BOY

7/ 20, 2003

The Eagle County District Attorney Mark Hubert has charged the- all-American boy Kobe Bryant, the NBA
superstar, of having had raped a nineteen old white young woman. The twenty- four year old Los Angeles
Lakers guard entered the team's arena accompanied by his ravishingly beautiful wife Vanessa. Holding tight
to her right hand was his preliminary statement, projecting an image of a loving husband. He was in a mission
to eagerly defend himself.

"I love my wife with all my heart," the player said at the opening of the conference.

83

"I know my husband has committed adultery but he is innocent, it was an act of two consenting adults," said the loyal wife, who was dressed conservatively. She looked quite a lady in her beige dress and her calm tone left every man to dream, for a moment, of a sweet woman like her. Was she sweet or just well coached by a shrewd lawyer, who dreamt of a big chunk of the NBA superstar's fat fortune?

Whether a lady or a publicist; the betrayed wife had her personal interest at heart. She wanted to salvage, as much as possible, the clean image of her husband that had landed him many lucrative contracts' endorsements. Once dust settled, she will be heftily rewarded. A long vacation in an exotic land with her darling will tell that her body was still more desired than that of the other woman. Besides, in today's materialistic culture, it is better to be the betrayed wife of a superstar than being the wife of a faithfully loving ordinary working man.

In spite of hard work to embellish his image, the falling star still remained in the swamp where many aggressive serpents were crawling under his feet. Soon they will ascend to bite his pocket. The battle has already begun. Yes, Satan had spoken to the white young woman; she must be compensated. And the superstar had spoken to Robert Shultz. His appearance in the Cathedral undoubtedly won him the sympathy of thousands of the infamous Preacher's white herd. In return, the black player would reward the white preacher with a million dollar, I presume. Such a sum could be used to raise the Cathedral's minaret a few hundred feet closer to the heavens. Are we not rebuilding the Babylonian tower?! Well, America lives under the achy adage: "scratch my back, I scratch yours," even at the expense of morality, I must add. And God will have no other choice but to break both backs and that is divine justice.

-- In Washington, Basem Youssef, the FBI's highest ranking Arab-American agent, has filed a racial discrimination suit against the Bureau, claiming, because of his ancestral background, he was kept out of the Sept 11, 2001 hijacking's investigation.

--Jeb Bush, the darling little brother of King George Bush Junior, has been twisting the arms of those politicians who disagreed with his medical malpractice new policy that puts a cap on the punitive awards.

-- A charter pilot has resigned after a video tape surfaced showing him asleep during the flight from Nassau / Bahamas to Fort Lauderdale/ Florida.

-- Some Americans are migrating northwards; they thought their country was growing too conservative; believing that Canada is more inclusive and less selfish society. Indeed, Canadians have often chosen different policies: establishing universal health care; maintaining diplomatic ties with Cuba; imposing tough gun control; legalizing same sex marriages and an initiative already on the table to decriminalize the use of marijuana.

-- The Moscow orthodox archbishop has informed the world that the 1150 pound bell of the St. Basil's Cathedral started to tilt. It is a "sign of the Lord's discontent for the planning of constructing a new subway in Moscow that will disturb the worshipers," explained His Eminence.

--If all the above-mentioned events are tragedies that plagued others, allow me to report one of my own: Marla, my wife, has discreetly slipped into son Javier's mouth a piece of nestle crunch, thus ignoring my craving for chocolate. Are we not living in the latter days?!

I despise preemptive wars and nations that produce nuclear bombs, sleeping pilots while on duty, the arrogance of superstars, marriages of interest and the discriminatory chocolate treat. ------But above all, I despise the attempt to create "*the Death Switch*." Professor Thompson, a Canadian biologist, believes that it will help fighting the human diseases. "When the switch is on, cells die. When it is off, they grow and proliferate," explained the Scientist. But who wants to prolong his/her stay on this earth, where our butts are roasting in the fire of lies; manipulation; negligence; hatred; superstition; arrogance; indifference and discrimination? Am I becoming a whiner who complains about everything, including the colors of the alphabet cereal?!

GOD'S UNFAILING JUSTICE

7/ 22, 03

Today the American troops engaged in a fight with some Iraqis inside the home of a wealthy contractor. After three hours of fire exchange, the big dogs rushed into the demolished home to pick up their most dreamed of prey. They became high at the smell of the dead bodies of the sons of Hussein the tyrant. Unfortunately, the children have to pay for the crimes of their parents. Yes, I'm thinking specifically of Oudeh's son, may God have mercy on the innocent soul of that young victim. As for his father and uncle, may they roast in hell! The same wish goes to the fourth victim, who might have been a health care provider to the crippled Oudeh; one cannot serve the devil and expect to be in the company of holy men, anyway.

The death of the two great thugs has brought a political relief, and even jubilation, to the Bush and Blair Administrations. It also has enforced my deep conviction that only fools can ignore God's justice.

-- A great parade was launched in Palestine, a small town in West Virginia, in honor of Private Jessica Lynch. American soldiers, tipped by an Iraqi nurse, had rescued the twenty year old Jessica captured by the Iraqi army. The week's ordeal and the inflicted wounds have elevated that humble town girl to a national fame, attributing to her the pride statement: "I am an American soldier," so they said she had told her capturers.

85

Why not? We all dream of a moment of fame and soldiers are the most deserving of it, they pay the highest price, their lives. However, the sign that read: "God is still in the business of miracles making" hasn't cheered me a bit, although it was a thanksgiving statement for Jessica's safety. I'm dreaming of the day when man gives thanks to God, not for escaping the claws of an enemy, rather for throwing himself trustfully into his arms, a sign of acknowledgement of our brotherhood.

--In spite of the many depressing news of the day, I was greatly impressed by the interview of one of the nine miners, who had risked their lives to earn the bread for their families; they were entrapped in a caving mine, a year ago.

"I'm still doing the same job I'd been doing for the last thirty years; I've a family to support," said the devoted husband. For a moment I questioned my level of devotion to Marla and her son Javier. Exalted by the devotion of good husbands, by the news of the death of the two thugs, but a bit depressed by the death of the young boy and slightly annoyed by my own shortcomings, I began to think that life is a theatrical play that exposes man's deep longings. I claim no power to redeem humanity, rather I long for the day when man will recover his sense of responsibility toward others. On that day his redemption will becomes certainty.

HALL OF SHAME

7/23, 2003

A former political opponent has shot a forty one- year old black council member, as both were walking in the New York City Hall of shame. At his turn, the white assassin became a victim of his own violence as a security guard shot him to death. Ironically, that day the black council had submitted a proposal to prevent violence at the workplace. Let the human mouth speak, but if the human heart does not say amen, all words, eloquent as they may be, will be the heritage of the wind. Goodbye council James Davis, the man known by his smile; may God's angels smile upon you as they lead you to meet your Creator. Frightened be not, you are above and your assassin is down. No longer can he inflict harm upon you; heaven and hell do not have intercommunication lines.

-- Today violence has also cast its heavy dark shadow over San Antonio, Texas, as a middle- aged man started dispersing bullets at his coworkers. Two women were dead and a man was severely injured.

Please take me back to the peaceful mountains of West Virginia. But, if they're no longer a haven of peace, then drag my corpse into one of my country's pyramids. There I want to lie down on a cool mastabah, where I can listen to my ancestors instructing me about the exalting journey to eternity; weary have become my days in this agitated planet.

--Not all crimes are equal. Some of them perpetuate death and others prolong suffering. I find the latter more brutal. The hypocritical laws have sent Sam Waksal, the CEO of "Securities Investment Firm" to a federal prison in Pennsylvania to serve seven years and three months. Mr. Judge, have you seriously thought of the many sufferings that thug did and will continue to inflict upon the thousands of investors? Yes, he had stolen the cow, slaughtered it, ate its meat and sent its manure to the farmers. His Honor such a soft punishment encourages thieves to keep up steeling our fat cows, even during their short confinement in a prison cell. It's about time to slaughter the fat cow; numerous are the deprived. Instead of slaughtering the fat cow, you have sent her not to a lesser green pasture. As CNN displayed the jail's entrance, I thought it was a door of a country club. Still, I hope that the working hours there, from 7:30 a.m. to 3:30 p.m., will remind that thug of the agony felt by those men and women whose savings he had unscrupulously robbed. Could the sentencing to pots washing, lawns mowing and floor- scrubbing be a theatrical act, another way for the powerful to sly the weak? With the stinky notion of reward for good behavior, that thug will be released in less than three years.

--And the sexual abuses of delinquent children while in the custody of adults, who were supposed to protect them from the world's cruelties. Dear Lord, may I dare to ask: Where does the buck stop? You have hired them to labor in your fields. Look what they had done to the seeds. Could that be a ground for me to rebel? Have you hastily created man from nothingness, but didn't provide for his moral evolution? Lord, pardon me to have entertained such a thought; you are incomprehensible and my ignorance is thick. Once this heavy mask of ignorance is taken off my face, then I will see you as you are, all- merciful, all –wise, and all- caring.

-- Last but not least, fifty- one years ago today, I was pouncing up and down in the court yard of the Coptic Catholic Little Seminary at Tahtah (Thebes).Yes, I was overwhelmed by joy, my beloved country was no longer under King Farouk's grip. Lord, do remember Egypt, my native country. Although no longer it has a King, I am still waiting for the day when it becomes a true republic. Until then and forever praise be to your holy endurance and please forgive my erratic insanities; I am an ant that has failed to reach the top of the mountain of your divine wisdom. Thank you, Lord, for the sporadic joys in my life.

INCUR NO MORE KARMA –MASTER YOGI

7/ 24, 2003

"**Life** is not a tragedy; life is a performance of self," said Master Yogi.

Then he went on to ask, "What is the purpose of life?"

"To elevate all, be big or small," he replied.

"What is the reality of life?"

"Incur no more Karma, you want to be free," said the wise man.

Since I claim no higher wisdom than that of the great sage, allow me to put it in my own words: life is and will continue to be a tragedy until man finds himself. Once he has found himself, it becomes a canticle to all God's creations.

How could one find that most precious pearl?

To answer this question, I must follow the master's line of thought. Yes, through alleviating the sorrows of life, our own and those of others. We must pour ourselves into every empty cup we encounter on our path. If there are so many empty cups, it is because they are a few generous waiters.

Throughout my writing I leave the impression of being fixated on tragedy. One might even accuse me of having a perpetual love affair with that old toothless witch. I do, indeed.

"Why?" You might ask.

"Well, let me draw you a rapid itinerary to my own: At the age of eleven I was confined into a religious Seminary. There I stayed till the age of twenty-six. During this period (long or short, to each his own perception of time), I was dreaming to become a savior, just following Jesus' steps. However, at the summer of 1966, I sacrificed that dream and left the Seminary for a woman whom I have loved and married two years later. We lived a relative happiness for ten years. Then tragedy struck; my wife has fallen into coma, right after the birth of our twins. I had to give up my pursuit of a Doctorate degree in philosophy to meet the immediate needs of our four children. To give them the motherly love, I got remarried, four years later. My second marriage was a total disaster. Disappointed at the world, or maybe at myself, I became a Casanova, a big time womanizer. Although I enjoyed the company of many women, I have not loved enough any of them. Hence, the saga of my lack of commitment continued until I met Marla. She looked fragile and innocent and to her I delivered my heart. Soon after our marriage, Marla revealed herself to be anything but innocent and fragile. I often rebelled against her heartless behavior and several times I forced her out of the conjugal bed. That was my emotional journey.

As for my intellectual and professional journeys, they were no less disastrous, due to indiscrete outspokenness that was interpreted as arrogance by my flathead bosses. In summary, I was thrown out of many institutions. So, the life of Sinbad was a tortuous journey on all fronts. Now that I am in my autumn, I realize how yellow my leaves are, I had failed to water the tree of my soul. Yes, I was a victim of fleeing sensualities and revolt has greatly ravaged my soul; I had lacked to ask God to walk by my side.

For so long I have sought but not found salvation in the traditional religions. Now I am convinced that God exists ultimately in man's heart and not between the lines of any scriptures. God is not a writer, rather a sculptor. Lord, in the twilight of my days please have mercy on my soul. Help me to join my voice with those of birds to welcome your light. Show me that the road to peace and happiness starts from you and ends in you. Teach me how to give it all and expect nothing at all. Expecting nothing from the world is a sure way to have it all from you. Today let me pour out myself into the world's cup and may you bless this cup so it will not poison anyone. You are the wise One who gives a taste to the true joys of life. Through your self-sacrifice, you have poured yourself into my cup. In return, help me to fill in those of my fellowmen, I need to communicate with you; I am already worn out by the mundane.

A WORLD OF LIES

7/26, 2003

Today was Amerigo's funeral. I called Noemia, the wife of the defunct; she was not at home. I contacted the office at the Saint Cecilia Church to find out at what time the funerals will be.

"At 9:45 a.m.," informed me a female's voice. Well, I must attend, breaking bread with someone obliges.

"Could I accompany you?" Marla asked.

"Sure!" I wanted her to experience at firsthand the vanity of life.

When we arrived at the Church, the officiating priest was preaching the sermon.

"Our beloved Amerigo was a fervent Catholic and I am certain he will be warmly welcomed into our Lord's mansion," with those words he concluded his homily.

What a lie! The defunct was a fervent Mason and a hostile critic of the Catholic Church, I thought; remembering some of his comments whenever we discussed religion. Elevating the defunct to sainthood, to which he himself would have objected, is a clear indication of the tyrannical force of money.

After those negative thoughts, finally I got a grip on my distraction. Recollected, I followed the funeral rites with no negative thoughts. After all, life is too short and one must accept its transient afflictions.

After the mass, the director of the Moss Feaster Funeral Home has instructed: all those who want to accompany the defunct to his final rest's place, please put your headlights on.

I had one headlight functioning, the other was broken and needless to add that my car was the ugliest and the oldest. Well, the thought that death is the greatest equalizer was a comfort for me. The funerals cortege proceeded slowly to the Largo Cemetery. There we have been instructed to take different directions to park our cars; only the black limousine was allowed to be close to the deceased's destined tomb- it was carrying Noemia and the few members from the immediate bloodline of the defunct. At the grave's site, the priest turned toward the mourners to remind us, for the last time, of how pious of a Catholic the deceased was. "May our Lord and his angels welcome him into heaven and may his death serve us as a reminder of how short our lives are on this valley of tears," said he. Closing his book of the dead, he faced the casket to sprinkle some holy water, it was a hot day and the defunct needed all the cooling he could get.

"I sincerely apologize to the Costas family, the grave isn't open yet, we will lower the casket at three o'clock. Meanwhile, those who want to comfort the family of the deceased, may go to the Portuguese Club, I've maps to give upon request," suddenly erupted the squeaky voice of the opulent funeral director. The wife started shaking like autumn leaf, heavy was her disappointment; the grave was not ready to receive her beloved husband.

Marla, her son Javier and I drove to the Club. Right at its entrance stood the shrine of "Nossa Senhora de Fatima- our lady of Fatima." I stopped for a moment to silently revere the most Blessed Lady. Attracted by the good smell of food, we rushed into the club. Javier, his mother and I sat at the round table. Soon an elderly man dressed in a black suit joined us.

"I am Jacques," he introduced himself.

"I'm Max; my wife Marla and her son Javier... Mr. Jacques, what is your relationship to the defunct?" I asked for the sake of entertainment.

"No relationship whatsoever, I'm the limousine chauffeur for one of the Moss Feaster Funeral Homes. There are ten of them in the Pinellas County."

"That is a good way to kill time."

"I'm not retired yet, I work fulltime. I have been working for the same company for the last eight years. I love every moment of my job. I send to the Lord, at least, two people on a daily basis," said Jacques, with some pride.

"Soon or later everyone will have to leave this world," I said, reminding him, indirectly, that there was nothing worthy of bragging.

After the hot meal we were reminded that the casket will be lowered into the grave at three p.m. A few of us went back to the Largo Cemetery to say the final goodbye to the deceased.

The son of the defunct was joking and laughing as if he were having the best time of his life. Why not? Father had left him an inheritance of ten houses. If asked, my humble opinion will be: the defunct should have left his wealth to benefit the Humane Society, animals are more grateful than the majority of us.

"Goodbye, my dear husband, we're only separated one block away," said a tearful wife.

Well, apparently the old man did not want to let go of her either. What a perfect marriage. Personally, all what I want is a grave in another planet. Apart of my first wife, who died after ten years of our union, I have failed to tame any of my other wives to become my true soulmate. My wish to have an unknown burial plot is well-founded: I do not want any of the three ex-witches to have easy access to my grave; they might disintegrate it and perhaps with some justification.

I approached Noemia to hug and offer her my sincerest condolences. I even promised her to be in touch, something I had not done when her husband was alive. She gracefully thanked me.

HUNTING FOR BAMBI

7/ 27, 2003

Hunting *for Bambi* was the title of an article I have read in the St. Pete Times on July 20. The ad was the enterprise of a certain Michael Burdick. Advertising on his website for women hunting, somewhere in one of the Nevada's ranches, he detailed:

Spend four nights and three days hunting for nude women; just for the small amount$10,000.

Locals will enjoy our big discount.

The hunted deer will be paid $1,500, if hit by a pinball.

The missed target will be rewarded a sum of $1000.

Afterwards, understood, the hunters will drag the hunted into the morality slaughterhouse, where their dignity will be skinned off. A good sex- session was a pleasurable reward for the hunters and a lucrative means of earning a living for the hunted.

Would I be pleased to be a hunter in one of the Nevada's ranches? No, thanks, I prefer being dressed in a gentleman suit while roaming a Moroccan marketplace. There, I'll try to seduce a veiled woman. If she presses my hand, I know that I am her favorite suitor. She will hand me her address wrapped in a perfumed handkerchief, thus inviting me to her parents' house to ask for her hand. Ah how I do long for the doves' playfulness! That is what I call civility. As for the ritual of Hunting for Bambi, I leave it to the brute Westerners.

Mr. Burdick, how cruel you are! You wanted us to hunt for nude women whom you do not allow to wear even a helmet. Your explanation was: you wanted the ritual to be as natural as possible; deer do not wear helmets.

Sir, deer do not run nude either, they have their hair to protect them from the hostile elements of nature. Are today's women less worthy of our respect or at least of our compassion? Ah, where could I find that lioness from the women's liberation movement, I would like to see her striping you of any piece of cloths and make you run with the wild.

Mister, you wanted to be rich, and I hope soon you would get the law's attention. Hunting for Bambi is not a sport as you claimed; it is a modernized form of prostitution and a savage one. The traditional form of prostitution leaves women with the basic protection guaranteed by four walls, and their clienteles will be incriminated if they leave a physical injury on the flesh they would have enjoyed. Conclusion, you and your hunters are sadists, and for that only you must be severely punished. I suggest that you be taken to the Florida's Alligators Alley. There you will be thrown into one of its narrow canals, and let's see how much fun you would have with the hungry. I hear your loud voice defending the ethicality of your enterprise: It's a mutual consent of adults.

Again, make no mistake; it is a cruel form of prostitution. Not all is your fault, Mr. Burdick; guilty as well is the State of Nevada that had licensed you to degrade women.

And to you, all the Bambis out there, who exchange their dignity for fast cash, I recommend a visit to Mother Theresa's grave in Calcutta. There you will learn about the worth of a woman. Dear America, I must remind you of the fate of the Roman Empire, whose constituents had found great delight watching beasts and slaves engaging in a fight of annihilation. The Romans was fascinated at the destruction of the flesh; Mr. Burdick and the likes are nowadays fascinated with the destruction of our morals.

GOODBY BOB

7/ 31, 2003

Bob Hope's life ended Sunday after having spent one hundred years on earth. "Goodbye Bob," as your then-young son used to say whenever you had to hit the road. For sometimes he has refused to call you daddy because you have frequently been on the go. Being a smart, noble and responsible father, you began taking him along, as much as was permitted. For that awakening you have passed the test of good fatherhood. Your sense of a responsible parenthood was colored with your high sense of patriotism: you have brought America to the military when they were fighting far away from home.

Millions of your admirers certainly will miss you; I am one of them. Yes, when I heard of your death, I felt some hollowness in my heart and I knew America has lost a piece of itself. The memories are great healer and thanks for the good memories. As we say goodbye to good people, we are glad to see others arriving. Thank God for the continuous cycle.

--The recent showdown of violence between the gay community and the conservative far- right politicians was quite disturbing. Gay marriage in America and elsewhere is looked upon by the cons as a menace to the very foundation of what constitutes a family. Yes, holy Procreation is the ultimate ground for marriage, cry those hypocrites. My question to them: why then do you promote racism, hunger, war and ultimately death? Your fake ultra- religiosity is nothing but your evasion from your evil selves. You are incurably corrupt and your passion for sin forces you to take a plunge into the hot but shallow waters of your notion of free redemption. Ignorant and greedy, Redemption is forgiveness. But how can you expect to be forgiven if you continue to judge others? O you, hypocrites, get over your false piety, God will always be holy and no man's deeds, evil they may be, can diminish His sanctity. So, please join me and enjoy the human circus ... Yes, laughter, laughter… If you cannot laugh, do not expect me to hand you a handkerchief, I need it; I am drowning in my own tears for a humanity that has lost its compass. Indeed, hypocrisy is your greatest tragedy. Lord, I thank you for the deeds that celebrate our greatness. As for those that reveal our weakness, I ask for your mercy. You have not failed us, nor have we failed you. Falling short of your grace is not a denial, rather a reaffirmation of it. Yes, we acknowledge it as we stumble through the dark labyrinths of our lives.

MOKING THE MOKERS

8/ 2, 2003

Pity on you, Governor Greg Davis of California, your policy of compassion has subjugated you to mockery from the cold lips of the cruel and greedy conservatives. They've spent millions of dollars buying signatures to depose you. Well, weep not; soon the strong sun of compassion will shine again on the Golden State. When the light spreads, it will discolor the sheepskin and then the wolf will reappear.

Mr. Greg, be not frightened, the sky is not that gray; you're just competing against 359 clowns. Indeed, America is and will remain a country of great opportunities for all: One just needs $3,500 dollars and sixty-five signatures to apply for the governorship position.

Woe to you who deny funding the kitchen soup to feed the homeless! You deny the poor a bowl of soup while you nourish yourselves from their fleches; carnivores you are born.

-- Jerry Springer, you have rejected the possibility to live in the governor's mansion, just to keep up running

93

your show of the human moral degradation. Yes, the glamour of nudity; the throwing of angry fists to deform faces and send hard kicks into fat butts are favored gestures of the populace. Congratulations, and keep up entertaining the insane and mediocre.

--Finally, my sympathy goes to you, young woman of Ohio, you are the least understood of all the benefactors. The puritans have accused you of obscenity for having had breastfed your toddler in public. They have dragged you into the court of justice. How wicked is their sense of justice. Be consoled, I do share your sense of morality. We must build shrines for women like you, who display publicly the tender motherly gift of breastfeeding. Reason is simple: the baby will grow up to be gentle when nursed from the motherly milk under the auspices of men. After all, men once were babies. Are we less loving than animals? Worse, have we become so puritans that we are ashamed to display such a sublime act of loving? Bottled milk raises wolves, breast milk raises angels. Just look at me, how nice and gentle I am, thanks to having had been nursed by many women in my village. And that is why I hold no grudge against anyone, except a deep despise for the neo-cons and tyrants.

--If all fail, we must be consoled by the AAA (Alcohol Anonymous Association) report. Yes, 40,000 of us annually meet their death and three millions become injured. What a way to slow down the human insanity. Thank you, Henry Ford; you have given us the ultimate medicine for our most stubborn disease- passion for speed. You have primarily invented your vehicle to move us from one point to another. And here you are moving us so fast from the world of the living to that of the dead. What a success story! Please, Sir, don't feel guilty; it is a race and some of us want to arrive first at all cost. How foolish they must be.

A KISS FROM A REPTILE

8/ 6, 2003

Today I posted this sign on my house door: "Writing is in progress, please don't disturb."

While plunged in the thought of how man has become so irrelevant to man, I heard a harsh knock. I tried to ignore it, but the knock persisted. Definitely, he is the one; he might be in a worse situation than yesterday, I said to myself. I pulled up the Persian shade, opened the window and shouted through the dusty screen: "Who is out there?"

"Me," said Gary in a feeble voice. In the past his voice was strong and assertive. I stopped writing and rolled down the narrow stairways.

"What's the matter, Gary; don't you know how to read a sign?"I spoke harshly.

He uncovered his left arm and calmly said, "Look at this birthmark."

"What happened, has an enraged dog attacked you?"I asked with some compassion. I even felt guilty for having been so rude to him.

"No. It's just a kiss from a reptile... I had approached that big alligator, thinking I could take it by surprise. I needed a kill, I was hungry. Quickly it jumped and grabbed my arm. We wrestled for a good while. I shouted for help; no one was there to help. Finally I decided to bite its neck. It was the only way to free my arm. The alligator ran into the lake and I started digging the ground, I needed to stop the bleeding. Yes, my friend, dirt is a cure, a great cure; it is even more effective than the Mease Hospital emergency room. Dirt didn't cost me a penny, just a knife stab into the heart of the ground ... I really wanted to kill that damn alligator...Oh well; he who is willing to kill must be ready to be killed."

"Wise saying, Gary, but please next time do remember all creatures, small or big, get quite violent if they feel that their lives are endangered. I'm really starting to feel sorry for you."

"Save this sorry feeling, you need it more than I do. You have a woman controlling your life. No one controls mine; I am a free man... Yes, my friend, chasing a woman is a good thing until she catches you, then the good thing turns to be very, very bad." The silly Gary giggled like a happy baby.

"I don't understand."

"Simple, when you chase a woman, you're a player; but once she catches you, you're a dead duck." He let out a malicious smile to add, "Just think of your own situation... Man, every time I look at you, I feel how lucky I am."

"Well, Gary, I'm glad to see you in such a great spirit and nothing else must matter."

"Yes, something else matters, you're my friend, and I want to see you real happy."

"Gary, do you think you have a happy life?"

"It is as good as can be."

"No regrets whatsoever?"

"I have none. I am my own boss; no one controls my life. Yours is in the hand of any female that wears a tight skirt. Yes, every step of your damn life is drawn by the hand of a woman. For me, only the wind is my companions... man, get a grip on your life."

Deep inside, I found myself drawn to Gary's philosophy of total self- surrender to the wind. Nostalgically I remembered the admirable words of the Spanish Poet, Antonio Mancha: "Camino no hay Camino, al andar se hace el camino – I walk there is no path, I create the path as I walk."

I went into the kitchen to prepare a sandwich for Gary. I gave it to him wrapped in a napkin and said: "We must separate now; I need to finish up my today's writing."

"I, too, have a mission to accomplish, I must do something stupid to be arrested… it has been too long since I had left college," -Prison in his language.

"Let it be, if that's the desire of your heart, goodbye, Gary."

"Just give me one extra moment of your precious time, great thinker of the Del Oro Groves Estates (our neighborhood). I simply wanted to tell you that last night I've found myself drawn to a brother of yours. The nigger and I spent great deal of time, sharing some good and bad experiences of our lives. Finally we've agreed that the secret to happiness is to be free from all laws… screw society."

"Don't be surprised, if society will screw you, it's a mutual feeling of indifference."

"Well, it's our constitutional right to pursue happiness or misery."

"True, now we must go our separate ways."

"Goodbye, you know where you can find me, if ever you need to talk… Yes, I still have no hard feelings toward the jungle nor its wildlife; I even look forward to another encounter with the alligator that had left me with this big kiss…Go, go back to your papers and ink, but do remember the world is full of two things: shit and papers. I use tree leaves to wipe my shit, you use papers and that is the only difference between us… No big deal; still we have this thing in common… shit."

"Goodbye, Gary, and say hello to the alligator that almost ate you alive."

"You, too, say hello to Marla, the alligator that is eating you up slowly but surely."

Thanks, Gary, for the entertainment, I needed it as much as you did. And from now on, please try to read the signs on doors.

"And you, too, don't forget to read the signs of time." He walked away firing a loud laughter into the air.

MAY GOD BLESS OUR CHILDREN

8/ 9, 2003

I woke up at 3 a.m. to get ready to welcome the arrival of the first caravan of my children, scheduled to arrive at four at the Tampa international Airport. I ran to embrace Tameri and Nailah. They looked healthy and happy.

"Good to see you, Dad," was their expression as the ritual of embracing ended. Truly it was a moving moment. We went home to wake up Amon to take breakfast at our favorite IHOP (International House of Pancakes) restaurant located on U.S.19. Soon as we sat, a familiar server female came to our table. With big smile she said: "May God bless them, your children are growing wonderfully; I've been watching them since they were little." She looked genuinely happy to see them.

"That's the effect of time; it makes the small big and the big small."

"Well, you, too, still are looking good," she complimented and that instantly increased her tip by 50 percent. We ate our breakfast in the mist of joyous laughers forgetting, for a moment, our life's trials. Who, anyway, could be exempted from them as we journey through its unpredictable surprises?

After breakfast we returned home to crash in our beds until the hour of 3 p.m. We had to get ready to return to Tampa International to welcome Nafré and her son Takaya; scheduled to arrive from Barbados at 4 p.m. Since we did not make it on time to welcome them at the gate, we went straight to the luggage platform to wait for them at the foot of the electric escalator.

Soon as Nafré and Takaya appeared; an emotional Nailah shouted their names while bouncing up and down with loud giggles that got the attention of the many.

"No doubt twins share one soul that inhabits two bodies," I said to soften up the unfriendly looks of a woman, who seemed to have had been annoyed by Nailah's uncontrolled excitement. The middle aged- woman smiled and I felt a certain self-gratification, I have succeeded to turn her disgust into a light smile.

Soon as we arrived home, Nafré opened a luggage and said; "Here, dad, this is a small gift for you." It was a straw box containing Barbados cherries.

We chatted for a good while. Afterwards, Tameri took the motherly task to prepare an elaborated early dinner for all. As we sat around the dining table at seven for dinner, the dull walls became bright again; the spirit of the family had penetrated them. I've felt great joy as my children ate in uninterrupted giggles.

"I wish if Ammo (uncle) Femi were here," said Takaya in a sad tone.

"Ammo Femi will be here tomorrow and then our family will be complete," mother consoled him.

"Mom, how much do you like Ammo Femi?"

"A lot..."

"Why?"

"He is my brother."

"Mom, are you going to make for me a brother?"

"Why?"

I, too, need a brother to love," replied Takaya without hesitation.

I then remembered the sad story of a murderous Cain... How he has missed all the joys of having had a brother to love. Ah jealousy, it takes away from us the true joys of life to plunge our hearts in the deepest of sorrows. Well, I might have done a better job than Adam. This thought gradually grew within me as I observed the great love that bonded my children. It was God's grace bountifully shed upon us.

NOSTALGIC

8/ 10-19, 2003

Finally the impatiently awaited tomorrow has come. The whole family went to Tampa Airport to welcome Babafemi arriving at 9:30 p.m. The plane came a bit late. Soon as he saw us, his arms spread wide like the wings of a young eagle. Marla and son Javier were then in their native Colombia to spend a few days with her gravely ill sister Carolina.

"Here this is for you," said Nafré, presenting a bouquet of gardenias to a smiling brother.

"Are those from our father's garden?" Babafemi asked with nostalgia as he detached himself from the arms of the Queen Sister to smell their strong aroma.

"Yes, they're."

"Blessed are the laboring hands of our father."

"Dad also has planted eggplants, cucumbers, tomatoes, zucchini and watermelon. They are quite healthy because of dad's hard work," proudly reported Nailah.

"Wow! Our father has become a true farmer. It's a good thing to plant one's own food," commented Babafemi, the vegetarian.

Suddenly I became aware that his hair has noticeably receded. Ah, the pass of time! I then recalled the moment when I saw, for the first time, his hairy head. To hide the crime of time, he has created a hairdo that was slightly successful covering up his balding forehead. Soon as we arrived to our white house, he noticed that missing loquat tree (we had six of them). In a saddened voice, he asked, "dad, where is she?" He called it a she in association with his mother. Yes, that tree had given him a second chance to life as mother had given him the first. A decade ago, he had fallen off the second floor as he was painting the house. Having landed on its branches, he came out unharmed.

"Well, son, insects ate its trunk; I had no other choice but to pull it out."

Tears escaped our eyes.

"Darn it! Time is more damaging than I ever thought. It has taken away my mother, my hair and my tree."

Tears escaped our eyes.

To cheer everyone up, Babafemi promptly added, "Thank God, you are still here, dad... you look good, man.

It seems that the gods have injected their blood within your body so that the pass of time leaves the minimum effect on you. For that we all must rejoice." He turned toward his siblings and nephew to ask: "how does the Abdou tree feel about its trunk?"

"Apart from his colored gray hair, dad is still the same since I've known him for over three decades now," replied Tameri, the eldest. Although I rejoiced for my apparent endurance, deep inside I knew it was a mere vain flattery; we are horses that cannot get into the race without the mark of time, flagellation. Yes, time is a painful but necessary whip as we race for wisdom, the only virtue that outlasts time.

"Hurray, Grandpa is not going to die soon. I need him to stay alive so he can buy me a car when I grow up," shouted Takaya the pragmatist. The reason behind Takaya's wish for my longevity was anything but flattering. It made me even praise the work of time, destructive as it may be. Early the next morning, I heard a repeated knock on the closed door of my bedroom. Quickly I sucked in the few drops of the bottled alpine spring water. That did some good to my throat; no longer did it squeak, and I answered:

"Who is that?"

"Me, grandpa, let's play ping pong."

I opened the door to contain Takaya for a moment between my arms.

"Did you have a good night sleep?"

"Yes. Grandpa, let's go play."

We went to the Florida room where the ping pong table stood enduring; in spite has been often used as a playground for capricious squirrels.

"Hurray! Hurray!" Takaya shouted as the wildly hit ball zoomed through the curly white short hair of my skull. It was a random shot celebrating a game he had just won. I was happy to see my grandchild a winner. I embraced him and pulled a dollar that was stored in one of my pajama pockets to rest it on his right hand.

"What's for, grandpa?" asked Takaya, a bit surprised.

"A reward for your winning," I replied smiling. Yes, grandson, a job well done must be rewarded." I wanted to be that proud grandpa celebrating his grandson's small victory. After all, the greatest victory is made of a series of small victories.

"Thanks, grandpa, I will win all the games I play with you," said he in a victorious tone.

"May you win the ultimate game of life," I murmured and then hugged him.

After a long day of excitement and storytelling about our separate lives, finally, at 10 p. m., we retired. I spent a few minutes watching the stars from our sundeck. The mosquitoes were then quite active; but the gentleness of the shining stars and the warm memories of the family made me forget and forgive their pinches.

Next day, after breakfast we visited an American landmark, Sam's Club. There we shopped for cheaper food with a relatively good quality. We even bought a guitar for Amon. A guitar and plentiful food make a good melody of life. O God, how I miss the flute; with it comes the freedom of skipping the hills with the herds of sheep and goats while chasing the wolves that endanger their lives. Nostalgically I remembered the home of my childhood, especially that scene of my father herding his into the barn for the night. And they say that only laughter and speech are man's distinctive characteristics from animals, and nostalgia I must add.

Between the 11th and the 19th, the Abdous took every opportunity to enjoy themselves. We frequented the local cafés of Pinellas County and made our presence quite visible to the goers of the Clearwater Beach. My children took advantage of the evenings to visit their old friends. It was a time for me to reflect and savor the joy of being the father of such great children. I was extremely thankful to the forces that surrounded and governed our lives, in spite of all its tragedies. I was grateful for having the opportunity of raising them in America, despite my persistent displeasure of the invasion of Iraq. True, America is not the land of angels, still it is a great country to live in; many lands are infested with villains, thugs and despots. May God bless America!

GOD HAS NO RELIGION

8/20, 2003

As we returned home, after saying tearful goodbyes to the Abdou's young ladies, the left behind three males of the family sat face- to- face in a tribunal format for breakfast. Amon and I sat on one side of the round dining table and Babafemi sat on the opposite side. Suddenly the eldest began questioning his youngest: "Tell me, brother, do you believe in God?"

"Well, and what's the reason anyone could have for not believing in Him?" answered Amon with the blind faith his ultra-religious mother had breastfed him.

"Brother, it's a fine thing that you believe in God. I, too, do believe in one; not the same as yours though…" Babafemi stopped for a moment to reflect, and then explained: "a real God must manifest Himself to man's physical as well as to his spiritual reality. However, history has proven more than once that Christians are full of violence… just think of the Crusaders and modern Christianity, exactly right now, who is invading an Arabic county?"

"Son, one must separate the content of any religion from the ugly behavior of its followers," thus I interfered.

"True, dad, it's a big mistake to hang onto a Jewish, Christian or a Muslim God. Like a spider webs, the human conscience keeps up spinning, gradually moving toward universality. It's the law of life. Ultimately, we will have a solid God whom no external force can destroy. If we all could share this conviction, it will be no more devastating wars to satisfy the human greed for money. Yes, if man rejects this false god, humanity will become a giant tree on which all birds of heavens gather to sing to the Ultimate Creator, the universal conscience, the one and only song, the song of peace," thus Babafemi philosophized.

"Son, war has its deepest roots in man's desire to impose his own will upon others and that's treason against oneself... I mean man's ultimate task is to dominate himself and not his brother. It's a matter of looking inwards rather than outwards. A fulfilled self is the only force capable to prepare the coming of the true God, the One who embraces all," thus I presented my own philosophical jargons.

"Well said, Father. And you, young brother; in whom must you ultimately put your trust to safeguard your walk in this dangerous jungle called today's world?"

"I put my trust in God," firmly replied Amon for whom God is above any other self.

"No, no, brother, we should put our trust in our ancestors. I have faith in my mother, my father, in the big giant one called Abdou, who had lived a hundred years ago.... ultimately this faith culminates in me and you. Yes, brother, we are but the extension of our ancestors and the land they had inhabited... That's the god we must seek and trust; other gods create deadly divisions amongst brothers... well, little brother, you are excused; you haven't reached the age of reason yet."

"True, Son. As we grow older, we gain a better understanding of life."

I opened: *"Le petit poche de philosophie"* to read and translate to my children the following sentence: "l'homme doit avoir juste assez de foi en lui – même pour avoir des aventures, et juste assez de doute de lui – même pour en jouir – one must have enough faith in himself to have adventures, and enough doubt of himself to enjoy them." (Revue Européenne 1942) G.K. Chesterton.

"Father, you're a well-educated man, and your enlightening opinion is well taken: Should man have a religion at all and if so, which of the traditional ones?" Babafemi asked, looking quite anxious to hear my answer.

"Son, the problem with all the world's religions is that each one reserves the truth and the whole truth for itself. We need to reflect a bit about the sad consequences of the Babylonian Tower. It was those men's dangerous search for the whole truth that led them to confusion... they should have accepted the ambiguous, the partial truth of their innocent childhood. It is man's pretentious appropriation of God that leads him to his own downfall."

"Well said, father...By the way, do you have the Qur'an?"

"Yes. I do have the Scriptures of the world's religions. In fact, I've a fair knowledge of them all."

"I want to learn about Islam so I could have a better understanding for Leila (his twenty two- year- old Palestinian girlfriend for the last three years). "You know, father, women do not turn easily my head, but Leila has just the right stuff… Some nights my eyes remain wide open, watching her dancing on the clouds… Father, do you know the classic Arabic story: "magnoun Leila, Crazy for Leila?""

"I understand you quite well, son. Your mother, too, was the only Leila for me. Since her death I searched for another Leila but haven't found one as yet… Maybe that's why I've been roaming many sentimental jungles."

"That is very sad, father. For me Leila is the one. However, there is this big problem: her parents will not approve of our union because I am not a Muslim. I told her that we must breed for the race and not for any religion. We both have the right stuff to have children who will advance our race." As Babafemi spoke, sparks of excitement flashed through his face. "…Strange, Leila's father is engineer who works for a company owned by a Jew." He stopped for a moment to add, "I guess only in America can one find his true identity… I mean to be race- blind, universal and all- embracing…But if a Palestinian can work for a Jew here in the good old USA that means Jews and Arabs can get along very well if they want to. Why can't they do the same over there?"

"Son, you have had already your answer."

What was the answer, dad?"

"They can get along very well if they want to." Isn't that what you have just said? Yes, they can; it's just a matter of goodwill and that is the key to true peace."

Babafemi opened his eyes wide, as if he has discovered the whole secret of life.

"Dad, you have made a great point. In fact, Leila and I have many Jewish friends. We both are race- blind and that is exactly what we all must pass to our children."

"Let's hope that your generation will bring to completion the peace initiative the few good- willed amongst our conflicted peoples had launched." I smiled but unaware of the reason behind my smile. I then stood and went upstairs to look for the copy of the Qur'an. A Pakistani accountant had given it to me, when, a few years ago, we had attended a lecture about Islam, delivered by the Indian- born minister of the Unitarian Church in Largo. I also brought along a copy of the Bible, containing the Old and New Testaments. With the Holy Scriptures resting against my chest, I rolled down the stairs. With big smile I handed them to Babafemi. He immediately returned them to me and said, "Here, dad, please write for me in Arabic something dear to your heart."

And I wrote: "dear son, 'do unto others as you would have them do unto you'. This is the ultimate criterion of all religions."

That's beautiful, dad, from now on I shall live by this mighty code of ethics. I will even preach it to Leila, so we could teach it to our children. Here, dad, write for me in Arabic the following: "Babafemi, follow the heart your father has given you."

I took back both Holy Scriptures and wrote in their first pages the desired expression. He looked so happy but suddenly there was long silence.

I also handled him a folded paper that read:

"Just keep in mind, son, God has no religion, rather a heart for all."

He smiled and stood to gently rest his head against my chest to whisper: "In daddy's heart I have found my God."

"Son, may your spiritual endeavor be not to have God in your heart, He is always there; rather may you work hard to be in His heart!"

To my great surprise, suddenly Babafemi looked sad.

"Son, you seem to have deep secret eating you up?" I asked with some anxiety.

"Well... I was thinking of my encounter with Ali in Egypt .We both were then eighteen. We had a lot in common and looked very much alike physically. We even could have easily passed as twins. We enjoyed so much being together until..." he sounded a bit tense.

"Until what, son, speak out, words have their healing power."

"I told you about it, don't you remember?"

"Not really, please do refresh my memory." I knew exactly what he was alluding to; I just wanted him to retell the story that has deeply scarred him.

Taking a long breath he said: "...until Ali asked this silly question: 'are you Muslim or Christian?' I replied: "If the fact that we are both Egyptians is not good enough for you to be friends; then we have nothing to say to each other. I stood and walked away without even saying goodbye to him." Babafemi spoke with the mixed feelings of anger and regret. "...I really miss Ali," he added.

"I am sure he, too, misses you. However, I must say, both have been a bit careless."

"How is that, dad?''

"Well, have you been tolerant of each other's way of looking at the world, you could have been friends for life, and Egypt would have been proud of you. Apparently Ali has found his identity in religion and you in patriotism. Neither has been wrong, nor has been right, just you haven't made enough effort to understand each other. It was a lack of tolerance on the part of both and that where the carelessness lies. But don't worry;

there was no malice, just short-sightedness that time will correct."

"Please, dad, elaborate."

"Whatever one values most, one must look at it as a flower. To save the flower, one must accept, or at least, tolerate the thorns surrounding it. Your differences were those thorns, but you have forgotten that thorns are needed to protect the flower and keep its fragrance fresh. Both you were negligent for not having deeply understood what you were cherishing most; respectively Islam and County."

"Wow! That makes great sense, dad."

"Well, I am glad you didn't say goodbye to each other, because you remain always bound thanks to the mysterious power of patriotism. The fatherland is a powerful source of positive energy."

"Wish I could see Ali again."

One could have easily detected sincere remorse in Babafemi's voice.

"Well, son, any shortcoming can be redeemed so long we learn a positive lesson from it."

"Thanks, dad; it is always great enlightenment and pleasure talking to you."

"Welcome, Son, just keep the faith alive."

"I certainly will."

Nietzsche could not have been more right when he wrote: "quand on a la foi, on peut se passer de la vérité – when one has faith, one can overlook the truth."- The little truth of the mind I must clarify.

During the course of the painful conversation that had dealt mainly with Babafemi's emotional and intellectual anxieties, Amon listened attentively and delightfully as if he were having an intellectual gourmet meal paid by the courtesy of the years of his father and big brother. After that tedious and long philosophical discussion, we crashed on the floor. While lying down, bewilderment and nostalgia overwhelmed me. I bewildered why our house of joy had turned into a territory of painful thoughts. I remembered those fresh memories when my daughters were there, and how they had filled the house with joy and laughter; legitimate children of the heart. How torturous the intellect can be! It is the heart that ultimately leads to peace, heaven; the mind is a one-way ticket to conflict, to hell. Yes, wars are born from the thoughts of shrewd Politicians, and executed by blindfold generals. I prefer being a wanderer in a jungle, searching to befriend its ferocious animals, than being a general in a battlefield, commanding my men to kill our enemies.

TAKEN CAPTIVE

8/26, 2003

The USA forces have captured TahaYassin, Saddam's Vice President. What a victory for the Bush Administration! Finally a big fly has landed into the hungry mouth of the King of the jungle. The President stopped swinging his golf bat to joyfully shout: "We will continue to haunt them and bring them to justice one by one."

--Not all news was good for the self-anointing savior of the world; the roadmap to peace was thrown into the flames of violence as a Palestinian bomber has exploded himself in a bus in Jerusalem. Most of the passengers were Orthodox Jews coming from their Shabbat prayers at the Wailing Wall. Twenty people were killed; the youngest was a two months old baby. Over eighty were wounded; some of them have suffered serious injuries. O Jerusalem, city of the abundantly shed blood; have mercy on your confused children. They are all convinced to have the exclusive right to your motherly breasts. Why can't they understand that love can be shared without loss?

As usual, the Hamas militia claimed that the attack was to revenge the killing of one of their leaders. Other Palestinian factions gave a broader reason: The continuous Jewish occupation of our land leave no room for us but to fight the occupiers. And the cycle of violence goes round and round and they all fall down. Whatever may be the reason(s) presented by the conflicting parties, I give one word of advice: Peace. Yes, peace is the least costly and most beneficial to all. Palestinians and Israelis, you need to grow up. Till then, you will continue to act as restless adolescents.

"My wish to the U N is to continue its humanitarian work in Iraq," those where the last words of Sergio Viera de Mello, the U N top representative in Baghdad. He was one of those seventeen victims killed today on an attack carried against the international organization. Indeed, what the Israelis and Palestinians need is the heart of Sergio Viera de Mello of the UN.

LORD, YOU GAVE US TEN, MAY I ADD ONE?

8/ 27, 2003

I watched the Chief Justice of Alabama, Ray Moore, standing behind a pile of flowers that surrounded the 2.5 ton monument on which are inscribed the Ten Commandments.

"Lord, remember the covenant you have made with your people," wearily prayed the clown. Having rested his head, for a moment, against the monument's cool marble, he raised it to discourse: "I will not remove from the yard of my court the Ten Commandments that acknowledge God as the foundation of my nation. It will be an intended act of treason I'm not ready to commit. The Supreme Court's order to remove the Ten Commandments is a sad decision in the history of our country, and we must defy it in the name of our Lord..." Deafening applauses mixed with the shouting: "Jesus is the Lord! Jesus is the Lord!"

Chief, you have nosed out the secular authority. Do you not believe in St. Paul's teaching that commands obedience to all authorities, religious be or secular? Judge, you're less than a godly man, you have ridiculed what you have pretended to revere. You must remember that true reverence comes through a heartfelt obedience to the heavenly and earthly laws, and not through a public display of false pity. You are a good clown and a successful mass agitator and for that the Lord has deserted your heart. His Honor, if you cannot submit to the laws of the land, I recommend you spend some time in one of Alabama's numerous jungles. There the wild might succeed training you on how to obey the communal laws. I warn you though; the training will be long and tedious. However, it will benefit you greatly in case you would decide to join the lawful society, afterwards. Truly, chief, you are a fox that roams the jungles of Georgia. I know you are howling for a seat in its Senate Chamber, or maybe a- soon- occupation of the Governor' Mansion. If you are honest enough about it, I would be willing to impregnate a redheaded Georgian woman to procreate a dummy, who will vote for you in whatever capacity your ambition might lead you to. Until then, meaning: until you are governed by genuine honesty, shut up, take a hike and let the Constitution be. It's God and the people's will that must prevail over yours. You and your neo-cons, by mocking the millions of us, who do not share your religious convictions, have mocked the same God you claim to honor. How would you react if the statue of Buddha, Moses or Mohamed were to be looking upon your court? Would you not protest? Certainly you would, because it is the god of the others. Why then do you push your beliefs into our throats? Ah! How the power of the Jordanian River has greatly diminished; had Jesus not plunged Himself deep enough into the cold river?! Has He not shed enough of his blood?

Agitator of the masses, if the blood of Jesus is unable to cleanse your heart, a dive in the holy Ganges River in India might. Chief, allow me to remind you of your oath to justly apply the laws of the land. If this is not convincing, allow me to remind you of the eleventh commandment: Thou shall not get on the nerves of others to promote your personal beliefs. Indeed, some of us are great dividers and that is why the planet is dying. What is next for a site of destruction, heaven, perhaps?! Could it be that the gods are so naive to allow themselves be manipulated by brutes? How I dream of the day when the Western man accepts to be just a human. Otherwise, his complex of superiority might force history to declare his irrelevance. Moore, you are not the noble Gandhi of India, you are serving no higher cause other than yours, and many are your naive followers. I shall blow fire and pray not for your salvation; only the fire blown from the mouth of a dragon can redeem your hypocrisy. A reminder: I am, too, a Christian but of a breed different than yours. I pray to my God in the darkness of the night; you parade in the light of the day in the hope to be seen by the God whose existence you doubt. Woe to you all the religious fanatics! A true God is the one who fills the depth of the seas and the crevices of the valleys and mountains. He cannot confine Himself to a monument in front of a Georgian court and still be the God He is. Your desire to confine Him in such a small space is your hidden desire to negate His divinity that contains all and can't be contained by any. In confining Him to 2.5 ton monument, you are caging Him as if He were a bird to sing whenever your heart's itches arise. Chief, may you remember that the human heart is the safest and most sacred place to welcome the true living God!

IS AMERICA MARCHING FAST TO HELL?

8/28, 2003

--**Oh** godly people, march fast to hell. In Milwaukee, a Pastor of a small church has brutalized an eight -year-old boy. Mother held her child's feet and hands while the Pastor sat on his chest to cast, what he called, "the evil spirit,"- simply because the poor kid had failed to memorize the biblical verses assigned to him. The spirit was forced to leave prematurely his body; it could not survive the madness of this crazy world. So quickly the murderers surrounded the dead body with flowers of many colors. Men of God, you are well- trained murderers and the stubborn devil that lives within you is so conning. Rest assured, God will not be conned by your flowers and only the damnation of your souls will serve His justice.

-- In the Windy City, Chicago, a dismissed Latino employee has entered the warehouse supplies company and killed six coworkers-the boss and owner of the company arrived late that day. I am sure the assassin's only regret was having not been able to kill those two men who had fired him. - -Regretfully, I must submit my request to those foolish scientists who are working day and night to slow down the process of human aging. Please do disregard my desire for longevity; I am reserving a seat in the first rocket leaving this mad planet. Thanks for the consideration.

--Well, why picking on small people and places. Let me report about the state of crimes in our great nation. I copy the headline in the Saint Petersburg Times- Monday, Aug 25, 2003:

Crime rate drops again.

"Summary: crime at a glance (type of crimes and number of victims in the United States in 2001 and 2002, according to the Bureau of Justice Statistics."

Type of Crime	2001	2002
Violent Crimes	5,743,820	5,341,410
Rape/Sexual Assault	248,250	247,730
Robbery	630,690	512,490
Assault (aggravated/simple)	4,864,880	4,581,200
Property Crimes	18,283,510	17,539,230
Household Burglary	3,139,700	3,005,720
Motor Vehicle Theft	1,008,720	988,760

Notice: The above statistics represented only the reported crimes. If you consider the sense of shame, fear, negligence and laziness to report all the committed crimes, the above numbers would increase drastically. Now, America, could you please restrain yourself sending to many nations your smart bombs that penetrate their peepholes, all in the name of liberating them. Why can't you pay more attention to what is going on at home? Precision! Precision!

Is the end of the world a lot closer than anyone would have ever imagined? A loner fifteen- century visionary called Nostradamus has burned most of his numerous volumes that had foreseen man's uncontrollable madness. It was too much for his spirit that had often left his body. Thank you, Nostradamus, for having not told it all to us. Even your Hisler (so he called Hitler in his prophecy on World War 11) would have collapsed of depression had he foreseen it all coming.

Dear America, it is admirable that you want to share your freedom with others. However, the spreading of crimes in every stratum of our lives makes others rightfully question the value of this freedom you so desire to transport to them. Let's not overlook the saying: "charity starts at home."

THE EXECUTIONER'S EXECUTION

9/ 3, 2003

Today marked the execution of Paul Hill, a Presbyterian minister who, in 1994, had killed Dr. John Bayard Britton, his escort John Barrett, and had severely wounded the doctor's wife thus leaving her with a life in solitary confinement. Let me frankly confess that the act of execution was for me the bright side of the news. The sad part was that the killer has shown no remorse whatsoever. On the contrary, he has declared to the whole world that the killing of the unbelievers is a chariot ornamented with red flowers that will lead him to the arms of the heavenly Father. What a deformation of the image of a loving God. Delusional, let me ask you this simple question: How could you claim to love a father whose children you have murdered in cold blood?! You have said, "I'm expecting great reward in heaven for my obedience to the Lord's word." It's madness, rather than obedience that drove you to kill God's children. By killing two of His children, you have killed God twice. Dead pastor, rest assured you were not echoing God's voice or reflecting any of His divine qualities. Just remember, He did not get rid of Adam and Eve, who dreamt of equality to Him. Rather, after their fall, He sent a Savior to redeem, by the shedding of the blood of His only Son, their illusion of grandeur. Pastor, you have installed yourself on the divine throne to judge others, forgetting that only God can be the judge. By the way, what did you ask before you took your last gasp? If I am not mistaken: it was a big chunk of red meat, a sweet potato and vegetable salad. You have not even abdicated the request of an apple pie for dessert. That was your hidden desire to take earth along with you, apparently being uncertain of your dreamed destination. Yes, deep inside, heaven for you was but a dream garden where your maniac illusions strolled swiftly. Well, it is not my goal to negate heaven and give a greater legitimacy to earth; both are reflections of our true selves. Religious vipers, shed off your thick skin, then you will feel the tenderness of earth. Wolves you are born to this planet and wolves you will depart from it so may its valleys become safe for us, the lambs. We must continue grazing joyfully in the pastures of this mighty delightful and intriguing planet. By losing respect for earth, you have vomited heaven. You dream of heaven, forgetting that hell is its other side. Ah! How can you live your lives masked in such a thick hypocrisy? God forgives all sins, except that of hypocrisy. Reason is simple: all sins are born out of weakness; hypocrisy is a crime of stubborn conning. It inevitably leads to the following interpretation: I'm so smart to the point I can ruse my way to overthrow God and install myself King of earth and heaven.

Like Martin L. King, I, too, have a dream. Yes, I have a dream that one day the Western man will join the human caravan in its tedious march toward humility, the greatest of all virtues. Arrogance is eating him up, thus leaving him as a skeleton full of crevices where worms and serpents lurk. He must start developing a taste for God's grandeur, shown through a genuine respect to the diversity of His creation. This can happen only when he renounces his own false grandeur.

Dead Reverend, I certainly don't, and will not, miss your lengthy homilies about the fellowship of men and the love of God for all. You have uttered empty words to fill in, unsuccessfully, the deep hole of doubt in your heart. On the contrary, I miss that Pizza Hut deliveryman, who had received a bomb strapped around his neck instead of a tip.

O Lord, help me to have respect for mother earth and all its inhabitants of different races and creeds. I firmly believe we all are dear to your fatherly heart.

RETURN OF THE WEARY PRODIGAL

9/ 4, 2003

Today marks the humbled return of America to the organization of the United Nations. Before the break of war, a few months ago, the Bush Administration had propagated the notion of the irrelevance of that International Organization. It was a crime of arrogance born in Washington and raised by the great al Rushbo (Rush Limbaugh) and other smaller conservative talk show hosts.

Unfortunately, Bush's return to the United Nations with strings and conditions still has demonstrated unskillful, if not insulting, diplomacy. He wanted other nations to contribute with money and manpower without any serious concessions to them, political be or economical. Yes, his ultimate intention was to guarantee the whole pie for the American big companies, through the reconstruction of the devastated country. Oh you who hunger for money, I am not willing to sacrifice a cat for your wealth. If you are so consumed by the love of money, then be ready to pay the ultimate price, the blood of your own sons and daughters. To fill in your- ever- empty wallets, you cry for more accurate bullets and certainly fresh roses as a token of your sympathy for those whom you would have sacrificed on the altar of your greed. I dismiss your false sympathy. It's your conning way to appease the anger of the living, without failing to assault the dead by showing them false respect.

Before invading Iraq we had a few enemies in the Middle East. With the war we have turned the Arab masses against us. I have intentionally excluded their governments, they are but tyrant puppets. Besides oppressing their peoples, they don't represent their constituents' true sentiments, convictions and interests.

Let's promise ourselves never again will we deliver our great America to the hands of men of myopic vision. Short lives the victory assured by the might of arms, and tedious is the path that wins the hearts of men. America must get philosophical and not physical with the world. We must be vigilant enough to defend ourselves from our enemies abroad and at home. However, we must not put any longer our nation in the hands of those who adopt the dangerous doctrine that we are entitled to stick our noses in the other nations' affairs. Such a policy is ultimately designed for materialistic gains. Their insistence to convince us that we had invaded Iraq to liberate its people is a poisonous lie sugar coated by the notion of freedom for all. I firmly believe that freedom has a self- generating power. We must not forget that authentic freedom is a gift from

God to man. Is there anyone who can give such a precious gift more generously and graciously than He? I know our President had often rattled words in this line. However, in the same breath, he implied that we are the executors of God's will before all peoples. I accept the fallacy, but let's not forget that no seed can grow on rocks. We must first prepare the terrain, the human heart and then sow the seeds. Freedom is a heavenly gift to be received and not an earthy shot to be injected. Could it be that we are ultimately the executioners, rather the executors, of His will?!

Bush's agenda is far more dangerous. Besides catering to the greedy business community, he wanted to impose his religious beliefs on the rest of the world, an order he had received from the far religious right, a group of mad zealots, who declare that governing according to Jesus' law is the only way to save a world drowning in evil. Being a Christian myself, I initially responded well to this doctrine. However, soon as reason took over, I become obliged to profess that Jesus has many masks through which He manifests Himself to the world. He will ultimately bring all to Himself through His magical power of love; hence, there is no reason to worry about the fate of His kingdom on earth. I must warn the fanatics of all religions: you're not delivering God to the world; rather your bombs of hate and destruction. To redeem your madness, I declare today my determination to become the fox that digs deeper his hole to overcome this violent rapture you're working hard to hasten. Contrary to your belief, I need to take a solid grip on earth to insure myself a safe departure to heaven.

DIVISIVE

9/6, 2003

In the September issue of the Floridian Catholic newspaper I read Mindy Rubenstein's article titled: *Interfaith Panel discusses God, war and working together to fix the world.*

The NCCJ (the National Council for Community and Justice) had held this symposium on August the 27th. Before I offer my congratulations to, or criticize those so- called godly men, let's report how they proceeded. Every one of the four panelists spoke for thirty minutes about the uniqueness of his faith- mainly at the expenses of the other religions and denominations. At the end, the panelists took questions from the audience and defended their faith against the accusations made by the other representatives.

"Terrorism and war is the legacy of the Islamic faith," with those words Rabbi Basemen has raised his red flag.

"Terrorists use often the name of Islam as a way to justify their acts of evil. However, we must not forget that

Christianity and Judaism, too, had a history of no lesser terror." answered Dr. Sultan, the Pakistani.

Dr. Francis Dukes. Dubos, a Hungarian Holocaust survivor and a dear friend of mine raised this question: "Who killed Jesus?"

"Jews and Gentiles together had a hand in the killing," replied Fr. Bernard, the Catholic representative, as a public admission of guilt for all what have happened to Jews because of the long- sustained church's teaching that they, the Jews, were Jesus' killers. The priest was echoing the reconciliatory tone of the Holy Father, John Paul 11.

"We must call it flatly a historical crime because of the gruesome crimes that had been and still continue to be committed against Jews under the umbrella of that erroneous teaching," thus responded Rabbi Basemen.

The Lutheran Pastor James, fishing in the troubled water, declared: "To avoid damnation of others, we Lutherans draw our teaching from the Holy Scriptures and not from the mouth of one man." Certainly he was attacking the papal authority.

And the exchange of the attacks continued to poison the air. In the end, the host Rabbi Basemen, taking a reconciliatory tone, uncovered the ark to reveal the Torah scroll. It was a clever thing to do. After all, the five books of Moses have motherly nourished Judaism, Christianity and Islam.

Holy men, keep on anointing your faces with the oil of rightfulness and righteousness, and let the rest of us suffer our guilt and yours. Dividers, should we expect that one day you will be standing on mountaintops to shout: our superiority is worthier than the peace that dominates the valley, where the gentle sheep teaches its cubs how to walk gracefully?! I found no sheep amongst you; you all were wolves with old rotten teeth. You are not worthy to speak of the valley, rather speak of your natural habitat, the jungle.

Dogmatically speaking, I see no difference between the three monotheistic religions, rather different emphasizes on how to approach the one God they all profess. While Judaism and Islam have put a heavy weight on justice, Christianity has put greater emphasis on love. But justice and love are not contradictory rather complimentary virtues, meaning: the one can't withstand without the other. Justice without love is tyranny in disguise, and love without justice is anarchy in display. Can a true God be a tyrant or demagogue?! In sum: all the three traditional religions entail the virtues of justice and love, with variance degree of emphasis. In denying this factual truth to one another they end up destroying what they claim to hold dear, meaning: God. Unfortunately, their religious leaders continue to declare themselves, with great arrogance, to be the sole messengers of God's heart and mind. In so doing, they end up distorting the message they have claimed to deliver. If the worldly shepherds commit such a devastating negligence, their sheep would end up in the wolves' stomachs. May God have mercy on you all! In my humble opinion, you all deserved a

Grammy award for a poorly played religious drama.

The circus came to its closing when the panelists joined hands and silently prayed.

I must remind you that you were praying to the same God, the God you are constantly preying on. Yes, He is still alive and well, in spite your wolfish teeth have been and will be grinding up His heart. Only He can restore your morally bankrupted hearts. Shame on you, the so- called men of God! You couldn't spend thirty minutes in His presence without showing off the superiority of your faiths. Allow me to bring to your attention this humbling thought:

"Brotherhood can never exist unless all religions are willing to completely divest themselves of all ecclesiastic authority and fully surrender all concept of spiritual sovereignty." The Urantia Book (134:4.4)

Pardon me; I am just an agitated, confused and frightened observer. May He pour out tranquility, serenity and security into my heart and the hearts of all those who seek Him in sincerity and modesty.

.

TEARS OF THE TOWERS

9/ 11, 2003

Today marks the second anniversary of the Twin Towers' destruction. Hundreds of thousands gathered at the site to remember the dead. This heinous crime has shattered not only steel and concrete but also hearts and dreams; it deserves the condemnation of the whole world.

"I miss you, daddy," read the sign of one child.

"I remember I used to ride on daddy's shoulders," read the sign of a second.

The photo of a killed mother, attached to the carriage of her baby boy, spoke to my heart more than the tears of all the mourners. Observing him, for a moment, sucking the milk from his bottle, he transported me to the seventh heaven, to the breasts of my own mother. For both, it was a feeling of tenderness mixed with the sorrow of a lost paradise.

"Why can't peoples celebrate love instead of hatred? Aren't we all nurtured by our mothers, or have some of us been nursed by the wolves?" I found myself mumbling.

-- Thanks to the army chaplain who closed his prayer at the Arlington National Cemetery with these words: "May we work to make this world safe for all."

Those words were a temporarily balsam that spread on the deep wound of my soul searching for safety in an unsafe world. However, the aggressive and stern voice of the military has so quickly silenced that tender voice.

-- The chairman of the Joint Chiefs of Staff, Richard Meyers expressed the belligerent instinct of the beast. "We can't let the enemy destroy what we stand for…"

I ran to the kitchen, grabbed an apple and began destroying it violently. No apology to the apple, it is the law of hunger; I am a human, a violent creature.

After consuming the apple, I threw myself into the most consuming fire: Donald Duck started speaking. As is typical of his speeches, the Secretary of Defense spoke with assertiveness and arrogance. Conning politics overshadowed his arrogance as he praised the sacrifices of his armies. "A military is the one, who gives his life for a cause higher than himself,' thus he ended the brief speech.

Well said, Duck. But whose cause are you propagating? You aren't, in this case, asking the military to defend our country's honor. Rather, you are a leading force in promoting the fallacious and inhumane doctrine of preemptive war. You are no less of a mass agitator than Saddam. No wonder some dissident voices in Washington had called for your resignation; you are turning a country known by its civil government to a military regime. How could America preach freedom without being accused of tyranny! Yes, tyranny is the legitimate daughter of any preemptive war; just spend some time with history. Still, I am certain that America will remain the light of the world, in spite of an aggressive Donald, a myopic George and a delusional Dick. It is a government of a passing storm over "*a City upon a hill.*"

America, in your ups and downs we all have you in our hearts. We've seen your grandeur in the gentle soul of that gigantic man, who was shedding tears as dozens of children were reading the names of their parents killed in that barbaric attack. Our apology to you the dead, your beloved country will never forget you and may your precious blood redeem the arrogance of our present government.

A POOR STUDENT OF HISTORY

9/ 23/2003

King George has left Washington to New York; seeking help from the UN. Now the question to be asked: Why, Mr. President, have you bankrupted the U.S. policy? Your false sense of grandeur is killing not only Iraqis but also America's sons and daughters and those of other nations, whose leaders had decided to blindly follow your path of death. You and your conservative media had called wimps those who had opposed you. The day has come to bow before the mice you had crushed as you passed thus frightening all with your mighty roars. You have forgotten that sharing the jungle is the only way for the survival of all. Yes, I heard it:

114

you have asked the nations to unite in rebuilding Iraq. You had called your war a world's order; your opponents have called it a dangerous world mapping and I call it an attempt to Americanize history. A word or two of advice to you, Mr. President: History is the unrivaled power that leaves its marks on us. The only way we can leave our marks on history is to work within rather than outside of it. Read about the fate of Napoleon; Joseph Stalin; Mussolini; Hitler; and Saddam himself. In discarding history, you have added your name to the list of the unwise.

You wanted to improve the lot of the Iraqis, so you claimed, and you took the road of the barbarians to achieve your goal. Mr. President, war nowadays is a legalized violence, no matter what the reason(s) is/ are. Anyone claiming to reach peace through violence, by violence he will be repelled. For civilization to progress and not digress, man must engage in dialogue. In politics there are no deaf; only there are hard of hearing politicians. For those impaired, the civilized world must create hearing aids, clever diplomacy of patience and compassion. The whole Arabic world is tribal and dictatorial. Nations come to maturity according to the mental strength of their citizens. The road to true freedom starts when the oppressed begins to realize his oppression. Until this awareness is achieved, no voice is powerful enough to get their attention. We ride the modern means of transportation to move us from one point to another. However, to arrive to freedom, the desired destination, patience and understanding are imperatives, only those virtues can deliver true freedom to all.

Mr. President, it is irrational to destroy a whole country to get rid of its dictator. So doing, is like destroying a castle to kill a snake that lurks somewhere inside it. Yes, Saddam was that snake, why haven't you found a smarter way to kill the snake, meanwhile preserving the castle? Or was it your apathy for the castle and its inhabitants that had forced you to this criminal decision? To the lions of all jungles, I advise humility, because a dormant lion lies within every mouse, and lions must fear the awakening of the mice.

The question is not how long we can stand on our numbed feet before we start running again, rather; how well we have learned about the road as we stumbled. The back of the turtle is all what we need. True, the turtle is slow, but it knows the road better than all its travelers. Through its slow movements, it communicates with every inch of the road. In fact, its slowness carries within the road and a victorious arrival is to bring all the travelers to a safe destination. Mr. President, good luck asking for help, you had been acting like a restless adolescent. You had wrecked the car; you must accept the wage of a restless behavior. Let's hope that the first term will end your nightmarish presidency. There is no greater humiliation for a leader than to hear, through voting: we do not want your leadership any longer. In so doing, the people are loudly saying: You have come to us from the wilderness and to the wilderness we are sending you back for a job so poorly done.

And now that you are the biggest vulture in the jungle, fill it; many are the rotten victims. In case you would run out of illicit meat, eat your own tail; it is the last bite an unwise can taste under the auspices of history. Such a sour taste is a price paid for having not had been a good student and loyal steward of history.

It is the autumn in nature and it is the autumn in our nation. But soon spring will come to it. Then all its naked trees will flourish again, not only with new younger and stronger leaves, but also with matured fruits that will be tasteful enough on the tongues of all nations.

SAINTS AND FARCEURS

9/ 24, 2003

Race and creed divide men; still one common characteristic unite them: all are farceurs constantly playing tricks on one another.

Yesterday evening I watched the five finalist candidates who dream to replace the incompetent California's governor Greg Davis. It is thanks to similar clowns that the Golden State has become a muddy one. The candidates had already received the written questionnaires.

All claimed to have the right recipe to the State's many lingering problems. In fact, they have proven nothing but their ingenuity through plucking one another's feathers. To find the cause behind those attacks, one must retort to irony, just imagine five whores speaking of purity. And many thought that prostitution is the oldest profession! Yes, politics is the oldest. Let me remind you of the very first political debate: It took place in the Garden of Eden between the serpent and Eve. Look at our fate today: Most nations practice dirty politics. Let me substantiate by the following political event:

--The Syrian ambassador was at the CNN Studios to respond to the allegations of the spying activities attributed to a Syrian American sergeant in the Air Force in favor of his native country. He was then working as interpreter at the Guantanamo Base to facilitate the communication between the American military authority and the claimed al- Qaeda prisoners. The twenty years old sergeant was arrested for thirty counts against him. Having given baklava to the prisoners was one of them. Baklava is sweetness, the last thing the American military authority wanted to offer to a group of terrorists.

The Syrian ambassador has vehemently denied any tie between the accused and his government. I paraphrase the core of the interview:

It's impossible, according to some in our Congress that Ahmed al Halaby has acted alone, Miss. Costello, the program host, has challenged the ambassador.

Our country has a long tradition to raise our youth in the right path of life, he asserted emphatically. Those kind of false allegations are no news to us. Just a few months ago, your government had accused my country of giving refuge to many Baathists of the Saddam's regime. They are all still in Iraq. There are some elements in Washington who are trying hard to heighten the tension between our two countries, the ambassador complained.

I: Sir, you and your government are still denying the killing of al Hariri, the Lebanese Prime Minister.

--Well, the news about the children's predators, the organized crimes of the bikers and especially the judgment in favor of the telemarketing firms have stressed me more. In spite of the fifty million Americans who had signed up "*the do not call list*," still the presiding judge gave the marketers the right to call us while we are eating, sleeping, making love to our wives, mistresses or even to our... "It is the right of free speech," said our legal genius. I wondered where this judge had been educated. My apology, even in the jungle, animals respects one another's territory. Is this civilization falling into the deepest pits of greed and confusion?!

--Rejoice, O man of Nazareth; Peter Lexie is your true vicar. The Pittsburg shoe- shiner has given his heart to the Children Hospital where he had been shining shoes for the last two decades of his life. Before and after work he passed to distribute his smile to the bedridden angels. He made them laugh and kept the hope of recovery alive. It was not a show for him rather a mission. He even has saved and given 89.000 dollars from his hard work for their wellbeing. Indeed, he was not a showman, rather a godly man.

--Pope John Pall 11 Pope has elevated many good servants in the Catholic Church to sainthood, and more yet to come this October. However, Mr. Lexie will not be on the list. Mr. Lexie, I am sure Mother Theresa of Calcutta will be honored to see you sitting next to her in heaven.

--At the Lowery Park Zoo of Tampa, I had seen him recollected and calm. Leaning against the rock wall, he covered his face with two hairy hands while lazily bathing in the sun; chilling for him was the coldness emanating from humans. I pegged him to remove his hands and look at me for a moment. Instead, he emitted sounds that I interpreted: You are one of them; you humans are the ugliest sight in my world.

You might be right, Mr. Monkey. Sadly I withdrew, moving forwards. I felt great disappointment as I found myself walking alone; my wife and her son had walked away. Am I a propagator of cynicism, or just the shadows of despair are shuddering my world?!

ONLY IN AND THROUGH THEE

Our gross sins are weighing heavily on God's heart.

--A woman in Nigeria was condemned to death for having had a child out of wedlock.

--A Tyco CEO has robbed his investors so savagely to spend two million dollars for his wife's birthday celebration and had paid six thousand dollars for his shower curtain. Please, Lord, explain to me the reason behind the creation of such a monster? Are you trying to tell me: so I may know what does a monster look like? Well, thanks for the enlightenment; heavy is your food, Lord, and I am a man with a soft stomach.

--A man killed his two children so they would not be in the custody of his estranged wife.

--In spite of my enlistment in "the do not call list," recently signed by the President, many business institutions continued to send me unsolicited calls. They wanted to sell me things I didn't need and even if needed, I didn't have the money to pay for them.

 Lord, how about the Scientologists who keep on ringing my phone at least three times a day, in spite of my previously expressed resentment. I knew they wanted my scientologist wife to "cross the bridge." I wondered though what bridge is there to be crossed. Have any of them ever crossed one! If they did, what have they found on the other side other than the mighty dollar?

Lord, please allow me to shake off lingering dust. The disintegration of the so-called "evil empire" has created a greater world's instability, just look around and see how America is handling its exclusive super power. How could I accept the logic of my beloved America: destroy them now and rebuild them later? Even greater insanity arises when w have asked other countries to contribute in restoring what we have destroyed; otherwise our government ridiculed them. Why our President and his aides cannot have a better common sense? Could I speak up my mind without risking to be victimized by the Ashcroft's passion for punishment?!

Under the spell of fear allow me dear Lord to pray for the resurrection of another camp of power, one power corrupts; two keep the balance and three destroy it. Lord, I am looking for no corruption or destruction rather I am praying for balance. Could it be that I am looking for the right thing in the wrong time! If so, please, Lord, help me not to fall victim of my own disarray. Yes, I beg you to help me create this balance within myself. Lord, I know how rigid reason can be often times and how gentle the heart is always. This dichotomy between mind and heart stresses my soul out, Lord. How could a stressed soul find peace?! Only in you and through you can man find peace, his lost paradise.

BE MY BODYGUARD

9/ 28, 2003

Today my friend Gary gave me the following report:

A few days ago, a woman had approached and greeted him with good wishes and wasted no time to ask him to be her bodyguard.

"Who is frightening you?" Gary asked.

"The CIA… they're trying to kill me," the woman informed him. "If you accept to be my bodyguard, I will give you free lodging and a hundred dollars a day," she promised.

As they sat to know more about each other, the woman disclosed to Gary that she had bore and was forced to abort John Kennedy's child… She has barbequed with George Bus 41, and she will attend George Bush's 43rd inaugural ball, if he would win the presidency for the second term.

"Apparently you're a woman of the aristocracy but what happened?" Gary asked, pointing.

"Are you talking about these four missing teeth? …Well, I was a battered spouse of two New York mafia bosses and I'm actually bearing the child of one of them," she reported with some seriousness.

At my turn, I began sharing with her a moment of my own glorious life.

"I'm an ex-convict and a booze addict," I told her.

"No problem, so I am."

"Anyway, did you believe her?" I interrupted Gary's rattling.

"Why not, I'm a madman myself." Gary spoke with confidence and satisfaction.

"True. We all are insane to a certain degree and only through acknowledging our insanity that we become somewhat sane," I commented. Gary appreciated my approval.

"Tonight I'll be sleeping in a king bed with a queen beside me," he fantasized.

It was not a harmful fantasy for someone who, through his own choosing, had become homeless.

Gary and that woman shared madness with our President, I thought. For over four months of tedious search, still none of the alternating 1500 scientists has found Saddam's Weapons of Mass- Destruction. It is all in Bush's imagination. Or was it a fabricated excuse to conduct a preemptive war against Iraq? Anyway, such a war will be lost, even by its own winner, America.

--"Say no to TV, yes to books," was the advice the First Lady had given to the children of the third world during her goodwill tour for promoting education. Wow! Madame, what have you done for education here at home other than taking a few co-opted photos at some schools of the underprivileged?

Madame, you have said that you are glad to be away from the politics of Washington. In fact, you haven't failed taking Washington along with you. The only one you have left behind was your husband. Please, return soon, your birdie's feathers are being plucked unmercifully. Yes, the President needs your tender chest to lean on. Mr. Novak, the CNN reporter, has claimed that Ambassador Joe Wilson's wife, Valerie Plame, who once was a CIA operative, had expressed her reluctance to recommend her husband for a mission to investigate Iraq' arrangement to purchase uranium from Niger. The former Ambassador responded that the unfounded leak was retaliation for discrediting your husband administration of having a solid proof about Saddam's Weapons of Mass - Destruction. Indeed, Saddam is still on the run, as aloof and canny as the devil and his Weapons of Mass- Destruction are still as elusive as your husband's political skills. Mr. President, gross is your lie. So far, it did cost us 310 young men and women, 2.000 wounded and the count will continue for years. Well, Sir, do not worry about the destruction you have caused to those imaginary enemies, the Iraqis. But how about the credibility of our country?! Mr. President, may you join that woman, who claims to have close ties with your family, to share her feast of madness. As for Gary and I, we share different madness. Would you please allow us a dazed dervish dance in front of the gate of your isolated ranch in Crawford, Texas? For your consideration, Mr. President: when you have a conflict, don't try to solve it by creating another.

MY SON'S ULTIMATE DREAM

9/ 30, 2003

We are already over a week into the autumn. However, it is the first day that I felt the cool northern wind blowing on the Tampa Bay area. It had been a long humid summer and it is great joy to inhale the acidic aroma of lemons and the sweet fragrance of mandarins and oranges as they broke open in the middle thanks to the torrential rains.

While savoring the fresh breeze of the night and staring at a bright young moon, I heard the phone ringing. It was Babafemi.

"Greetings, father."

"I extend a warm greeting to you, too, son."

"Dear father, the reason I'm calling is to inform you about the demons and angels I've been lately carrying on my shoulders."

"That's not bad news, son. After all, who could live without demons and angels?" I suspected emotional

120

storm coming my way.

"Well, although energizing is the loudness of their voices; still I need, now and then, a moment of quietness."

"Why can't you grant yourself this blessed truce?"

"Well, father, I do feel I'm running out of time and my caravan must advance with the speed of thunder."

I observed silence for a moment; I was thinking into myself: Lord, should I add another madman to the list of the insanes?

"Father; are you still there?" asked the anguished son.

"Yes, I am here. I was just thinking that great things can be achieved only in a peaceful and clear state of mind."

"Who would disagree with a wise man like you? However, at times it is hard to slow down; lately my mind is running twenty- four hours a day... so many are the dreams and so little time to achieve them."

"Well, son, remember Rome hasn't been built in one day. Do you know why it took a long time to build it?"

"Why?"

"Because it was built upon seven hills; if you want to enjoy the sight of the valley, you must first climb up the hill."

"Father, what is the purpose for desiring the valley if one is on top of the mountain?"He challenged me; perhaps he wanted me to explain the relationship between the hill and the valley, the high and low.

"Son, the valley is the foundation of the mountain, and you must bow to the valley before you climb the mountain. And once on the mountain, may you forget not the valley; the mountain is but an exalted valley."

"Wow! That is quite deep, father. Let me then talk to you about the mountain I am dreaming to climb... Yes, I do feel a nagging urge to devote my whole energy for the cause of my race. In so doing, I will be honoring you."

"That's noble of you, son. In what capacity are you planning to serve the race?" There was a worrisome in my voice that even a simple-minded fellow could have detected. Yes, the word race frightens me. I believe only in the human race and that too disturbs the peace of my mind, at times.

"Please, father, don't take me wrong, I'm not a fool... weapons can't solve any problem. I just want to go to Egypt to promote the solar energy. I also plan to teach them how to cultivate the desert. Jews have done it, why can't our people do the same; are we a race of a lesser intelligence?

"Absolutely not... Although I don't know much about Egypt, I know they are already cultivating the desert."

"Well, if this is the case, I could divert my energy to awaken the dormant freedom within them. All humans are born free. That much I have learned from my twenty- six years in this planet."

"Well, that's even a higher calling, however, it's extremely challenging to promote freedom amongst our people, who for centuries have been living under foreign occupations ,and even those so- called national governments of theirs oppress them ruthlessly."

"Exactly, father, it's the lack of democracy there that gives me the burning zeal. I want to liberate our people from their tyrannical governments."

"Again, that's a noble goal, son. However, charity starts at home; you must wait until you are in a more secured financial position. Don't forget that you have a mortgaged apartment building to attend to."

"Nonsense, father, one must not waste his/ her life just chasing mediocre goals such as eating, sleeping and accumulating wealth. Rather, one should have a bigger dream and be willing to give one's own life for that dream."

"Son, survival must be man's first preoccupation."

"Father, there is no reality worth living for greater than pursing a noble dream."

I gave up trying to convince Babafemi who, for the last three years, had been consumed by the idea of helping his father's people to live up to the challenges of the 21st Century; he saw great potentials in their weaknesses.

"Well, what is Leila's opinion?" She has become his first true enduring lover and confident.

"Leila is a great young lady and I love her dearly. She shares your opinion, I guess because she wants us to get married and have children. Although it is a nice dream, it should not stand on the way of serving our race."

"I thank God for your zeal, son, but let me tell you a brief story. Exactly at this same age of yours, I dreamt to save not only my people but also the whole world. I was raised to become a priest with eyes on leadership in the Coptic Catholic Church... I have given it all up when your mother's love has stormed my heart. No regret. How could I regret a decision that resulted of having a great son like you? My most pragmatic advice to you is to ask for a sabbatical. Go to Egypt and see at firsthand how you could serve. Do not cut ties with your native America, in case you would need to come back. Yes, in spite of all its imperfections America remains the best place to be in; it is the last refuge for man-kind."

"That's a great advice, father," he said with certain resignation.

"Hope I haven't plucked one single feather in your wings."

"Not at all, father, rather I thank you for grounding me for a safer flight to my dream... Now I know what you meant when you spoke about the relationship between the valley and the hill. In fact, the hill is the valley impregnated by the sweet dreams of its inhabitants; it's the result of their labor in sweat and hope that can only go up."

"Well summed up, son. My heartfelt blessing," those words concluded our lengthy and mentally tedious conversation. Afterwards, I wanted to consult with the sage of the sages, with F. Nietzsche. Randomly I opened his portable; it was the theme of *"the wanderer."*

"... I stand before my final peak and before that which has been saved up for me the longest. Alas! Now I must face my hardest path! Alas, I have begun my loneliest walk! Whoever is of my kind can't escape such an hour – the hour which says to him: "Only now are you going your way to greatness! Peak and abyss – they are now joined together."

Indeed, there is no dichotomy between the peak and the abyss; both are the two facets of that same reality called man.

THE UNIFYING POWER OF THE HEART

10/ 6, 2003

It is in the heart that one can discover the serenity and tranquility of the human depth: love. Hate and death are but the fruits of the rigidity of reason. The heart is the guiding light to the true joys of life. A man in the China Town, Los Angeles, California, has established a grocery market that caters only to singles. Before shopping they must register for a match- up opportunity. Wow! Indeed, man's ultimate need is not a dozen of eggs, a bag of potatoes and a gallon of milk. Rather, he urgently needs someone to share himself with; sharing is what sustains and gives meaning to life.

--Ah the grandeur of the human heart! An American soldier in Iraq has fallen in love with a young lady whose father he had killed in the name of reason. Indeed, the limitations of reason ultimately yield to the overwhelming power of the heart.

-- The abundance of the heart's goodness has inspired a black preacher to be so creative: He has pledged to pay five dollars for every white, who will attend any of his Sunday services and two dollars for any service of the weekdays. In so doing, he wanted to see blacks and whites sitting next to one another in the hope that the physical closeness will bring out their spiritual one.

Yes, indeed, the grossest sin of modern man consists of giving too much attention to the wilderness of the mind at the expense of cultivating the garden of his heart. The heart invites; the mind divides, deprives and finally kills. Now that we know how far the mind can take us, let's embark in the heart's ship. It will take us to the other shore where the gods bathe nude. We all dream of that state of a healthy nudity, that absence of guilt. For so long the mind has misled, poisoned and divided us. It is about time to experience the curative and unifying grace of the heart. We saw it in Jesus forgiving his killers as he was taking the last gasp. It has been incarnated in Mother Theresa bending over the sick of Calcutta, without thinking of their religious affiliations. We saw it in the simplicity of San Francis of Assisi calling the donkey his brother and smiling at the birds perching on the palm of his hand for a feed. We also saw it in the Prophet Mohamed knocking on the door of his neighbor, who had failed that day to put his trash in front of his door step, as usual. The prophet might even have taken along some dates for him. Those are the hearts forged after God's.

Lord, today I beg your mercy to grant us a short memory for the atrocities of our enemies, so we can experience the healing power of your love. Help us to learn how to forgive others; so they may forgive us. Help us how to love them; so they may love us. Lord, may your grace control all our acts; it is in your grace that we find ours. In your name we pray, so may the gates of our hearts open wide to all! Only there can we find true security and everlasting love for ourselves and for others.

THE TIGER'S TEETH IN THE TRAINER'S THROAT

10/ 7, 2003

In Las Vegas a tiger's teeth were dug into the throat of Roy Horn, its long- life trainer. The sad news has dominated all the TV channels. How hypocritical humans can be! We are shocked beyond belief to see a beast acting as a beast. (By the way this tiger's loss of self-control happened only once during a period of almost half a century, the life of the show). So, in fact, who have the worst record of violence, humans or beasts? If honesty obliges, no one would hesitate for a moment to say humans. Just let's not forget all the killings between Arabs and Israelis. Violence has become the status quo that we get quite surprised if a day passed by without. How about the Iraqi insurgents and the coalition forces? They too are constantly after one another's throat. Lord, forgive me; I, too, have bitten my companion. Worse, the life of our companionship is less than a year. Yes, I haven't been in good terms with Marla for a whole week now. Although she had been acting irrationally, still I am guilty for not accepting the nature of the beast. Thank you, Lord, today you have led us to Saint Cecilia church. During the Holy Mass I prayed for the softening of my heart. For a brief moment of gentleness, I held Marla's hand while praying "the Paternoster, our Father who art in heaven…"I also gave her a kiss on the forehead as the priest said: "Let's exchange a sign of peace."

It took thousands of years before the wolf has evolved to a dog. Strong are the genes of the wild within all of your creatures; even the angels needed to be subdued. I can think of Lucifer, he, too, had gotten on your nerves by declaring equality to you. Forgive us, O Lord, for all our savageries and may you continue nourishing us from your divine table of gentleness.

THE CIRCUS IS OVER IN CALIFORNIA

10/ 8, 2003

The circus is over in the great State of California; we have a new- elect governor named Arnold

Schwarzenegger. Congratulations, Arnie, I hope that one day you would become the President of our great

nation. ..Wait a minute, there is a serious obstacle, you are not American- born, a constitutional block.

I am the terminator, I heard you howling.

"You mean you're going to squeeze the law as you had been squeezing the breasts of many women?"

I'm not a sexual predator, just a man of compassion; I wanted to feel their pain.

"Arnie, you did a very admirable job. Are you going to continue being consumed by the same passion for

compassion?"

Why do you ask this silly question?

"Well, I heard that you have a plan to give free breast exam to all women who will be working for your

governorship."

God wills.

"How about Maria's feelings; don't you think she might get jealous?"

Maria is a good wife; she will always stand behind her husband, no matter what.

"Ah, Arnie, don't worry she is a fragile creature and you're a hustler, I mean a wrestler. You are a smooth

wrestler though. I have been watching your successful campaign tactics... Gary Davis was kissing the babies

and you were kissing their moms. Is that how you came on top?"

Sacramento needs me on top.

"Wow! Good luck, big guy, you have been officially elevated to debauchery, thanks to the cons' chariot."

RELYING ON PRAYER

10/9, 2003

Flipping the pages of the Florida Catholic edition of October 2nd, 2003, I was struck by

Sister Gil Cottrell's article: *"Relying on Prayer"*.

It is the nature of God, according to Sister, to help those who help Him.

The nun was speaking about her successful fund-raising effort. Hmm! even God lives by the American saying: "scratch my back, I scratch yours." What an awesome God! We give Him a word of praise; he gives us at least ten dollars. Why not? He is a lot richer than any human. Besides, He is quite generous. Still, no thanks, I am not seduced by this commercial approach. Rather, I am looking for His spirit. Please, Holy Spirit, save me from those barbarians, the self-anointed people of all religions.

Enough of the religious poison, let's consult with the wisdom of the secular world. The CNN channel reported: a mother is seeking compensation from the Company where her son had worked before he has killed three employees and himself. Her defense: she has lost her source of income. What a great world we live in! Yes, kill others and yourself; your inheritors will reap the sweet fruits of your murderous acts. Now I know better, I must stop thinking to put an electric fence around my chimney, just in case a thief would decide to use it as a route to rob me at night. If injured, I might lose my house, my only earthly possession.

--Finally, thanks, Tom Ridge; you are the best homeland security's Tsar. I just wish if our drug Tsar were as effective as you are; our society is living high on a drug called frustration for the freedom you and the big Boss had stolen from us.

MISS. NORA'S FUNERAL

10/ 10, 2003

I accompanied Marla to attend Miss Nora's funeral. They both worked as food servers in the cafeteria of Dunedin high school. Nora Mae Davis' brief biography stated that she was born on the 6th of February, 1928 in Lafayette, Alabama. Yes, dear Nora, I have heard about your cries before the many injustices of the South and I have also heard about your struggles in face of those injustices.

You have proudly raised five children alone. I bet it was a tedious but rewarding journey for you. Rejoice, today your soul reposes in God's greatest justice and love.

The Saint John Primitive Baptist Church's Females Choir sang in your honor: *"He is a waiter..."* Indeed, He is a great waiter. He holds in His mighty palms all the sweet rivers and the limpid fountains. Today He generously extends His holy water to quench forever your thirst. Dear, drink; drink from the fountain that will never dry up.

Your family and friends reflected upon your life. A younger sister remembered you saying:

"If the children start misbehaving, Jack them up and send them to me." I bet you held Solomon's iron bar to straighten up those rascals.

Your son remembered you as the mother who never had enough sleep. I understand. Being a single parent is not an easy task. A good parent is like a shepherd dog that doesn't close its eyes; many are the wolves seeking to devour the flock.

There were also acknowledgments and resolutions in your honor. In all, they commanded you as a woman who had lived God's will, in spite of the numerous hardships of life. For that reason the woman of the white hats sang, *"It's only one heart, it's only one song... We love you and God loves you best."*

All was good and sincere until elder Benjamin Adams Jr. came to the pulpit. From the top of his powerful larynx, the Senior Pastor screamed: "I've lived dreaded days; I'm looking for a happy eternity. Oh yeah, my Father's kingdom has so many mansions. However, brothers and sisters, to enter those mansions one needs:

1. To work. No work, no eating, just give me a rock to suck on.

2. To suffer the devil's attacks. Oh yeah, give me a sword to cut the devil's tail.

3. One must worship God in the midst of all the trials. Oh yeah hand me the Holy Book, I want to dance with it before the Lord's throne."

Having elaborated lengthily each point, the Reverend closed his eulogy with these words: "Sister Nora, you have fulfilled all the three requirements, now enter victoriously into the Lord's mansion. We look forward to the day we will join you."

There was prolonged applause. He then raised the Bible high and started the Dervish Dance, the revolving dance around one's self; while waiving with the other hand a white handkerchief. In the peak of the Reverend's uncontrollable excitement, a faithful walked up to him and drove a punch unto his fat belly. "Halleluiah, Halleluiah! The Lord is tickling my tummy," the Rev. shouted. It was quite a show as the clown heated up his dazed dance.

"Yeah, Yeah, Yeah!" screamed the religion- intoxicated crowd. They, too, were jumping up and down. It was a kind of a religious orgy and everyone had his/ her separate climax.

The service lasted almost two hours; black people enjoy worshipping from the heart. Prayer for them is a time full of heavenly gains, unlike whites, who live according to the saying: "Time is money."

Finally, the funeral employees pushed the casket inside a black limousine. Why not, a little vanity could be a happy treat for someone who had lived, for so long, under the crushing yoke of poverty. The Eternal Rest Cemetery welcomed Sister Nora with a smile, no more hunger, thirst or pain. After the coffin was rested in the grave; the living were invited to a delicious lunch made of: chicken wings, rice, black beans; corn bread; apple pie and coffee. Yes, man must suck the breasts of mother earth until the day the real banquet will take place in heaven.

Although Nora's death was an opportunity to fill in my stomach, it has left a vacuum in my heart. With great nostalgia, I recalled those processions of the funerals in my childhood. How they were filled with mournful tears and melodic sad chanting. I love tears and reject frivolous laughter and dance, two emotions that dominate modern days' funerals. Could those two emotions be often a sign of our gladness to see the departure of someone we would have had hated so much?! Or are we just laughing at the vanity of life in general?! Whatever the motive (s) may be, it is not funny; death is a solemn occasion to reflect upon life; may God forgive our frivolities.

ADVISING MY DAUGHTER

10/ 11, 2003

The phone rang three peeps before I picked it up.

"Hey, Nailah How was your first date with Chris, after a long courtship through wires?" I was anxious; after all I am a father and fathers want to see their daughters settled down.

"You can't believe it, dad."

From the tone of her voice I detected that things didn't go well.

"What happened?" I, too, sounded stressed out.

"Don't worry, dad, it is just one of those instances of insensitivity that plagues modern day man."

"What did he do?"

"Well, I waited on him until 8 p.m., he didn't show up, nor did he call. I decided to call him. He called me back at 9:30 p.m. I had to cut short the conversation; I was tired waiting."

"What excuse did he give you?"

"He was busy preparing for a TV interview."

"That is a valid excuse."

"No, dad, still he could have taken a moment to call and let me know what was going on."

"You have a point here, but do remember that man's mind runs on different tracks than those of a woman's."

"Dad, no excuse, he just has failed to respect me; I don't need a man who puts me down. I have a lot to give; apparently he doesn't deserve me. It doesn't matter if he plays for the Minnesota Vikings; I'm too good to be mistreated."

"Daughter, I totally agree with you."

128

"True, he had apologized more than once; still I told him his apology wasn't accepted."

"How did he react?"

"I accept your decision," he said. "The fool didn't even bother to fight for me. O God; I'd wasted a whole hour before the mirror, just to look like a Cinderella for a beast like him. How naïve we women are; we dream of a prince to end up getting a frog…oh well, I guess there are more frogs in this world than princes. We poor women live in unjust world, but we don't have to accept its injustices." Nailah sounded quite determined to duel for respect.

"Basically we men don't want to hurt you, we're just careless. If you would allow me, I'll talk to Chris and let him know how much you're hurting."

"Dad, do you really think that I should give him a second chance?"

"Daughter, forgiveness is a safe net to land a healthy relationship."

"You might be right, dad; you have lived long enough to know this crazy world better than I do."

"It's a jungle out there; still some of its wild beasts can be tamed."

"Well, then call him. But please reiterate to his ears that I'm not one of those ladies who will tolerate abuse. I have a lot of goodness and love in my heart; I need a man who enriches the qualities of my heart and not someone who would suck them up dry.

"Absolutely…"

"Would you please let me now as soon as you finish talking to him?"

"Certainly I will."

I called Chris; there was no answer. I left a message and waited from three until 6 p.M., still no answer. Marla, Javier and I went to the Immaculate Conception Catholic Church in Tampa to enjoy the celebration of *"el savor Latino, the Latin taste."* The festival featured the popular dance and food of the central Latin countries. It was a pleasant experience. At midnight we returned home. Soon as I walked in, I heard the telephone ringing. I ran to answer.

"Hello, Mister Abdou." The voice was warm.

"Hello, Chris." Although it was the first time I ever spoke to him, I recognized his voice; his black southern accent was quite obvious. Briefly we spoke about his Carrier as the quarterback of the Minnesota Vikings. Then I turned to what concerned me dearly, his relationship with my daughter. Immediately I made it clear to him that Nailah is unique. (Nothing is new; all fathers feel the same about their children). "She is a straightforward, responsible, sincere and loving young lady and she demands from her man the same. She cares a lot about you; but if you don't feel the same toward her, please don't call her again." I was quite firm with the player. For a moment I thought that firmness might have frightened him. It did not; rather it was quite a force to get what my daughter wanted.

"I'll call Nailah and apologize again early in the morning," he said, apologizing to me as well.

"It's your decision. But do remember, my daughter's demands are non-negotiable."

"Yes, Mr. Abdou, and thank you for helping me to win your daughter's heart."

"You're a smart young man, a good heart is a rare treasure, if found, it must be cherished. Once again, good luck." We hang up and I had a hard time sleeping, I was anxious to know how things would go. I didn't want to call Nilah; it was too late and was afraid to wake her up. Next day early morning I called to update her about my talk with Chris.

"Thanks, dad, Chris came and we went to have an early breakfast in his mansion. It was an opportunity to let him know who I am, and what I want. He told me I'm more beautiful in real than in the photo I'd sent him. I felt quite flattered. Amway, I made it clear to him that I wanted a man to love, to bear his children and to grow old with. If you want the same, welcome to my heart; if not, hello and goodbye. I do not have time to waste; I am a busy young lady."

He assured me that he wanted the same. I certainly hope so, although I have some doubts about the level of his emotional maturity…Oh Well, it's hard to predict the future, anyway. One more final thing, I also told him we needed to take this relationship slow and time will tell. After this serious talk, we hit it on a light note. I made a funny remark about his jewelry. I told him that hundreds of thousands of meals were wrapped around his neck and wrists. Yes, the price of all these jewelry can feed a hungry third world village for a whole year. He laughed and promised to buy me some. I told him no, thanks. I don't need jewelry, I rather have your love and that can only be proven by respect. He promised me he would do his best to meet my expectations…Again, only time can tell. Thanks, dad, for giving my relationship with Chris a second chance. I really care a lot about him; he has this unique innocence about him. Unfortunately, again, he seems to be immature; but that too will be the work of time…We will meet again this evening; he had to leave for training in preparation of an upcoming game.

What humans need is good character, if character lacks, nothing can work properly," Nilah concluded with conviction.

"Absolutely, daughter, just let time works its magic; it shapes all things."

On this hopeful note we bade goodbye. Money doesn't move the world; hope does.

HAPPINESS IS CRYING BEFORE AND HEALING THE WOUNDS OF OTHERS

10/12, 2003

Toward midnight the phone rang.

"Hello, dear father...This is your twenty- six year old son seeking your guidance."

"Hello, Youhanna, how have you been?" I gave Babafemi this nickname because of his passion for the desert, just like John the Baptist.

"I have just returned from three-day retreat in one of the California's deserts." He sounded quite happy.

"Son, any new bats entered your head?" I asked sarcastically, bats of fire were the last visitors he had met in the desert, so he had told me a month ago.

"There are no bats this time, rather doves."

"Glad to hear about this new alliance; doves are associated with peace."

"Exactly and peace I've found as a result not only to my repeated visit to the desert but also thanks to the good advices I received from Nailah, Tameri, Leila and certainly my most wise father. Now I feel the kind of peace I'd always been dreaming of." In his voice I depicted serenity.

"Glad to hear the good news, son, finally you have arrived."

"Arrived no but I have the right provision to embark into my true journey."

"And where are we going finally?" I asked with some anguish.

"The same destination: to Egypt, the fatherland where monks play with snakes."

"You want to become a monk?"

"Father, the desert is a station to refuel the human heart with all the aspirations needed to go to the valley where we live and dream with our people. Individuals are nothing, the collective, the community is everything."

"Are we now trying to resurrect a dead communism?"

"Father, a few things are wrong with communism; many are wrong with capitalism. Just think what capitalism has given us... We kill for pennies. It's about time to share our hearts and minds."

"Please do guide me to your mind and heart, where are they now?"I knew exactly what he was alluding too, I just had a hard time to accept it; I thought my son was out of touch with reality.

"Where my heart has been for so long; God has put me in this world for the purpose to help my race. Yes, I must go to Egypt soon as I get the approval for a sabbatical from my job; I had already applied for it. I know they aren't ready for freedom; but at least I can introduce it to them. Besides I could help them building cheap houses with beams of steel; wood rots fast and Egypt has little of it, anyway. I also want to share with them my knowledge of the solar energy…And who knows I might even meet my lost friend Ali there. If I would be lucky enough to meet him again, I will never walk out on him no matter how different our world's views would be."

"But, son, Egypt is a very hot country; they don't need protection from cold."

"Exactly, father, I want to create comfortable dwellings to protect them from the heat of that burning sun." He then began talking about the various gauges that create and regulate moderate temperature all year round. He spoke about the non-contact thermometers, thermometer probes and sensors. Although his project was still incomprehensible to me, I admired his sincere concern.

"I know, father, I do sound like a dreamer but I rather float on a sea of dreams than to stay on the dry shores of reality. There is nothing exciting about having a job from nine to five; then go home to wake up the next day only to enrich oneself. The real reward, father, is to live for others, for a world greater than one's own."

"That is very noble of you, son. Follow your dream, go to Egypt and see how you can serve our people. I have a lot of relatives there; they could guide your march toward your dream. But please don't quit your job, just wait for the approval of your sabbatical."

"I will. I'm quite aware of the possibility of failure but even that must not discourage me; I want to break the chains of egoism; egoism is a deadly disease and because of it we have wars and destruction."

"Indeed, Babafemi." No longer could I call him Youhanna; he is not a mystic, an abdicator of the worldly commodities as I first thought. He is definitively an avid seeker of them and wanted to share them with the ones he loved most, his father's people.

Before we finished our tedious conversation, I reiterated my endorsement. After an emotional farewell, I too found myself dreaming. I reflected about the ultimate source of happiness. Yes, it consists in listening to a bird singing, watching a squirrel jumping from one branch to another, following the dance of clouds, howling at the moon, inhaling the warmth of the sun, dancing around fire and crying before and healing the wounds of others, even those of our enemies. Happiness is to see beauty in all and to cherish everything and everyone in the universe, not only one's own race. Yes, man's true greatness lies in discovering God's face, even in the mud and to see one's own as a part of that infinite and beautiful face of the universe. Race is nothing. I rather race toward the neglected of the world, the rejected, and the persecuted; it is in their arms that God lies with open wounds. I dream to drink from God's blood. It is the only drink capable to quench man's thirst. As for the quenching of the thirst of my beloved son, I prayed for more dried fountains, he has just started his journey; he was in a dire need to feel the painful thirst so he can open wide his mouth wide to the limpid fountains of a true fulfilling life.

THANKS DAD FOR A JOB WELL- DONE

10/ 14, 2003

My son Amon has turned eighteen. Although no more payments of child support, still I have to assist him financially. I don't mind to lodge and feed him, along all the other cares of life until he finishes his college. We provide the needs of our pets, after all. This evening the Abdou's kitchen smelled the odor of good food. The number eighteen was attached to a heart –shaped balloon and a birthday cake was hidden in the fridge. Amon, Marla, Javier and I sat smiling around the table; we looked like a happy family. Civilly we passed the plates that contained a variety of entrees. The young lad with a wolfish mouth ate like a gentleman; he even used utensils. A great amateur of photography, Marla took several pictures. I guess she wanted to document that happy occasion. We laughed out loud as we recalled some of Amon's past mishaps, and no one was more ironical about them than he. Indeed, it's great achievement to laugh at one's own sad past.

"Dad and Marla, thank you for the good meal," he said, looking very happy. He was so thrilled to have had landed safely at the age of reason in spite of a turbulent adolescence that had left him a bit scarred. The new life has promised the young lad pursuit of liberty, prosperity and happiness. That evening he spoke quite optimistically about a bright future he thought will never have. That day marked not just a nominal arrival to the age of independence; he also knew well that with maturity comes responsibility and responsibility he had gladly embraced the very same day he turned eighteen. It was the first day of his company's function. In that day the owner and President of "the Kings Pressure Cleaning company" had labored ten hours. The sores on his hand were the visible prints he can show to his benefactor, big brother Babafemi, who had wired him three thousand dollars to establish this small business. All great things start small, so I have lectured Amon. Thank God, he was ready to meet the challenges life would throw on his way.

With powerful breath and in the midst of the "Happy Birthday" singing, he blew out his eighteen candles. For that special moment Marla took more pictures.

"Dad, aren't you going to welcome me now to the real world?" a joyful shout flew into the air as the son wrapped arm around father's shoulder.

"Welcome, son, to the real real world." My repetition of the word real implied; yes, a lot of dirt will be thrown onto your face, just be speedy to clean up that smeared face of yours. I bet he understood that as he passed me a bundle of his business cards with a beautiful design of which meaning I could not decipher due to my innate weakness for the visual art. The card read: "Kings Pressure Cleaning: roofs, driveways, walkways, decks, pool areas, painting prep, kills grime and mold, environmentally safe: residential and commercial.

Cell: (727)420-7095. Licensed and Insured."Amon

Wow! Truly my son has come to the age of reason. Almost 3.5 his age, I still was inefficient and unprepared, compared to him. Thank God, our children are improvement of ourselves.

"Dad, what do you think about the cards' format?" He asked.

"It is very well presented."

"Do you mind distributing a few of them?"

"Gladly I will."

"Thanks, dad… Would you like to listen to my business recorded message?"

I dialed his cellular number while he was still devouring the last bite of his chocolate cake.

The message recorded: "Thank you for calling Kings Pressure Cleaning. This is Amon; sorry we have missed your call. However, your call is very important to us. Please leave a name and a number, and we will get back to you as soon as possible; have a great day."

Wow! How polite and responsible my son has become in such a short time! He even spoke in the majestic form: "We." It was just a week ago before that business revelation; his cellular recorded the somber message: "This is the city morgue. Listen to the following options:

If I owe you money, the check one day will be in the mail. If you owe me money, I am on my way to get it. If you are selling something, I do not want it. For anyone this recording doesn't apply, leave a message after the three beeps."

What a change of tone!

Soon as the young lad got my approval of his recorded message, he dragged himself to bed; the painful responsibilities of tomorrow had already weighed heavily on his shoulders. In spite of his tiredness, the apparent readiness to battle the world reflected his determination to win the future, just to make up for those many missed opportunities of the past.

"Son, hard work never kills; only laziness sends its subjects to prisoner," I has lectured him, and he has abided to father's wisdom.

Marla left to put her darling to bed, and I went outside for a walk under the bright stars that illuminated our neighborhood. "Thank you, Lord, I am now a free citizen and a proud captain who had landed his crowded ship onto the safe shores," thus I found myself murmuring. Suddenly I felt a slight pinch in my left shoulder from an invisible hand, as if it were reprimanding me for conceit.

"Why, Lord, am I not entitled to it; had I not done a great job?"

"You did. I just wanted to remind you that it was thanks to the efforts of both of us," I heard the mysterious voice.

Returning home, I answered the phone. It was Nailah.

"Congratulations, dad, now you're a liberated man; your youngest son has turned eighteen. Thank s, dad, for the long years of good care you have given us, a job well done. And please forgive us for all the heartaches we'd given you."

"Well, now I can close my eyes to survey the beautiful kingdom I've built," I joked.

"Indeed, dad, you have built a great kingdom by raising the five of us so well. We thank you for the hard work. We promise to be as good to our children as you had been to us. Your legacy of goodness and care is becoming our guiding light to this kingdom. In fact, you're our kingdom."

As I finished speaking to Nilah, I lay my head with large smile on my lips and my eyes were engrossed with tears; my struggles have not been in vain, after all. Swinging between my many failures and the ultimate success, finally, I fell asleep, dreaming of a bright future not for myself but for my five children and grandchildren. Our dreams never die, so long as they move into their souls. Yes indeed, man's most authentic life culminates in this divine breath, his children.

THE HUNGRY FOXEX ARE IN THE COOP

10/16, 2003

--**The** President went to California seeking Arnold Schwarzenegger's political support for his re-election. They lavished each other with false compliments. In vanity and lies Politicians can score higher than anyone else, rivaled only by the religious leaders, at times.

That day I saw Arnie's long nose stuck into the President's short ear before the bodybuilder introduced the Texan cowboy. Lord, protect the hens; the hungry foxes are in the coop.

"Arnie and I have a lot in common," said the President. "Just to mention a few:

A – "We are married well."

I: Let's just hope that Arnie doesn't have a half- dozen illegitimate children, I found myself murmuring.

B – "We both have been accused of poorly speaking the English language."

I: How true!

C – "We both love our country."

The President went on reminding the audience of his constant efforts of fighting terrorism, a theme that has become a litany of his administration. Would he ever find salvation before the liberal audience in reciting this litany? This might happen if a prostitute could pass through the gates of heaven just by hiding her face behind the thick veil of purity.

--Enough of the worldly news, now let's hear from the religious sector. Today His Holiness, Jean Paul II celebrated his twenty- fifth anniversary, reigning over the Sea of Saint Peter. Although the two men never met, history has created a hidden envy between them. His Holiness envies the dead apostle for having occupied the Holy Sea for thirty- four long years. Wow, nine years, so far, ahead of the most popular Pope. Certainly Peter, too, has his own reason of envy; he did not have the gala Jean Paul II enjoys today. Well, who can say that a longer and modest reign is better than a shorter but glamorous one?!

Let's concentrate on the Holy Father's achievements. The aging lion has brought down communism, so they say. He has climbed many high mountains and governed his flock with an iron bar that has been softened by his sweet grandpa smile.

--The Pope's Declaration that Anti-Semitism is a sin against God has made theological history. Indeed, all of us are responsible for having sent Jesus to the Cross.

--One more surprise: evolution can be proven through the examining of fossils, declared His Holiness. This latter declaration puts him in the age of reason, modernism. In spite of this apparent opening up to science, still conservatism wraps itself around the Pontiff's neck as a poisonous snake wrapping itself around the neck of its victim. He opposes women's ordination to priesthood. He is accused, and rightfully so, of being an oppressor of the catholic religious dissidents.

Unfortunately, now he can't walk and that is not of his own fault- just the human condition. Nevertheless, more than two hundred and fifty thousand faithful still gather every Wednesday at the Saint Peter's Square to hear the message and greet the charismatic leader. That is certainly another reason for envy as Saint Peter peek from heaven. Never the first Pope had audience larger than those desperate wiggling few fishes caught after a long vigil and trying to escape his net.

His Holiness, it is a capital sin to classify you as a dictator in your own reign. However, forgive me if I belong to the 82 percent of the American Catholics who disagree with you on several theological, spiritual and managerial issues. Yes, I am a catholic who follows his own conscience. By the way, I am a disciple of Sister Wanda who once called man: "The beast of a soft penis and hard head." You have made it clear, despite your slurring, that you will remain the leader of the flock as long as the Lord wishes. I know what this declaration implies: your hunger for power. Could this hunger be also the reason behind the failing of reaching ecumenical unity with the Orthodox Church?! Is this your kingdom or the Lord's?!

"You have taught us how to live; now you are teaching us how to die," proudly declare your faithful followers. And we knew of your famous saying: "don't fear." Oh, please, stop this old sophism. Are you not contradicting yourself by holding onto power?! I am not saying go die, far from that. All I am saying is: if you are plagued by arthritis, Parkinson's disease or any other serious ailment; keen of old age, please accept the human limitations and surrender that power to someone else. Just remember: Noah's children used a garment to cover up the embarrassing sight of their father.

Holy Papa, your face, twisted into your chest, pains the millions of your flock. Please retire, the visa of your residence on this earth will soon expire, and do not try to hold too tight onto the ephemeral, you have a whole eternity awaiting you.

In spite of this harsh criticism, we thank you for Mother Teresa's beatification. Certainly the humble small woman has made it big in heaven. You, too, can, just curve your appetite for the big crowd; too much applause could envenom even the holiest soul. Thank you, for the twenty- five years, so far. You have governed us with an iron shaft; we look forward for another shepherd, who would herd us with a bamboo stick. All wish your Holiness long and tranquil life. And thank you for great the memories.

MR. PRESIDENT, PLEASE COME TO THE AGE OF REASON

10/ 17, 2003

The President has dispatched the major members of his cabinet throughout the country. They all carried heavy bags of lies. The heaviest: go tell your fellow Americans that everything is alright in Iraq. Enforce this message or you will vanish from my court. Mr. President, all is well in Iraq, if one could ignore the daily vanishing of an average of two American military and a half dozen wounded. Forget about the hundreds killed Iraqis, those are mosquitoes; they don't count. One more thing bothers me: how could your military keep humiliating the Iraqi population in the most sacred places, such as in their mosques and homes?! Your military have often put men flat on the floor, and beat them before the frightened eyes of their wives and children .Even those desperate cries didn't save the dignity of the beaten.

You have been complaining, for a while, that the liberal media reported only the bad news: the killings; the robberies; the beatings; the burning and fair to summarize: the constant destruction. According to your view, they have ignored the opening of schools, shops and places of worship. Yes, Sir, we must acknowledge, at least, that the hospitals and oil refineries are operating, almost to their full capacities. Indeed, it could not be short of great achievement. After all, the wounded need to be cared for and the thousands of your military vehicles need fuel to run throughout the country delivering terror even to the ruins of Babylonia. Mr. President, by invading Iraq for the spoils of war, you have acted like a monkey that stuck his head into the jar, dreaming of the rice. You may have your belly full; still your head is stuck inside an empty jar. Good luck, but don't count on the prayers of the far religious right to save your presidency. Having had cheered you to execute this suicidal act, they need those prayers to keep the plates passing to doubting worshipers.

--Have you heard of that monkey who had fled his cage and waited at the bus stop to carry him to the land of his dreams, to his master's home? Well, Mr. President, just a simple advice: Please come home, to the age of reason. Enough of your mishaps; redeem your great mistake in invading Iraq and go sit down with that so-called mad leader of North Korea; a few hundred thousand bushels of grains could save the world from the curse of his fast- spreading nukes. You have expressed willingness that you will not attack his country, conditional to halting the production of his nuclear weapons. Why cannot you sit down with the enemy and look him in the eyes? Even the ugliest hides the wounded face of Jesus.

--The news is not any brighter here at home. The medical costs rose 13.5percent this year while the social security rose to 2.1percent. Hurray, good news for the rich; forget those who cannot afford medical insurance. And even those who have reached the age of retirement are now feeling the pain of the high medical cost. Yes, let suffering spread throughout the land.

--Ignore the urgency of curing our ailments and let's escape this garden of thorns to the Garden of Eden where all boobs, even the wiggliest, dream of standing upright. Yes, after eleven agonizing years of suspension, the silicone implants are now on the table for debate with the high prospect of a victorious return. Had they bribed you implementing a pair of them into Laura's sagging chest? Anyway, rejoice, O my eyes, rejoice, the big solid boobs are returning, and soon your earthly hunger will be satisfied.

Is this a great world or what?! All the late events are celebrating man's achievements. The plan to rebuild a devastated Iraq and the augmentation of women's breasts and the many other unknown accomplishments of yours, Mr. President, all make me shout: Halleluiah! Still I can't forget that I lack medical insurance. Thank God, I am 31 months away from collecting a meager social security. The Medicare will cover 80 percent of my medical expenses and certainly I will be eligible for Medicaid to cover the remaining 20 percent; I am as poor as they come. But, above all, I wish to enjoy the good health of spirit and body till the last breath. This is my main earthly hope. As for the big heavenly one, it will soon come true. Please, don't misunderstand me; no plan for suicide; just hope, hope and hope. Nobody dies by hope; let's hope to die in hope.

THE STINGER GOT STUNG

10/ 22, 2003

Today the small eyes of the little hunter have spotted the fat bear that had been roaming the jungle for so long. Shoot. Rush Limbaugh is the prey. It's the day for all liberals to rejoice, the mighty fat bear lay bleeding on the floor of morality. And why not laugh at his fall? For over fifteen years now he had been bombarding our ears by his unbending preaching on morality and hard work, and repeatedly condemning drug users. The lack of fully assuming one's own responsibilities was a crime in his vocabulary. No excuse, be it poverty or birth defect; still we are responsible to overcome the atrocities of life, often repeated the great preacher. His long monologues on righteousness and personal responsibilities and its merits have made us, the vulnerable, feel like a bunch of a-morals and damned failures. Yes, if you cannot stand the darkness of a cave, have a $ 35 million mansion in Palm Beach, Florida, like Rush. But don't hesitate to swallow $200.000 worth of pills annually. They activate your brain and keep you high while discoursing on peoples' miseries. Al Rashbo, according to the State Attorney's report, you had been stuffing your fat stomach with those illegal pills. Could we expect an honest explanation from you? Oh, forgive me for asking the impossible, honesty doesn't show in your guide of morality. Rather, hypocrisy is the dominating virtue of your conservatism. We are all humans, the leftists and the rightists; both parties fall short from the spectrum of morality. However, we liberals sin, acknowledge, and even enjoy our sins. As for you, conservative hypocrites, the story is more complicated; you sin with a sickening remorse. Such felt remorse is not for a moral code you would have violated but for having been caught while violating it. Indeed, you are suffering the shame of the moral oedipal complex. Self-righteous clowns, allow me to ask those simple questions: How could you see evil everywhere- if God truly reigns over your hearts? Where is your compassion for the human sufferings? Well, forget about answering those silly questions; empathy is not your virtue. You are always right; others are always wrong, case closed. Must I ask your forgiveness for the odor of my armpits? I advise that you take time to wipe the shit in your asses, though. In case you cannot smell, please open the telephone guidebook; there are too many nose doctors. But beware, choose not one of yours, you will be duped and condemned. Rush, you're actually lying somewhere in a drug rehab facility. Get well soon. But when you sit again your fat ass on the leather chair, holding your EIB golden microphone with your *nicotine- stained fingers*, please be a bit more compassionate; you, too, are subject to the shortcomings of anyone else. And just remember: you have built a financial empire attacking our weak spots. Indeed, they served you well.

Marta, wife of the very ferocious bear, upon you I implore God's mercy; you had been seduced by his glittering gold. Would you deliver this humble message from a cave dweller to your beloved genius husband:

a night spent under a bridge might help him to discover that all God's creatures, small and big, are worthy of respect, a notion he couldn't grasp in spite of his "*talent on loan from Gaadge-God.*" Yes, rich and poor, we all suffer the fragilities of the human condition. The human heart emerges pure only after having been immersed in the divine river of mercy.

FANATICS ARE IDIOTS AND ALL FALL DOWN

10/26, 2003

General W. Boykin spoke in one of the churches; he was stripping Islam from its divine message. "Islam is the religion of idolaters," he declared in the midst of the bigots' applauses.

A storm of reprimands from all directions blew up on his face. Some of the retired military have asked for his resignation- certainly for political reasons and not for the love of Islam. Even the Secretary of Defense, Dock Rumsfeld, was uncomfortable with his subordinate's indiscretion. General, do not worry, you have on your side the neo-cons who swear on the Holly Book that you are a godly man. Woe to you, devils, you worship division and propagate prejudice. Ostriches bury their heads in the sand; you bury yours in hate. I am, too, a Christian, and unto you I say: respect the belief system of others. Often times we all worship God for the wrong reasons. Please cry hard, you need purification; thick are the sins weighing on your own wicked hearts. You have brought shame on Christianity. Cry, cry, sinners, questioning other people's beliefs cannot guarantee the purity of your hearts; for that you need the good God who embraces all. For so long you have been busy accusing others of idolatry that you have lost sight of that true God. Stop courting the devil, then you will discover God's beautiful face reflected on all religions.

--Well, let me now lower my wings and fly over Washington D.C. As I flew over the treacherous City, I heard the news that the Senate Committee had awarded itself with $30.000 annual raise. Thieves, you're entitled to pickpocketing us with the same ruse you had used convincing us to vote for a war that serves only your interests tied to your masters, the lobbyists, even at the price of killing our sons and daughters. Millions of Americans have lost their jobs and have run out of their unemployment's benefits. Still, you have found justification to reward yourselves for a job poorly done. Could it be that our democratic government is a body of thieves elected by a herd of idiots?!

--Notorious men, who stand in the fast lane, I am glad that you no longer can arrive in three hours from London to New York; your sky goddess is now retired in an old hangar. That dizzying machine was the creation of the French and Brits as a bandage to cover the wound, after having been scientifically bitten by

140

that big bear called- America, the most aggressive and accomplished leader of technology. Ah! How I do dream to travel to infinity on the back of a camel; while enchanted by the hissing of the desert's serpents and the dancing of its playful cobras. I am not a fool to give up the tranquility of the camel's hoofs dug into the tenderness of the cool night- sand for the deafening noise of that super speedy machine, the Concorde.

STARVED TO DEATH

10/ 27, 2003

Lord, I feel guilty eating a good meal after I have read the story of those four foster boys in New Jersey. Their ages ranged from nine to nineteen and their combined weight was only 136 pounds. They lived on peanut butter and wall plaster. Sure, one cannot get fat on such a poor diet. The foster parents received from the government $30.000 a year to care for those misfortunates. They have given them no care, just abuse. How did that escape the attention of the supervising authority?! America, how can you pretend to feed and liberate the oppressed of the world and starve to death your own children? Indeed, Lord, man is a bizarre creature and you might have your own regret. If you would have to do it again, will you? Forgive me, Lord, for the dumb question; I am just a brute who has walked on thin ropes and slept in dark caves.

--What a senseless act. An Iraqi sniper has attacked the Red Cross Headquarters. He used a car marked, "Green Crescent." The tragedy resulted in 35 dead and over 200 injured. How about the losses of those needy the Red Cross had served with much compassion?! Is death the proper reward a beneficiary could offer to his benefactors?!

---Lord, forgive me; I need to bring more complaints to your table, just to show how troubled I am. Two men had started fire in Southern California. It has destroyed over 2, 000 homes and killed sixteen persons, besides the uncounted for and the fire is still raging. How destructive man can be. Still, you call him the prodigal Son. Indeed, you are a gentle father, who stands on the lonely icy road, always hoping that the lost might emerge from beneath the snow of ingratitude. Yes, you meet us where we do not expect you; may your warm love cure our cold insanity.

 Why then there is so much hate in man's heart? Ah! The wildest of all fires, the fire of hate that stands on man's way to accept his brother. I know the tale of Cain killing his only brother Abel. How terrible! Still I am waiting for a more serious explanation than that of jealousy.

-- Here is the today's most absurd news: Short and ugly people are less capable to earn their bread than the tall and handsome colleagues. Example: College Students give a more favorable evaluation for tall and better looking professors than to those short ones who are less attractive. Attractiveness! Is it not the heritage of the wind?

--And you, His Holiness Pope John Paul 11, please stop reiterating your long- standing that women can't be ordained as ministers in the Lord's Kingdom; (as if God has created a female soul and a male one). Wow! What has happened to the scholastic notion that the soul is asexual, odorless and weightless?

--Well, I must end my lamentations by a heartfelt weep. Yes, I am weeping for I have not seen in Cairo, Egypt, the traditional "Mawayed al Rahman, banquets of the Merciful." Why, Lord, have they forgotten it was Ramadan? I remember. Yes, I do remember, not too long ago, those banquets were established in every corner in the crowded City; offering free meals to the needy and hungry. Now that they are no longer held, how the poor would know there will be a big feast when the holy fast ends?! How I do miss my most compassionate Egypt of a half century ago! Indeed, the greed of the few often creates godless societies.

WHAT WOULD WE TELL THEIR CHILDREN?

10/ 28, 2003

We have invented the laser bomb to kill our enemies. The serious question arises: What would we tell their children?

Well, it is a big dilemma for me, although the answer is quite obvious for the many. Lord, I find myself standing alone, i.e., I am not one of the many nor I am one of the few. Yes, I stand alone on the ethereal road of truth that has no odor, weight or price. It is the lonely voice of God speaking to the wind. When the wind speaks to me, I shall shout: Rejoice, O my soul, rejoice, you have found your salvation. Where the heart sleeps, all the earthly treasures will be there to declare their submission to you. Now my disciple Bashir, don't ask me to speak to you about the doomsday of the fools; they will be trembling before their own shadows; the sun of truth had retained its warmth from their souls. Ah the power of the heart, Bashir! It can change the course of the stars and winds. We can lament the decadence of man; we can kneel down in reverence for his great ruins, all that is of no significance until we dive in with our hearts to restore his spiritual ruins. There is no religion or psychological treatment that can save him; only the change of heart can reserve for him a seat around the divine table.

How foolish humans are! Some mobilize their military power and others offer their money. The early are in search to conquer and the latter are in pursuit to seduce. Both are misleading and misled because the truth does not deliver itself to the conquerors nor to the seducers; rather to those who surrender unconditionally to the voice of a pure heart. For this reason, I stand alone on the lonely icy road; I am awaiting the rise of the divine golden sun in my heart. And I am willing to give away all the treasures of the world, just to be a worthy recipient of that prize.

"Pour chercher la vérite´, il faut étre seul et romper avec tous ceux qui ne l´ aime pas assez-seeking the Truth, one must stand alone and brake away with all those who don't like it enough." Doctor Zhivago. Chap. V

Yes, truth does not parade in the public places and refuses to appear on the television screens. Rather, it exists in the unknown dark caves, discovered only by the fervor of the hermit's heart. O holy Truth, today I bring all my fruits, my flowers and my sweat to offer them to thee. All are modest tokens of the fervor of my heart, accept them with thy white hands; they are all and uniquely for thy majesty. The change of heart is the true change; the change of time is a nightmare, if left untouched by the human heart. Although man is a drifting leaf on the agitated ocean of time, still he is eternal through the merits of his heart. The heart is the source of all the good that flows in the universe.

WITCHES AND GOBLINS

10/ 31, 2003

It is Halloween, the night of witches and goblins. At night I went to the New York nightclub where the county's most bizarre people gathered. How cruel time can be. That evening I saw a couple of women whom, ten years ago, my heart had so much desired. They looked tired and weary as wrinkles made themselves quite visible on their aged- faces. Their looks disgusted me and so I was disgusted, somehow, with my own; I too have been subjugated to the flagellation of time. One consolation though, it was that well- built young woman whose snow-white puffed breasts have emanated enough tenderness for all the anguished aged men like myself. Her unique sweet smile was the silver line that shone through the uninterrupted stream of smoke of stinky cigarettes. Surveying the whole club panorama, suddenly I saw him. A decade ago, he was the Club's Casanova, in spite of his advanced age and short stature. He had this unique charm as he gracefully and energetically swung women, young and old, on the dance platform. His movements were smooth and agile as those of an eagle. His agility had made him the most visible male on the platform. Most the club's males envied him- at least I did. His distinct vitality might have made women fantasize about his extraordinary sexual performance. In the past he wore a white suit, as if he were celebrating an interminable status of a groom. All that was then and this is now: He was dressed in a black suit. His head was covered with a flat black hat that hid his savage untrimmed silver hair. His nose seemed to have gone astray from his small face.

143

He looked more like an outdated clown than that image of the little prince he once had. Worse, his debilitated arms clunk into a pair of rusty aluminum- crutches that sustained his –now-weakened body. His slow movements forced me to think that he had finally reached the edge of his mortality. Aided by those crutches, he came to greet me. As I shook his hand, I felt the absence of that force once inhibited it. Yes, it was weak and dry. We exchanged a sad smile and then parted without saying a word to each other, as if we were two humiliated generals who have lost the war against a ferocious enemy called time. Certainly we both feared to speak about this defeat. I began to think of time as the wildfire that had consumed Southern California, over a week ago. Suddenly I felt irresistible sympathy for the man. Perhaps I was projecting that sympathy to myself; eventually I will look like him ten years from now.

The smoke rose high and I almost choked. I retreated toward the entrance. There I stood in a lonely corner, just to watch the incoming flock of the bizarre creatures. I saw that young lawyer with the slightly- twisted mouth, but extremely beautiful body. Her curves have noticeably disappeared and her twisted mouth has expanded; too many lies. Thank God, she had rejected me as I once attempted to befriend her and was hoping even for more. Then appeared that couple: The lady was dressed in a nun habit and engaging arm to arm with a guy who was dressed like a Franciscan monk. She held a box of cigarettes in one hand and a big lollipop in the other. The male companion held a Bible in one hand and the other was closing on a brown beads rosary. Shortly after, gloriously arrived that nurse with the voluptuous boobs. Ah, how I desired to be her Patient. Her Patient I could not be, the boobs were reserved to another woman.

I was glad to be married, although unhappily so. Finally, I took off, with a lot of bewilderments on my mind. I thought how Halloween, the traditional day of camouflage, is the day of a bad rap. If thoroughly examined, in spite of all its disguises, it is a regular day like any other of the year. Modern man is the mask of all masks. Truly thick is this mask. It is so thick that even God's head could swallow as it tries to pierce its opacity. Indeed, Halloween is not the day of the witches and goblins, it is our day, our everyday's treat; we are the witches and goblins. And this is quite bitter. So waitress, please be generous in sugaring my lemonade, since I can't handle the hard liquor; I am here for treat and not for trick. O humans; trick or treat! You have often accepted the trick and neglected the treat. Still, the choice remains yours.

WHAT IS WRONG WITH YOU ALL?

11/2, 2003

The Iraqi insurgents greeted the world with death; a missile had hit an army CH-47 Chinook helicopter. The downing of the US aircraft resulted in sixteen deaths and twenty- one injured; fifteen of them have suffered serious wounds. What a sad day for their spouses, children, parents, siblings, relatives, lovers and friends. Although I am none of the above, I felt sad; the universal soul connects us in spite of the repeated merciless stabs into her heart.

Consequent to that sad event, the Secretary of Defense held a brief conference. Surprisingly his opening statement was indirect condemnation of the invasion: "The existence of foreign troops on foreign soil is unnatural," he said.

Ah, how I wished he and his boss had seriously entertained this thought before having thrown themselves and the world unto the hellish fire of war.

"... Violence is expected under those circumstances," he added, telling us the obvious.

"...We will not run away from the enemy; rather we will confront and defeat him on his own territory," the Secretary assured his audience, thus restating his familiar arrogance.

Well, it is a jungle out there and the beast with the strongest teeth will continue to chew on the flesh and bones of the weak. However, the philosophy of violence jeopardizes any hope for peace. Seductive is the eloquence of the demonic wisdom that states: peace is often the legitimate child of war. In so believing, we find justification to unleash our worst instinct of aggression. Dangerous is man's violence; it ends up reclaiming him as its ultimate victim.

Mr. Secretary, may I submit to your meditation the words of the renowned spiritual leader J. Krishnamurti- in his work: *the book of life*:

"...when you are violent and have the idea of nonviolence, you are essentially violent."

Could it be that one has within the same dictator?!

In simpler words: stop issuing ultimatums to your enemy. In so behaving, you are awakening his worst, but most legitimate, instinct of auto- defense. Shouldn't charity start at home, meaning: one must first destroy the monster within before chasing the neighbor's cat that disturbs our sleep?

Mr. President, You have opted for war because you lacked imagination, patience, listening, compromising and other diplomatic skills of negotiation; all are distinctive qualities of great leaders. Unfortunately, small leaders are short of Patience, uncompromising and ill tempered-qualities of children and beasts. I cannot call you beast or child, you are my President; but certainly I am convinced that you are still a novice, who desperately needs the diplomatic maturity to play a constructive role in the international arena.

It's your parents' fault; they have introduced you, at an early age, to the cowboy culture. They failed to train you to roll over hills and to have a chance to taste the mud. And certainly you have missed the pleasures of chasing butterflies. Deprived of these simple natural innocent activities, you have become a warrior, acquiring the -ever- sour taste of destruction. Being a spoiled brat born to a rich family, you have learned to sacrifice others on your altar. You are a false god, who craves for the worthy reverence of the true one.

In my humble view, the only means for peace is peace; other means are doomed treacheries. It is man's unrivaled stupidity to believe that the price of war is less costly than that of peace.

Since the buck stops at your office, Mr. President, history will remember you as the man who had failed to use the various diplomatic channels with Saddam. I hope that you would not commit the same mistake with other dictators.

--Forgiveness, I have been carried away; today I am obliged to reflect on the precious but lost sixteen young American lives. One of them was supposed to travel that same day to attend his mother's funerals. Apparently mother was awaiting him on the other end of the road. Young American soldier, may your abducted life help us to understand the meaning of life. To you, the other dead ones, how I wished to know a bit about every one of you. However, I am sure of one essential thing: Your sacrifices will forever live in our memories. I thought of your spouses who dreamt that one day they will go to the hairdressers to appear beautiful before your eyes. I thought of your children who will wear their best dresses, suits, purses and white cute hats to run and hug you upon your arrival. I imagined what would be your reaction to the warm reception of those loving spouses and innocent children. All these human sentiments would have the power to heal the remorse deeply rooted in your hearts for having had killed strangers. You were quite aware that they, too, were loved by their own as you were by yours. Unfortunately, the strong wind of violence has swept away all those gentle dreams and sweet sentiments. Beloved dead parents, wives, brothers, sisters, sons and daughters; may the true eternal peace embrace you all. Along the reposed souls of my beloved ones, I remembered you today in my prayer. Innocent lambs that have been offered as sacrifices on the altars of our vain ambitions, may you rest in peace. Do not forget to breathe mercy on us; we are lost as we journey toward eternity. Please, do pray for our safe journey; you have safely arrived. You're now in the company of our most merciful Lord; may your ultimate sacrifices redeem our vain ambitions.

AMERICA ROCKS THE VOTE, OR THE VOTE ROCKS AMERICA?

11/ 4, 2003

America rocks the vote thus read the headline of the Anderson Cooper's show. The title has seduced me but the content was quite disappointing; I should have known better. After all, they were politicians and politicians are robots programmed with ambiguous clichés and empty promises. The nine Democratic candidates gathered in Boston to deliver everything but candor. I liked though the humor of some of them, especially that of Al Sharpton. His great sense of humor redeemed his funny hairdo and cheap suit that did not fit him well. As they finished giving their foxy answers to questions posed to them by journalists, they were more than anxious to take questions from the audience. I paraphrase.

A white young man: Mr. Sharpton, what would be your first thought as you wake up the first morning in the White House?

 I make sure that George Bush had packed up and left. Second: I'll change all the locks to make sure he can't get in, in case he would come back." The amused audience applauded aloud. Another: Senator Kerry, what do you think of gun control?

 I'm a hunter, I eat what I kill.

That, too, was an evasive answer. What else could one expect from a politician, anyway? The questions and answers fluctuated between the serious and the funny and that was entertainment in its dramatic best.

A black female: "Senator Kerry, what's your plan to create jobs? Apparently she was unemployed.

Well, jobs are hard to come by nowadays, joked the Senator. Certainly he was attacking George Bush. "Now, let me be a bit more serious, I'll make sure that every young man and woman in America will have a job."
 He received a warm applause from the young and naïve in the audience. Mister, you couldn't be more comical.

Another: This question is addressed to any of you: Who of the candidates would you like to party with?
They all raced to jump onto the wagon of leisure.

If my wife would allow it, I certainly like to party with that young lady who has asked the question, replied old Senator Joseph Lieberman.

I'll choose Mrs. Kerry, replied Al.

I was going to choose Carol (the only Presidential female candidate), but since I need to keep an eye on my wife from Al, I chose the Reverend, replied Senator Kerry, the wounded Vietnam hero.

For a change came the question of race. They all dreamt then to become instant stars as each started telling how close he had come from that shooting one, Martin Luther King.

I'll create a colorless society, each one of them answered and all were lying. Prejudice is a universal disease that has no cure by the power of the human mind; only a pure heart can cure it. However, the purity of the heart is a rare product in the market place of the commons; only saints and angels can practice and promote it. Well, am I then promoting racism, at least, by despair? No. Rather I am warning of the seriousness of the matter.

A white young man: Has anyone of you used marijuana?

This question has divided the candidates into three camps. The Camp of the Puritans made of: General Wesley Clark, Joe Lieberman and Al Sharpton.

In the liberal camp, appeared Howard Dean, the former governor of Vermont, John Kerry, the Senator from Massachusetts, John Edwards, the Senator from North Carolina and Dennis Kucinich, the Senator from Ohio. All of the above candidates have confessed to have had used the soothing drug.

Carol Moseley Braun, a former Ambassador, and presently a representative of the District of Columbia, abstained to answer; she might have had thought that the question was trivial.

From the audience's bodily gestures, it became apparent that those who have confessed to have had used drugs have found favor before the young. Yes, the lonely and desperate always look to identify with someone bigger than themselves. Indeed, vice craves for company, perhaps, more so than virtue. However, virtue has the power of self-fulfilling. It even finds itself secure in the caves' crevices.

Finally came into play the question of the confederate flag.

"It must extend hands to those who raise high the confederate flag in their pickup trucks," said the erratic Howard Dean. This answer was a deadly shot aimed at the heart of his political career. The seven other candidates jumped on him, not out of sincere conviction, rather they dreamt to take a big bite from the already slaughtered opulent cow. Until that unfortunate moment, the Vermont Governor had high hopes to be the front runner, who will face the incompetent republican George W. Bush running for his second term in the 2004 race for the presidency.

"We believe in dreams; Mr. Bush believes in hallucinations," was Al Sharpton's closing statement. "Because of those dreams, I remain loyal to the Democratic Party, although at times it, too, has difficulty to differentiate between dreams and hallucinations," he rightfully added.

LOWER RATING, SO DAMN THE HOMOSEXUALS

11/6, 2003

George W. Bush's popularity started to slip away, at least temporarily, amongst the Conservatives because of his failed adventure in Iraq. Those thugs have fast forgotten they were the ones who had waived the red blanket to arouse the bull's thirst for blood. For control damage, advisors suggested invigorating the debilitated by politicizing the ban on the late-term abortions. The President had invited a dozen of prominent neo-cons to represent and let the rest of the monsters know that he is forever the obedient servant of their values. Surrounded by the insanes, he signed the bill and for that he received well- merited prolonged applauses. After all, who can, in good conscience, claim to be civilized and still call for the ultimate barbaric act of aborting an embryo that would have had struggled against death for six months? To such a brave warrior, life must be his /her prize. Any opponent of life must not deserve to live. After all, the life of others cannot be less valuable than one's own. In legal words, a policy of a double standard is a policy of discrimination; it must end. For that act, I, too, applauded you, Mr. President, in spite of your unjustified war in Iraq. Now that I have applauded you, I must raise those same hands to heaven to solicit cure for your sick mind. You have won the battle for $87.5 billion to spend on your most perilous adventure. You are delusional thinking that through piles of money you can guarantee freedom to the long- alienated Iraqis.

Your- ill-conceived policy dreams to expand beyond the geographical boundaries of the Mesopotamia. You're dreaming to democratize the whole oppressed nations of the Middle East. In your sweet dreams, bitter nightmares are awaiting you. You will awake in the glacial winter- nights of history to find yourself swimming in a bath of sweat, secretions of your delirious mind. We all love freedom but not the instant kind. Unlike you, Mr. President, I believe that freedom is a caterpillar that must endure the process of a long metamorphosis before it becomes a butterfly that sucks the nectar of the changing times. Only through the caterpillar's endurance in the hostile environment of rocks and mud will be born the butterfly whose multicolored wings enchant our eyes and hearts. Mr. President, tonight I listened to your brief discourse about your plan to democratize the Middle East; forgetting that God had inscribed His gentle laws on the human heart before He has revealed them to the Prophets, who have delivered them to us on scrolls. It's the heart that guides man safely to his final destination, freedom. I, too, dream of freedom for my oppressed people in the Middle East, but the kind of freedom that will grow in their own soils. Like human development, a true freedom emerges from a tedious process. If we truly seek it, we must allow it to grow in a natural, human environment. Only God can say let there be light and there light be; humans must labor hard and long to discover and make use of the light. Therefore, Mr. President, slow down, modesty is necessary in this case. Your manufactured freedom leads to greater alienation. I prefer walking toward freedom as a turtle rather than as a fox; galloping never creates rapprochement, rather estrangement.

A BITCH CALLED LIFE

11/ 10, 2003

It is my 63rd birthday. Happy birthday old horse and worry not the mountain is only a few miles away. Once atop, you will burst out into laughing. No, I am not talking of joy rather of irony. Joy you never thought, but the undulations of snakes excite every fiber in your flesh; your ephemeral skin has carried the valley to the mountaintop. Let the shadow of death distract you not, rather in prayer you must wait to hear the ultimate song of the living mountain. Soon your mouth will be freed from the reins and then you will neigh and the echo of your neighing will make the mountain tremble. You are a voyager and your hooves have always been filled with small rocks, you have thought higher dreams for them; you have wanted them to become part of the mountain's peak.

Old snake, the dove you have eaten will form your wings that will land you unto God's hand. And when man is in God's hand, he will overcome death and all its sorrows.

Happy birthday old owl, it's through your aging eyes that the gods will pierce the heart of men. And when man's heart is pierced by God's grace, then the womb of earth will burst out with truth.

Happy birthday old eagle, you have built your nest in the clouds and the clouds are God's tears; your tireless search for the sun has moved God's heart.

Happy birthday stubborn old man, all the CEOs of Wall Street cannot pay the price that will seduce you to trade your soul. Your stubbornness is great witness to your taste for the divine. Happy birthday old sage, you scorn all what empowers man, you have been drinking from the cup of the gods and you have no taste for the drinks of the commons. They drink honey and milk; you have chosen to drink mud and myrrh. It is from the mud that the gods have molded man and from the myrrh they have promised him salvation. He must succeed making out of mud the mascara that will beautify their eyes and from the myrrh he must fill up their cups.

Happy birthday great rebel, the rebellion of your youth has composed the song of the gods; surpass yourself or else you will join the fast- aging caravan of the mortals.

Happy birthday old turtle, your slowness has revealed the secrets of earth to your rocky stomach and your scorn for the hopping of rabbits has always gained you the bewilderment of men.

Happy birthday old warrior, you have heroically dueled the gods; it is of no use to fight man. Man is your domain of compassion; the gods are the field of your fighting passion.

Today the gods toast you, would you please raise your cup and drink from their poison. Drink, drink from their poison, and once poisoned you will rise to the occasion to become God. Yes, their poison will fortify you and, at your turn, you will inject your humanity into their veins. They will become you, after you have become them. In such a fusion there is no loser, all are winners of promises made and well kept.

For the sixty-three, and the years to come, I have been and will be a moth attracted to the light; I want to gradually melt into the light. I have rejected darkness, that heavy garment of ignorance. I am the one who fears heights and has an exquisite taste for depth. It is in depth that man finds God; heaven is an upwards landmark for deepness and those who fear deepness have no taste for the gods.

Today I declare that all the above- mentioned strifes are truly mine. Still, under the oath of life, I beg you not to rush revering me. Like you, I have cheated and been cheated; lied and been lied to; defeated and been defeated; rejected and been rejected; duped and been duped; praised and been praised; criticized and been criticized. I have rose my feet exalted by the big dance, pulled up my hair out of sorrow and gnawed my teeth out of rage. In sum: In spite of my divine aspirations, I remain a villain, like all mortals are. However, my struggle must continue to elevate the villain within me to the stature of God, who awaits me on the mountaintop.

As I journey toward the mountaintop to encounter my God, I must continue flirting with all shadows spread on my paths. I fear not the mountain wolves; the wolf within me is more ferocious than anyone of them. Meanwhile, and in spite of the unprecedented qualities, I declare that I am a horseman of a carriage ridden by a bitch called life. I must submit to all her caprices and shall always love her. In case of failure, I still will have the satisfaction to say that I have tried and so hard have I tried. So, today from the top of the mountain, I scream: O deities, dwellers of the holy mountain, throw me into the depth of the dusty valley. There I want to embrace the ashes of my ancestors; their ashes are God breathing on me with hope.

TAP DANCE IS NOT RECOMMANDED TO THOSE WHO DON'T HAVE FEET

11/ 11, 2003

Today seventeen soldiers from the Italian regiment and eight Iraqis were killed; a loaded car had exploded into the Italian compound. No surprise, it is business as usual. The market of killing is up and down as if following the erratic behavior of Wall Street.

--Let's go to Saudi Arabia: Twenty were killed and 122 were injured, mostly Arabs. The perpetrators wanted to force the royal family to come to its senses. For decades, it had governed its people with tyranny and injustices; while showering the Westerners with the spoils of oil to keep their machine rolling, most often to intimidate Arabs. Worse, say the terrorists, the royal family had betrayed their people by allowing the loose Western morals to infiltrate into their godly society. Ultimately, in the terrorists' eyes, the House of Saud is a house of evil and it must fall in the name of Allah.

On this day King Abdullah 11 woke up, not to pray as usual, rather to complain:

O most merciful Allah, why have they done this to my Kingdom?! Don't they know that last month I had announced elections for the municipal offices and regional elections are scheduled to take place next year? Moreover, I had approved a televised coverage during the deliberations of the counsels' assembly…Oh well, I'm not the only troubled ruler; on the other side of the Ocean our colleague King George has his problems as well.

His Majesty, the appointed members of your counsels' assembly are nothing other than your own shadows. Therefore, your sleep and rise still govern the nights and days of Arabia. His Majesty, true freedom comes to man when he walks with God and not in the shadow of another man. Rulers must govern their peoples with justice and respect; otherwise sooner or later their ruling blood will stain the marble walls of their palaces. And now it is your turn, Mr. George W. Bush. Please allow me to remind you of what your previous rival presidential Democrat, Al Gore, said: "…It makes no more sense to launch an assault on our civil liberties as the best way to get at the terrorists than it did to launch an invasion of Iraq as the best way to get Osama Ben Laden."

 Mr. President, some Iraqis would like to save you the last dance but have no feet; a bomb had exploded from beneath as they were walking to buy a loaf of bread for their starving children. Thanks Saddam, Osama and Bush; you are all princes of death and darkness. Indeed, your graciousness has rendered the eclipse of the sun a frequent occurrence; you have failed to see the freedom of others as a part of your own. Oh well, let's stop insulting the so- called big boys of the world, certainly we need to offer some hope to the world's orphans. Let's pray: may God pour out mercy to cure our insanities that confuse your minds and steel the tenderness of your hearts. And may tomorrow's world be a better place for you and all the helpless.

MY GOD! I WANT TO BE A GORILLA

11/ 13, 2003

It's a day of a thousand follies. Let's visit the house of all the houses, Washington, D.C., the world's political capital. A few days ago, the genius ones, the civilian and military leaders have agreed to promote these three words: Iron, hammer, Iraqization.

What is meant by 'iron hammer?' It is a military tactic to mercilessly hammer the Iraqi insurgents, a way to let them know that we, too, are bad boys just like you. To achieve such a noble goal, Hawk helicopters are most effective weapons of annihilation. And the Chief prays:

 Fly, fly over Baghdad and let our bombs hit a thousand or two of those thugs. Tear off their fleshes so the hungry dogs of Baghdad can feast on them. Their wives and children's tears are soft music to our ears.

O pilots of mighty power, as you fly over Baghdad, seeking the destruction of the enemy, I beg you to remember the sleeping children, the old, the women, the disable and the rest of the helpless majority.

'Iron hammer?' What's for? To build ultimately iron bars around the heads and hearts of those we pretend to liberate? Why humans cannot use properly their exclusive gift of speech? Could it be that speech is a curse pronounced uniquely upon humans?

'Iraqization!' is another genius decision that comes from the dead brains of the Right –Wing gangsters. Hurray! Miss. Force wanted to show the goodness of her heart to the whole world by dreaming to liberate the Iraqis. Unfortunately, she had forgotten that freedom is born out of the psychological state of the oppressed and not out of the caprice of the strong.

Mercy upon you, O Mesopotamia, so much have you suffered. Thanks to Saddam's revolution and Bush's delusion, you are now the land of the forgotten dead. Warmongers, allow me to get your attention to one of the many kindnesses practiced in the animals' Kingdom. A dog named Ginny has devoted her life rescuing strayed cats from dumpsters, air conditioning ducks and other dangerous places. Sometimes, she has rescued as many as eight cats a week.

Have you heard of that grieving gorilla? Yes, Madame Koko had cried for two days when told of the death of her pet cat. Should we erect a statue for Miss. Ginny and another for Madame Koko? We must, but first we need to destroy yours. Feeling! Feeling! Feeling! The world would be better off, if animals dominate it. Those two stories and many others performed by animals make life worth living. I just wish humans have revolved and not evolved. You might ask: who are you and to what kingdom do you belong? Frankly I do not know; nor do I wish to. All what I know, I am a rooster. Unlike the other roosters, I do not chant the birth of the day. Rather in the silence of dawns I pull the wagon carrying the hens. And here we go to the jungle where humans are absent. Are you a hen? If so, hop in; we want to arrive there before the sunrise, we need to welcome the light. There we shall kneel down next to Madame Koko the grieving gorilla and Ginny the compassionate dog to celebrate life. Yes, we will spend the rest of our lives praying day and night for the renewal of the human heart.

LORD, HERE I STAND CONFUSED AND HELPLESS

11/ 19, 2003

Rain, rain, O heaven, rain mercy on us; we need it to wipe away our sins. Lord of rain, sun, of bones and stones, please take me for a stroll into your divine garden. Lo and behold, lays before me the perilous journey

153

into man's logic; wars and strifes are in every front page.

--Today the Massachusetts Supreme Court has approved the marriage of same sex. Some have hailed it as a victory for the human rights; others have viewed it as surrender to the new age's a-moral spirit.

Frankly, Lord, here I stand confused and helpless. I want to extend my hand to the two opposing camps but it is too short to reach both. Lord, help me to bless the one without cursing the other. I welcome equality to all. Brothers and sisters of the different sexual orientations, I may not have a taste for your behavior but you are not here to sweeten my tongue. Yes, man must find a way out of his egocentrism by acknowledging the rights of others. The old adage says: "Live and let live." It's the golden Rule that must govern nations and societies. It can be transposed to: "Think your way and let other think theirs."

To the straights: I hope you wouldn't accuse me of trying to derail your train; I am not in the business of derailment. However, I believe it matters not if we travel in separate trains; at the end we meet in the grand station, in the mighty arms of God. Lord, destiny of all travelers, today I rejoice for the kisses and the exchange of tenderness between my brothers the gays and my sisters the lesbians. To you complainers, I say: Stop raising grievances; rather begin finding praises in all and for all. God gives a taste to everything. His cup does not only contain, it also has the power to purify what is contained, poisonous as it may be. Do you believe in God's power or are you gratified in glorifying your own weakness?

--I grieve for the acts of that youngster who has killed an eighty year old woman after he had raped her. I grieve for the acts of that school principal. She was in her mid-fifties; he has just turned eleven when she began her pervert journey unto his heart. She showered him with gifts, cuddled him behind the closed doors of her authority and finally led him to her bed. It is the copulation of the devil with the angel. I grieve for the acts of that Tampa social worker who has abandoned her husband and four children to marry a prisoner, who had slaughtered five of her species.

I grieve for my own lust. Mad at my wife, I began fantasizing about the other women of my past.

Forgive me, Lord, I am, too, a sinner. Until I recognize that all rest on you and in you, I shall remain a hypocritical whiner. Lord, take my hand, lead me to the fountain of understanding and help me to drink from that fountain of self- negation. It is only when I negate myself that I affirm you. I need to celebrate your victory; mine is a passing shadow. Lord, help all to accept the fact that the standard of morality doesn't lay within us; only in your Sacred Heart can we rest and find balance.

YOUR BREATH CAN MOVE A MOUNTAIN

11/ 21, 2003

Today President Bush, his wife Laura, Secretary of State Colin Powell and Political Advisor Condoleezza Rice were guests of the Buckingham Palace. Aged wine was toasted and generous compliments were exchanged in spite of the uncertain outcome of the war in Iraq. King George, you may swallow whatever amount of wine your stomach can tolerate but you are not going to succeed convincing some of the international community to swallow your insanity. The majority of the world refuses to toast you; your restless war policy has made the world more dangerous.

Well, may God have mercy on the King and the Queen! The guards didn't insure the security of their palace in spite of the fortified walls and doors. Having had struck a deal with a tabloid magazine, the perpetrator has managed to penetrate the palace delivering pieces of chocolate to the queen's guests in their bedrooms. Indeed, he has succeeded to prove his point: the only security of the palace was its insecurity. This adventure has made him an instant celebrity.

It has been reported that the Queen is considering going to court versus the intruder. If that would happen, it makes the Western democracy worth dying for. Had this assault occurred in the Middle East, the intruder would have been decapitated soon as caught.

--Pity on you Michael Jackson, king of Pop. Your interview with Martin Bashir, that sly British journalist, has put your reputation in in a negative light. You confessed to him that you had slept in the same bedroom, but not in the same bed, with young boys.

"That's love and the world needs more of it," you told him.

This interview has alerted the local authorities to keep watching eyes on you. Mike, if you continue inviting youngsters to your Neverland, it might soon become the land that never existed. But don't worry, in case the system would take away your infamous ranch, below the San Francisco Golden Bridge you will have a bed, where you can lay with the certainty of nothing to lose. My sincere sympathy, Michael, I know your sliding from the king of Pop to the suspicion of being child molester has earned you vulnerability in all fronts. May the Lord throw some red roses on your long rocky road!

--Lord, it is not over yet, more tragedies are flying from our earth to your heaven: Today violence has shown its ugly face in Istanbul, Turkey. Two trucks carrying bombs have exploded near a hotel, killing twenty- six and injuring at least forty- five people. The terrorists were aiming to kill Jews. It seems that violence has become modern man's appetizer, instead of savoring the very subtle taste of peace.

Lord, my mind is troubled; may its troubles shake not the peace of my heart. I thank you for that gentle passage of the morning breeze whispering through the stripes of my Venetian blinds. Thank you for the unexpected melody. Lord, I ask you not to take away my bitter chalice; rather help me to find you at the bottom of it.

-- Lord, the return of Rush Limbaugh to the airwaves makes the air a bit thick for my lungs. May you breathe into them, so I may survive Rush's poisonous thoughts. Also, a gust of your holy spirit blowing into Rush's direction certainly will do much good to humanity .Please, Lord, breathe into Rush's lungs from time to time, if possible.

--Forgive me, Lord, for my own sins. Just yesterday I had slept with the blasphemous thought that there is a ferocious competition between you and Satan. However, deep in my heart I know you still hold the universe in the palm of your hand. All the sins of men are but drops of evil floating in the ocean of your goodness, and your divine breath can move a mountain.

HELP ME TO BELIEVE IN MAN AND TO PUT MY TRUST IN YOU

11/ 27, 2003

It is Thanksgiving, a special day in the American Calendar. In this day we reminiscent and create memories as well. Most of us stare at the food with one eye; raising the other to heavens and say: thank you, Lord, for the year's blessings.

Lord, I also thank you for the children at the Washington Airport as they anxiously await the arrival of their mamas and papas. When the- so- much- missed parents appear, their anxieties disappear. Thanks for the return of the children's emotional security. Thanks for the tears of the visiting parents who will hold, for the first time, their babies born while they were killing others, certainly not of their own choice. Thanks for the safety of that Oklahoma 1 year old boy who had undergone twelve hours operation; four alien organs were integrated into his small troubled body. Thanks for the President's surprise visit to the fighting troops in Baghdad, although his advisors had seen a high political score. We know politics is the erratic pendulum of all politicians. Although history will judge them by the outcome of their politics; your parameters are quite different: You will judge them by the measure of their intentions while making those policies.

Thanks for the friendship between the American soldier and one of Baghdad's strayed dog, they needed each other.

Thanks for that Iraqi council member leaving a kiss on George Bush's cheek. True, it has caused anger among some Iraqis, but also has created hope in the hearts of those who are less consumed by their hatred for the liberal spirit of the West.

Thanks for the love and union between that Iraqi doctor woman and the American soldier. They have shown us that with goodwill even enemies can find peace, harmony and love with one another. Thanks for the agitated womb of mother earth, I am quite certain with your blessing it will deliver us a son called the Redeemer. Oh yes, it had already, His name is Emmanuel- God with us. May He be our companion as we travel the perilous roads of our lives!

Lord, may you become my mentor when I speak to others. Today I have been anything but kind to Marla. I have quarreled with her for her son's behavior of being wasteful of water and electricity. You know, Lord, the underlying reason: it is that anguish caused by shortage of money. Or maybe my true poverty lies somewhere else: my lack of faith in you. Why, Lord, have I forgotten that you are the one who had fed thousands with five loaves of bread and five fishes? And still abundance remained; all was the work of your miraculous hands. So, Lord, today I ask you to bless my poverty; a poverty blessed by you is richer than all the treasures of man. Forgive me for my lack of faith. Were not you who have promised: ask and you will receive tenfold? Lord, let your hand touch me, and I shall find a cure for all the ailments of my flesh and the anxieties of my soul. As I walk in darkness, please guide my steps, not to the fountains that will dry but to those that will forever overflow with your goodness and mercy. It is man's command upon man to calculate; let your command be upon us to believe. Lord, I believe in your goodness; in spite of all the evils of man, in your wisdom; in spite of his madness, in your light; in spite of his darkness, in your justice; in spite of all his injustices, in your harmony; in spite of all his confusions, in your gentle and quiet healing power of peace; in spite of all the noises of his Weapons of Mass Destruction. Ultimately, Lord, I believe in your love, in spite of his hateful acts. Thank you, Lord, for the nourishing thoughts; my soul needed them to rejuvenate; for so long it had followed the path of doubt. It is only when we communicate wholehearted with you that we find the right answers to our questions and concerns. Help me to believe in man and to put all my trust in you. Man has the pencil and you have the eraser; you're the one who draws the last draft of all the mortals' journeys.

THE SUPERMAN IS MARRIED TO A SUPERWOMAN

11/ 28, 2003

I watched with great interest Paula Zhan's interviewing the injured great worrier, actor Christopher Reeve. It was his first interview without a ventilator. How uplifting to hear him speaking.

157

"What is next, Christopher?"

"I shall soon walk," shouted your brave spirit and that is liberation. A wink of an eye must be a celebration of life," you added. How ungrateful the majority of us are; we take God's gifts as given rights. Yes, we must be grateful for every breath we take, every move we make, every thought we entertain and every sensation we feel. All are God's special gifts and we must receive them with great gratitude.

Christopher, I heard you saying that one day you will take apart your wheelchair and run with your youngest son in a baseball field; may God soon grant your wish.

Paula asked you if you miss your pre-accident activities.

"Being is better than doing," was your graceful answer. At that moment you became for me the true superman, superior to the one who had floated on thin and thick air.

She then asked:

"What is your ultimate dream?"

"I dream of normal life," you replied, eyes filled with hope.

She went on to ask about your swimming competition, and you reported a winning. You are a raw model for the disables and able as well. You taught us that man's soul can fly in spite of all the ailments that enchain his body.

Having given such inspiring answers that revealed your spiritual strength, I might report those moments of despair that had visited you early after the accident. Yes, you had even thought of suicide. Your wise soulmate has advised you patience. You have accepted her advice; you have valued her womanly intuitive wisdom. Indeed, the superman is married to a superwoman.

"I love you the same," Dana told you. More than eight years now have passed since the unhappy accident and still you are here; she has been nourishing you with a lot of love. Indeed, love is a great healer; it makes life worth living.

"What have you learned from the accident?" Paula asked.

"One must stay focused on whatever one is doing," you replied. It is your philosophy of a full commitment to life, shown through your commitment to work and family.

That accident has widened your horizon; you are now a stubborn crusader to find a cure for paralysis. Your wisdom says: "hope is a product of knowledge and the power of projecting this knowledge into the future." In the most devastating accident you have found opportunity. You have seized this opportunity and have flown over the icy mountain of the life's trials. Strong are your wings; may God keep fortifying them; we need a superman like you to show us the way to the warm sun of perseverance and hope.

AMERICA, HOW AMAZING AND AMUSING YOU ARE!

12/ 1, 2003

Here you are, O December, month of coldness. In many places your snow covers the valleys and mountains; slapping young and old faces with your pinching winds. Although you make us weary, still you offer us unique warmth. After all, you are the month that records Jesus' birth, the month of hope to humanity wrapped in the thickness of despair. I am not being a whiner, but I have lived long enough to be aware of man's madness. Lord, how could I overlook the scene of that heavy-set young woman who was knocked down and crushed; all were rushing into the Wal-Mart to buy that newly- released DVD. What a missed opportunity of civility. Thank God, the majority of men still hold the door for ladies.

America, how amazing and amusing you are! If the whole world were to be captured in comics' videos, you be the funniest of all. Today I noticed an ad placed in a community magazine that read, "Save the Manatees." I was moved and wanted to be a part of that noble cause. True, manatees are ugly but cute in their own way. I called to find out how I could help. Surprise, surprise! It was an erotic operation. I hung up, a bit disappointed. Shortly after, the phone rang. I did not want to answer; I thought those obscene manatees might be calling me. As the phone continued ringing, I decided to answer; it might be one of my children. None of the above; it was a vendor.

"Good morning, Sir."

"The same to you," I replied in an impersonal manner.

"My name is Wanda."

"Sadat." I didn't want her to know my real name.

"Wow, the great leader of Egypt!"

"Already dead..."

"My sympathy, Sir…"

I had nothing to do with it," I replied dryly.

"O, well... Mr. Sadat, do you have a bird?"She asked in a birdie voice.

"I love birds and always wanted to understand them in their own language, just like the wise Solomon did."

"That's admirable, Mr. Sadat. In fact, we have the greatest season's gift for you."

"And what is it?" I asked out of sheer curiosity.

"Well, Mr. Sadat, we have a giant sale of birds' diapers. Besides the low prices, we maintain the highest quality for our products and they come in many colors with flowers embroidery. We…"

"Please, Miss., I hate to see you consuming your saliva for nothing; I no longer have any kinds of birds... I used to; then they served well their purpose. In fact, I used to talk to them and conversing with them was quite delightful. Now that I am old, I talk to myself; no time to communicate with any other creatures."She broke into faked laughter.

"Mr. Sadat, do you know that pets and birds have the greatest healing power for the sick?"

"Miss., I'm not sick, I am just disgusted with the world. Now we must disconnect."

"If there is anyone to be disgusted with, it must be yourself; Goodbye, Mr." Disgustedly she hang up on me, certainly she has made my day. To recover the lost joy, I should have thought assistance from a bottle of Vodka. Since I am not a drinker, I treated myself with a pot of hot coffee with milk and that did hurt little Javier's chance. How cruel of me to have caused discomfort for a poor Colombian boy who prided himself of drinking daily a gallon of milk. And I wandered, afterwards, could man ever find the balance between consumption and redemption, between cold and hot?

Disgusted, I laid down. Yes, let manatees be sex objects, let birds wear floral diapers and let me talk to myself; I need to know the stranger. It is all human, too human.

SANTA, SANTA, PLEASE BRING ME A WARM GIFT FROM THE NORTH POLE

12/ 3, 2003

Since it is the season of cheers; I must go light commenting on news. O piano man, please play me some happy tunes of Christmas. *"Jingle Bells…"* will do for now. And please, save me *"Frosty the Snow Man…"* for a better mood later. As for my stomach's need, just give me the day's appetizer: a reindeer will do it. Santa, Santa, please bring me a warm gift from the North Pole. Well.., a check of five hundred dollars will pay my water and electric bills. With the remaining amount I can afford buying a Christmas card for everyone of my five children and a six one for my wife; thanks, Dollar Store.

Please, Santa, do not worry about those fancy treats such as: ham, sweet potatoes, eggnog, gingerbread and the many other traditional Christmas treats. May God bless the ministries of the Tampa Bay; we have their promise… That's what the ad said on most of the channels of the local TV stations, anyway.

Santa, some minor grievances though from the other eleven months are still weighing heavily on my heart. (I know kindness during this month is a must, in honor of the divine child born in a manger). Yes, I despise the emotional brutality inflicted upon my sensitivity by those who go to the Oriental Hotel in New York City.

They have no problem spending $5,000 a night for a Presidential suite. How insulting. Jesus, even you could not have been able to afford it. Is that why you have spent your first night on earth in that cold manger? Well, a village in your days could have lived comfortably with $5000 for a period of a whole year. Yes, I am talking about supplies of herbal medicine, food, clothing, warm shoes and even woolen scarves wrapped around the shoulders of its elders.

THE UNFAMILIAR FACE OF LAW AND ORDER

12/ 4, 2003

"**Sir**, do you know why I stopped you?" the black police asked with gentle smile that assured me a happy ending.

"No, Officer."

He pulled out of his pocket a notebook and ripped off a sheet to draw the U-turn and its conjuring street. In a kind tone, he explained why one cannot make a U-turn there. "Besides, it is a Holidays Season; many people are on the road, and your driving could have easily caused an accident," he added. Sincerely I apologized and my apology paid off.

"I'm not going to give you the ninety dollar ticket, just drive carefully and have happy Holidays," he said, extending his hand to shake mine.

Was that a sweet dream or what? Wow! He did not give me a traffic violation ticket. Instead, he offered me happy holidays' wishes and even a handshake. I was going to say only in America but suddenly a feeling of disappointment overcame me. I remembered that black man from Cincinnati, Ohio. Three days ago, he had died in the hands of four brutal police officers. True, the video has shown the man attacking one of them; the arrested might have been high on some drug. Although attacking a police officer is a felony, in some cases and a criminal mischief in others. The question remains: did the suspect deserve to be beaten to death? Why didn't they content themselves subduing him? After all, he was unarmed. Well, to be fair, I must stop making any further comments about this tragic incident, since I lack knowledge of all the details. I drove back home with the good memory of that policeman. Soon as I opened the door the phone rang. It was Miss. Gloria; from the Flag, headquarters of the Scientology Church.

"Happy Holidays" said she.

"Happy Holidays to you, too."

"Sir, you, Marla and Javier are invited to our White Castle Christmas celebration. Several choruses from

161

different denominations will be singing Carols of the season. Would you, please, come and celebrate with us?"

 I knew very well what she meant: pull them out of the Jesus' net; we have plenty of salt to erase the stinky convictions in their reactive minds; they need to embrace ours.

"Certainly we will; thanks for the invitation." As I hung up, I found myself murmuring: there is no celebration as long our hearts are entrapped in the mud of false superiority."

Lord, it's my genuine wish that one day we all will abandon the caves of fanaticism to ascend to the mountaintop of tolerance; only a nude dance on a glacial mountain can save our entrapped souls.

COUSINS BY BLOOD AND ENEMIES BY MISUNDERSTANDING-AVRAHAM BURG

12/ 7, 2003

Peace to all men of goodwill, they are the inheritors of the earth and true messengers of God. The co-opted photo of Avraham Burg, a former speaker of the Knesset, and the Palestinian Chief Yasser Arafat was a heavenly sight. They were embracing one another on December 1, after they had agreed to work for the revitalization of "the Oslo Accord." This sight has convinced me that all conflicts between Israelis and Arabs were not born out of hatred; rather lack of empathy. Some Arabs and Jews have interpreted this encounter as nothing but a self- pumping gesture. In other words, the meeting had no political gravitas. Yes, it did have that heavy weight men of soft shoulders and impure hearts cannot carry. True, this meeting didn't and can't seal a solution to the -long-standing conflict. However, it was a conscience awakener meant to keep the Oslo Accords alive.

 I remember my encounter with Mr. Adara (means: noble in Hebrew). I was then seeking to rent an apartment while enrolling in the PH.D. Program at the prestigious New Graduate School for Social Research (several of the founders of this institution were former professors at Columbia University).

"I'm Egyptian," I said, extending my hand to shake his. He held mine for a moment and with a serene smile covering his face, he replied: "A very warm welcome to you, cousin."

I smiled and didn't know why though. Maybe deep inside, I, too, considered him a cousin, or at least a new-found friend.

"Yes, we're cousins by blood and enemies by misunderstanding," Adara emphasized as he finished telling me the story of how the Biblical Abraham had fathered the two sons: Isaac and Ishmael. Although I had read several times that story, I didn't allow its deepest meaning to penetrate my heart. Only at that genial

162

encounter I understood it. I then became sure it was the cry of the blood and that cry I have heard in Adara's sincerity as he was lively telling the story. With a sustained smile, he led the way to show me a vacant apartment in one of his many buildings. In a few minutes we closed the deal and parted with the good memory of each other.

And today I can say, dear Adara, indeed we are cousins, without forgetting that even cousins can kill one another. After all, Cain killed his only brother Abel. However, although committing murder in a moment of passion is human, perpetuating premeditated killing is a crime that must be stopped at all costs. We know that most politicians are more interested in creating problems than solving them. It is their peculiar strategy to hold onto power. We, the people, must not sacrifice the future of our children by listening to those false leaders; they do not have our best interest at heart. Great political leaders see the image of their peoples in their thoughts and deeds, but those are a rare breed.

If conflicts are the doing of politicians, finding solutions to those conflicts must be the peoples' tough task. They are responsible before their children to dismount that heavy burden so they will not have to carry it. After all, it is peoples who benefit from finding, or suffer from not finding, a solution for the conflicts between their nations. They pay it all, and not the few governing elites, who ultimately surrogate the damage to them. Governments are the necessary evil but restraining this evil is the peoples' duty. Strong reins can control the wildest of horses.

Again and again, my sincerest advice to you, Israelis and Palestinians, is to accept one another unconditionally. You are both a historical reality to the disputed land, and neither party can deny it to the other and still can claim to sincerely want peace. The wise create peace, the foolish perpetuate war. We honor our politicians and generals who conquer the enemy's land. It's about time for us the people to honor them when they conquer the enemy's heart.

Friends, seek not the direction of alien powers to bring you peace; they will mislead and harm you, in spite of any apparent claim to your favor.

And beware of the ambiguities of the road-map. There is a map but what road are we mapping? One must first define the road to take, and then one can accurately draw its map- since an authentic knowing requires an object; otherwise knowing and hallucinating have the same face- value. The road is a map waiting to be drawn and not vice versa; a drawn map is nothing but a pragmatic tool to cross the road. But if there is no road, what one would cross?!

Since a true road is a- well- travelled one, a humane one, it results that man's acceptance of himself is rooted in his acceptance of the other. A true road is an open one that nobody can rightfully appropriate to himself; it is a communal one. The claim to the exclusive ownership of the road is the absolute negation of it.

One can't travel in the vacuum of selfishness and still expect to reach the mountaintop for a dance with God, a dance that celebrates a shared life. Embark on the road, and the road will embark in you. You must carry the road in your heart, and the road, at its turn, will carry you to the hearts of the other travelers; and all to the desired destination, to God.

The other may carry a bag of a different content; still you must be tolerant enough to accept your differences. He may travel on his feet or on the back of his beast of burden. That must not be an insult to your modern means of traveling. Long, tedious and dangerous is the road for all. However, exhaling is the destination. The ultimate victory is not who arrives first and with what; but whom one would have carried along to safety. You cannot say I have arrived if you would have had left a dead or injured companion behind. The road of sacrifice and sharing is the only road to safety for all. Ultimately, all travelers will be rewarded with freedom, a legitimate child of a road well travelled, well shared; a humane road. The best of all our privileges is what we share with others; their freedom enlarges and limits not ours.

To achieve a true peace we need more than empathy; we need the divine patronage. Politicians speak about maps; good-willed men await the coming of God to fill in their empty cups. Only God can quench our thirst and enable peace to grow and prosper in our hearts. Peace is a gift from God given to men of goodwill. It is a leap of faith, the lack of which is the most destructive weapon of the human aspirations. Politicians draw maps but maps are misleading and confusing. On the contrary, compasses can take man-kind to the wondrous land of brotherhood and peace. Nations can draw maps to temporarily divert wars, only men of goodwill, nourished by God's grace, can find their way to a lasting peace with themselves and with others. We can achieve peace when we integrate them into our aspirations, ourselves.

Just today I read the story of a rabbit that was destined to be dissected, for a learning purpose in a high school's lab. Strayed, a car has hit it. Out of hurt came sympathy; the whole population of that school has planned get well soon party for it after a week of rehabilitation in a veteran hospital. You, too, Israelis and Palestinians, fear not the historical hurt, your sacrifices for peace will ultimately save your precious lives and those of your children- just remember that can happen only through empathy nourished by God.

"We are one, after all, you and I; together we suffer, together exist, and forever recreate one another."- Pierre Teilhard de Chardin.

DAD, WHY IS MY COUTRY IN THE BUSINESS OF KILLING?

12/ 8, 2003

Today I prepared breakfast for Amon. It was a well- deserved treat; yesterday he had labored hard and hard work must be rewarded in some form or another. The owner and President of the "King's Pressure Cleaning Co." has lived under the constant pressure of the real kings, the rich. Bowing to their orders and wishes, he must clean well their dirt, a job that supplied him money to maintain the lifestyle of a young man who drove a decent reliable Japanese car. After all, young beautiful ladies do not have the muscles or the will to push a junky car off the road. Amon's breakfast was made of four slices of buttered bread, two eggs and two fingers of Italian sausage. He avidly ate at the sound of sipping on a jug filled with Colombian hot coffee. One would have thought that a hungry wolf mountain has descended to the opulent valley.

"Dad, why is my country in the business of killing others?" Suddenly Amon broke a long silence. We were then watching the early CNN news. Last night the US Air Force had killed several Afghans, most of them were children, in a building suspected to hide Taliban fighters. The sadness of this event overwhelmed me too; I am a father, after all. To avoid pursuing the sad conversation, I clicked to the Walt Disney World channel. The theme of the cartoon was well fitting. It dealt with the benefits drawn from our differences. How hypocritical adults can be. We teach our children to celebrate our differences; yet we kill one another when differences arise. Indeed, we are confusing them. May God help me to understand man; depressing is the dichotomy between his words and deeds.

Having finished eating, Amon left to school. I remained glued to the dining table, still sipping my hot coffee. I was alone and felt peaceful; Marla was in her son's room to open his eyes on the obligations of the new day. For a brief while I relived the tenderness of those memorable dawns when mother woke me up to watch her milking a cow or a goat. Ah, the lost paradise! There was then no CNN channel news; all was peaceful in my village. The rare most tragic news was a fox has invaded a chicken coop and carried one of them into a hole dug in the low shoulder of the mountain veiling our village. Looking through the kitchen window, I noticed a blue jay perching on the orange tree whose blooming branches have touched that window. My memory carried me to that day of December 8, 1954. I was then celebrating the Immaculate Conception holyday with my fellow seminarians in a vast orange groves field that belonged to Yassa Beh (Beh: is a social title equivalent to Count), a Catholic feudalist in Upper Egypt. That day my brother Dmitri has stopped to see me; he was on his way back to his army Casern, after having had spent a few days with the family. I cried to see him escaping my sight. That sadness lasted only a few moments; so soon I have found consolation in that magical Swiss watch he had given me (it was my first watch). As the tender past was caressing my memory, I saw my now dead brother smiling at me. It was he who had planted all those lovely trees that enriched, perfumed, embellished my garden, enchanted my sight and delighted my tongue. May all the pleasures of the heavenly Gardens be yours, dear brother! Cheers, to you, brother, and to all those who plant the good seeds in the rich soil of the human heart.

TROUBLED

12/11, 2003

It is that time of the year, a wish of happy holidays to all, and a special sympathy to those who are suffering. I specially thought of those three children drowned by the hands of an insane mother, assisted by her abusive boyfriend. Gentle wishes to you families of the military, and please ignore George W. Bush's lecturing about the elusive phantom of exported freedom. He is brainwasher, just like Ben Laden, the one hiding in the crevices of the Pakistani mountains. Both are ultimately endangering the world's peace. They are troubled men: the one is desperate to be re-elected to the White House and the other is desperate to be abducted to an imaginary hall of fame. The caveman had more security living under the menace of ferocious animals. No comparison, it is safer to be pursued by ferocious animals than by desperate men.

--My sympathy goes to the families of those workers killed in a printing plant in California. He was fired. No longer able to put bread on the family's table, he has decided to shoot randomly, killing four.

 --I wish a peaceful eternal rest for those innocent Afghans who were reduced to ashes while they were sleeping. The CIA had mistakenly identified them to be Taliban fighters, America's most actual eager enemies. They weren't so when they were fighting the Russians. They had even gained the status of friends; a well- deserved title; they were doing the dirty work against our archrivals, after all.

--Kim Jong-Il of North Korea, your nukes have surfaced in a time we are busy killing somebody else; it could not be of a worse timing for us. If you do not back up, you will have your day in our court of demolition. Let me understand, Junior, if I have correctly heard: you wanted to break a deal with us. Did you say you will suspend all projects of producing nuclear weapons, if your demands were to be met?

 "What are those demands of yours, dictator of the high heels?"

I will suspend the production of my nuclear arms, if the U.S remove my country's name from the list of terrorism and lift all the economical blockages.

"Sir, you are falling miserably to understand our simple logic: We want to starve your people to death; you are a communist nation; you are a bone stuck in our political throat. Still, Sir, we are willing to reconsider giving up calling you names. As for the lifting of blockades, don't worry, once your starving people are in their deathbeds, we will send some medications and a few thousand tons of food; we have abundance of both basic necessities."

If this is the best your government can do, then I'll work even harder to speed up the production of my nukes, said the man of circus stunts.

"Sir, let it be clear to you that we had already struck a perfect deal with the Chinese: partners, take care of that stubborn short dictator. Reward: we will accept all your products, just for showing him your fist on our behalf."

Dear China, could we give you half of our country in partial payment of the heavy debts we own you... Would you give us a break so we can keep the other half?"

Sufficient!

Thank you, great benefactor; a half is better than nothing. After all, we have a gigantic country. However, if we were to exercise our clever diplomacy we might even succeed convincing you to accept the offer of our largest five States we had captured from Mexico. Ah you smart Mexicans! The white man had developed those stolen States, and you have come to reap the benefits of his hard work; he is too busy sticking his nose in the affairs of other nations. Oh, well, take back what belonged to you; it's a fair deal, after all.

Lord, have mercy on me; I am constantly being tortured by Bush's policy of preemptive wars.

Besides the great devastation the grasshoppers of war had caused to our opulent pasture, there are many other serious problems weighting heavily on America's shoulders here at home. May God fortify your shoulders, dear America, the tender mother of my five children and my generous benefactor! I enumerate a few:

1. How could we control the deadly use of drugs amongst the nation's teenagers? My great sympathy goes to the local Miss. Fritz; the tragic suicide of her drug addicted twelve year old son has deeply touched my heart. Drugs are deadly, indeed.

2. How could we control the ever-accelerating births of children born out of wedlock?

3. How could we prevent the daily road rage killings?

4. Thanks, credit cards, we are not worried about your high interest rates. We have no intention to repay you back, anyway; inflation is eating up fast our earnings. Just let's live like kings; we aren't worried to die like beggars.

5. Although the wasteful death of our sons and daughters saddens deeply my heart, the ignorance of our teenagers makes me very disturbed. Just yesterday evening I was in the East Clearwater public library. The

thorns of ignorance of those two white minors had pinched me bloodily.

"Have you ever heard of that man they call Rev. Jackson?" the girl asked her male companion.

"I think he is a nigger and he preaches Jesus to his brothers, the monkeys," replied the well- informed teenager.

"Young man, who taught you to be so prejudiced?"

"But who are you, old fool; we need to send you all back to Africa," replied the hate- stuffed bomb.

"What a pity! Too young to be so prejudiced," I murmured into myself and walked away, saddened. If our society lives on thorns, how dare we preach the aroma of flowers to the world?!

WE GOT HIM

12/ 13, 2003

"**We** got him," shouted the American administrator, Paul Brenner, to the military gathering.

Yes, we must rejoice, they had pulled the butcher of Iraq out of a hole. He is the vicious spider that had weaved a very complex web of problems for his people and the entire world. Thank heaven, finally the divine justice has shown its face; may fire reduce the thug to ashes.

This early morning I saw Saddam, the self-anointed King of the Mesopotamia, looking like the most miserable homeless on the planet. False lion, you have emerged from that hole like a rat. You looked extremely tired, humiliated and dazed out. The wild hair growing in your beard and head gave you the look of a cave dweller, or have you always been one?! You have shamelessly identified yourself as the President of Iraq. The question to you, delusional, is: have you ever been a true leader? What did the word leader mean to you? You had foolishly adopted the policy of killing and humiliating your people; today is your doom. You are finally in the iron cage, a price paid to the liberty you had, for so long, denied to your nation. You have miserably failed to recognize its beautiful face whenever she had presented itself to you. You have always thought that force is yours to inflict upon your people. No, idiot, liberty is a divine cup that a true leader must offer to his people in honor of the ancestors; so may all drink from it together in thanksgiving. Instead, you have turned to the power of the sword, and by the sword you will lose your head. Today your people and the whole world are rejoicing for your capture, except the few tyrants like yourself; the majority of whom are in the Middle East. Indeed, they are lamenting their own inevitable tragic fate; they see themselves in you. You are they; they are you and to each tyrant there is a doomsday, sooner or later. Yes, no one can escape the divine justice.

Tyrants of the Middle East, your hearts are filled with hatred toward your peoples. You hate them because you hate yourselves. How could the leaves part from the tree and still remain alive?! Today Saddam's capture must be more than a wake-up call to you all, bastards. It is the last warning voice you must hear, or else you will soon perish. If you do think this is a mere scare tactic, then consult history, that is if you have time; you are always busy flirting with your own self-destruction. Are you true Muslims? I'm sure you claim to be. If so, have you ever heard the Prophet saying: "If God wants to destroy some people, He lets them live in confusion." However, if you are so stubborn to acknowledge your confusion, because you refuse to hear a voice other than yours; then continue living in your confused world and certainly you will die wrapped in illusions. Never had you sought the truth and the truth has always refused to unveil its beautiful face to you. She is so pure; you are too impure. O you, who long for the absolute power, learn the hard lesson of your predecessors. You must not flirt with the curse of tyranny; rather seek the graceful walk to the divine fountain of freedom with your peoples. Only then and there you can quench your thirst and theirs. Blood never quenches, rather creates new thirst. Forget not that you are extension of your peoples and not their exterminators. You must share your power or it will exclude you. The beauty of power is in its dynamism. Once rendered static, it explodes; its nature is to expand and not to contract. Pray that you may govern others with mercy and yourselves with austerity. In so doing, you become energizing force to your people and not paralyzing one. You are powerful by being forceful and not vice versa. Strength is yours when you lead your people with respect and care. However, if you cannot see the true connection between power and strength, then it is mandatory that you visit history; there lies the destiny of all the rising and falling. To all the tyrants of the world: seek security not in killing your opponents; your greatest security lies in killing the tyrant within yourselves.

PAPPY, WE NEED TO PEE. HOW SWEET!

12/20-28, 2003

As the year was folding up lazily the fringes of its garment like a wise aging King, I found my heart flooded with mixed emotions and my mind crowded with contradicting thoughts. Still I rendered grace to a force superior than myself. Although we are history makers, we must also recognize that history makes us. Having stated this, I hear the protest of the few: O false prophet of the thousand follies when and where have you buried your egocentric views? What curse has transferred you from a restless rebel to a desperate resigned? You have always bombarded us with your rebellious spirit, why has your fire died out? How in such a brief

169

time have you withdrawn yourself from the list of the few elite rebels to become one of the docile sheep of the large herd?!

And I humbly reply: Friends, I have not asked for fortune or fame. Rather, I have fervently prayed for peace, not for you though, nor for the world, rather for myself. I have found that peace, at least momentarily, as I embraced my children who came from different points carrying their heavy luggage. They were seeking to revive the child buried under the foundation of the family home. They have come to feel that warmth and tenderness the world had denied them. Yes, I have found peace as I walked among the scattered articles of their clothes, shoes, cosmetics, books, notes and their bottles of vitamins. Having listened to their accomplishments, I realized that my life was not in vain; in spit the pains of my age. Noticing the shortness of my breath, they comforted me as much as they could. And the magic of their comfort worked better than any of the medications modern science has made available to the aged and sick. I have rejoiced as I heard their giggles echoing against the white walls of the family home. I have found peace even in the noise of their radio transistors blasting with the savage beats of the hip hop music. Although a shilling noise to my ears, it was elevated to the rank of music in my heart; it was the satisfaction drawn from seeing them happy.

The daily visitation to the neighborhood Starbucks coffee- shop was a holy ritual for them; apparently they were in love with the variety of its flavors. I have often chosen the delightful taste of chocolate cake. All was divinely sweet, especially their chat with a childhood friend. Incapacitated, after a car accident, the- now twenty seven year old Mat Miller reminisced lengthily about the past. He recalled the thousands of consumed grilled cheese sandwiches and the delightful sucking on sugar canes I had provided them. Ah how sweet were those days!

Then Christmas Eve came, and the Abdous went to the Espiritu Santo Catholic church to fulfill their religious duties. There the children sought to drink from the fountain of their childhood's church. In a deliberate act of revisiting their childhood, they have chatted sporadically, laughed and finally decided to go to the bathroom. "Pappy, we need to pee," they spoke in a childish language. Is there a better place than a sanctuary of worship to get rid of the heavy bags the world of adulthood would have laid on our shoulders?! On the 28th my children departed, leaving behind the strong aroma of the family's happy memories.

A TERRORIST ON THE PEW

1/1, 2004

Marla, Javier and I left home five minutes prior to the ten o'clock morning mass held at the Holy Trinity

Greek Orthodox Church. There I sat next to an old woman. She was fat and her gold jewelry has shown an equal obesity. For the first thirty minutes she sent me, now and then, some friendly looks. I flattered myself thinking she has found in me a gentleman pleasant to look at. Or more probably she was a widow and even an eighty year old man could have gotten the same degree of attention. Anyway, so soon the curse of the race's bad reputation has descended upon me. It was when confessing the Apostle's Creed. All the parishioners recited it by heart; I might have been the only one who read it. My inability to recite it by heart in Greek was a sure signal to her that I was not one of them and therefore I was an Arab terrorist- since there is great physiological similarity between our two races. Yes, her changed looks led me to this unhappy conclusion. They were hard, suspicious and persisting. For comfort I thought to myself: well, that's her problem; she needs to ask her priest what it means when the Creed reads: "I believe in one God, the Father almighty, creator of heaven and earth..." In spite of all her suspicious stares, I continued to perform successfully the religious rituals and my glued forehead against the pew testified to certain piety. For better or worse the mass ended; and old Fr. James Rousakis commanded the faithful to sit down for the cutting and distribution of the Vasilopita- the St. Basil's bread. He took a few minutes to explain its history. "It commenced in the last half of the fourth century of the Christian era. It was initiated by St. Basil the Great, bishop of Asia Minor; when he commissioned some women to bake sweeten bread. He arranged to place gold coins inside it; thus the poor families in his diocese in cutting the bread to nourish themselves were surprised to find the coins. It was his way to distribute money to them, so as not to look like charity to preserve their dignity."

All was good and noble until Fr. Rousakis started calling to the pulpit the privileged parishioners by name to receive their pieces of the Vasilopita. He even called them by the order of the importance of their functions in the Church. The list was too long and boring. Finally I understood the reason behind their distinction; they dropped envelopes in a basket as they were receiving the blessed bread. I thanked God for being anonymous; those envelopes might have contained fat checks and I couldn't be one of those contributors. The proud parade of the privileged ended and the timid march of the populace began. Why not, even the populace has a place in God's heart. Timidly the commons proceeded. Realizing there was no point of return, without becoming a subject of harsh stares, I continued, with great discomfort, to advance toward the podium. Soon, and in imitation of the others, I found myself unconsciously kissing old Rousakis' hand as I was receiving the meager piece of the blessed bread. A sudden roar of rebellion rose within me. Was it worth to kiss the hand of a mortal for a piece of bread, sweetened and blessed as it may be?

You shall eat your bread with the sweat of your forehead, said the Lord.

And you shall eat your bread at the price of your humiliation, said man. Wow! Indeed, since God has spoken to Adam, it has been an unbearable increase in the cost of living. The good Lord had made a beautiful world and man has transformed it to an ugly one.

Men of God and shrewd profiteers, Jesus has washed His disciples feet before He gave them the bread of eternal life, and today you insist that we kiss your hands for a piece of bread that will vanish in hours. Could that be our ultimate punishment for having had crucified the Just One to deify the mortals?! It is about time to crucify the criminal and glorify the just. That might be the achievement of the generations of another two thousand years in the Lord's Calendar.

COURTESY OF OUR WELL GROOMED AND GENEROUS NATION

1/5, 2004

The Secretary of Defense and his Chairman of Joint Chiefs of Staff briefed the nation:

"We have captured forty of the fifty- five most wanted thugs of the Baath Regime of Iraq," said the Secretary. Indeed, Mr. Secretary, we have captured Saddam and most of his company. We've checked their heads for lice and shaved their beards, courtesy of our well groomed nation. But would that safeguard our civilized world?

"We have been steadily oppressing the Iraqi insurgency," sang the Chairman.

That might be good news for the Iraqis, in spite of the ongoing daily killing of the innocent. As for the demolition of their habitats, do not worry, General; we count on the goodness of Jimmy Carter, he still can hammer, just to redeem the evil of your "Operation Hammer."

- -An earthquake in the Southeast of Iran had swallowed 45.000 alive and the count continued. The good news, they have pulled out alive a 97 –year old woman.

Before the human sufferings in Iran, the Bush Administration has proposed to send a rescue team. It was made of well- trained detection dogs to pull out the buried under the collapsing buildings and, perhaps, find some of the suspected Weapons of Mass- Destruction as well. Yes indeed, there is no better excuse for a camel to get inside his master's tent than to speak of a sand storm.

"We are strong and sophisticated enough to pull our people from beneath the debris," responded the Iranian President.

"It is better being buried alive than to be pulled out by the infidels," shouted the assembly of the Iranian clerics.

Well, we didn't mean to save you, rather to screw you up. But don't rejoice, our failure is only temporary;

smart bombs will do a better job; human compassion can, at times, mess things up. This menacing thought might have visited the sick minds of the three advocates of violence in Washington. Yes, I am referring to Mr. Bush, Dick and Ron. For you Miss. Rice, I reserve a bit of sympathy, you are only a political puppet, like the majority of State Secretaries of all nations. But who knows, if the masses' disgust keep rising against Ronny's arrogance, you might become the next Secretary of Defense. So far, you have proven yourself, through tough talks, to have the teeth and willpower to bite on a rock, just to please King George. I even predict that you will become a more visible puppet in the King's Court.

- - Martha Stewart, wish you no good luck in your trial. I hope you get thirty years and more in prison, a lesser sentence will be detrimental to the reputation of the notion of justice for all.

-- And you the mother who has drowned her three children, I wish you one way ticket to their grave; I am sure they cannot wait to see you, filial love.

-- Princess Diana be consoled, the daily news "Mirror" (the most feared tabloid in London) has published the letter you had written ten months prior to your blowing up along with your Egyptian lover. In this letter you had expressed fear that your ex-husband, the balding Prince Charles was planning your murder by car accident. Apparently, it was a promise made by a prince and princes rarely break their promises.

--Aside of reserving sympathy for those who suffer, I remain susceptible of overdoing it.

Yes, I feel your pain, Serena Williams, the tennis star. You have experienced great disappointment when Nike had offered you only thirty- eight million dollar contract. After all, it had awarded your big sister Venus, also a tennis star, with a contract of forty- five million, doing the same advertisement. How unjust the world is! However, not being a victim of greed, I settle for three millions, three thousands, three hundred or even three dollars. I am, too, a star on my own right; I just have no audience. Not even my own shadow wants to follow me; my intellectual honesty has created this hostile environment for me. That is fine; intellectualism is a poisonous advertisement to modern man, anyway; it jeopardizes all their greed.

--Yes, I am most envious of Reverend Pat Robertson. The evangelical Clown has lately claimed that God had spoken to him about the end of the world. Well, let's just follow the trail of basic logic: God is the Creator of all and He equally loves all His children. I am one of them, how could He be constantly talking to a Reverend of such insignificant piety, and not even once to me, who is not less pious than the Reverend?! I began to wonder if God is not anti-Arab. Certainly He is not. Conclusion: Pat Robertson's claim is pretentious, if not false.

Let me try a more forceful approach: my God, my Lord and my Father, how come you never talk to me? Forget about that childish jealousy of Abel. Aha! Now I understand. Lord, may you forgive the rebellion of an adolescent… You mean old Robertson is so dense that you are constantly talking to him as a way of showing your fatherly love for a mentally challenged child? Yeah, yeah, now I understand; dense people cannot see you through your marvelous works. Thanks a million for informing me about the curse, mistaken for privilege.

 --Good Lord, may I ask: if the re-election of Mr. Bush is on your mind, would you please reconsider your decision; it is a messy world out there and he is a very confused leader. Or could it be to purify earth you need to send, now and then, terrible earthquakes and bad leaders?!

--Thank God, I am not envious of, rather grateful to Princess Anne's dog. The Princess has sent it to a psychologist to avoid having it euthanatized after it had attacked a royal servant.

"I am sure it is just a dog who is feeling a bit out of sorts about something, perhaps, pain of old age and was feeling a bit cranky on that day," explained psychologist Roger Mugford. If this is a valid reason, then the world must forgive my constant biting; I'm, too, suffering the crankiness of old age. Hence, I expect, at least, not to be euthanatized. Thanks, great psychologist, for caring enough to save the life of old canines. So, please kindly allow me to bite you, though I have untreated rabies, unintended negligence, just lack of medical insurance. Don't accuse me of lying… I know I live in the richest country in the whole world. Yes, the President's erratic behavior is sinking our beloved country into a poverty rivaled by the Third World Nations. That, too, shall pass. We shall recover economically, that is if we could recover morally.

IS JESUS A MALE- CHAUVINIST?

1/ 7, 2004

 Forty- seven young men dived today in the lake of Tarpon Springs, Florida. They were in competition to pull the Holy Cross from the bottom of the cold lake. The tracer will receive the blessing of the Greek orthodox Archbishop Demetrius of the New York Diocese. As for you, the remaining forty- six young dreamers do not despair; your empty hands will still be holding unto God's hand where all blessings rest. Also, may those special blessings rest on the palms of young women; in spite the ecclesiastic orthodox authority prohibits their participation in the ritual of the Holy Epiphany. Should one blame it all on Saint Paul, or is it just the Mediterranean male chauvinism?

-- May those visible and invisible blessings of our youth be the redeeming grace of the sins of our robbers. Yes, for three days a man has been robbing grocery stores in North Pinellas, Florida. The first day he was arrogant as he performed his mission at gunpoint, and was dressed in a three- piece suit and a tie. The second day, humble and discrete, he was dressed in a chicken suit and holding a toy pistol; timidity obliges at times. In the third robbery he decided to look like a normal citizen. He got away unharmed in his consecutive three-days operations.

-- The thirty- one –year- old Gerry Jones of Ringer, Georgia, has gunned down his- in-laws and his ten month old daughter. Afterward, he kidnapped three young girls, two of them were his.

"My only regret I didn't kill the bitch. I am not a bad husband though; I was planning to put flowers on her grave. She is a bitch; still she is my wife," he wrote in a note left behind. The poor woman had left him to escape his daily terror. And they say that Arabs are terrorizing America!

-- Mercy upon you the eleven year old girl of Miami, your mother has forced you to sell heroin in a transparent night gown to maintain living with her sixty- two year old boyfriend in a comfortable home in South Beach.

-- In the flats of Cleveland, Ohio, two black women were disputing the ownership of the 162 million dollar lottery ticket. After a brief investigation, the police concluded that one of them was a professional robber. What a shame! She should have consulted with that robber from Florida.

-- There are small sins and capital ones, and do not blame me for being a conservative catholic, at times America's capital sin is the closing of the Levi's factory after 150 years of glorious manufacturing of the infamous blue jeans that had made even old men look like great studs. Well, many other companies are being exported to those cheap labor countries. Indeed, the simple principles of economics are at their saddest application. Mr. President, why don't you consult with those Chicago boys, the most infamous economists in the world? Your Administration needs them to learn about the basic principles of strong economy. In case those bright scholars frighten you, take it then from the rebel's uncontrollable mouth:

 If the greedy owners keep moving their companies out of the country, Americans must rise to their responsibilities. Yes, they need to repeat the old glorious revolt of the Boston Tea Party. In this party, we need to dump the bad politicians and not the taxed- tea.

-- Well, it is not all bad in America; Britney Spears has wedded her childhood sweetheart. The flaw in this good news is that seven hours later, the young pop star has announced her intention to divorce him. Aha! Could it be that the old seven years itch has been reduced to seven hours because we live in the supersonic age?! The present generation might have to live under the Britney's curse of the seven hours itch. And if this trend continues, marriage in the -not-too far future will become a fashion of the past.

-- America's ultimate consolation is to be found in technology, its sweetheart.

"Ladies and gentlemen I give you Man," thus proudly spoke O'Keeffe O'Neil, the NASA manager as

"Discovery One" landed in one piece, unlike the previous rocket.

Today I dream of a rocket that will land us into ourselves. After all, what good for is an opulent harvest, if cancer is eating up our stomachs?! Yes, the most authentic grandeur of man is when he succeeds launching a rocket of morality into his own god's -given- depth, his soul. Until then, all worldly accomplishments remain heritage of the wind, and wind inheritors cannot insure for themselves the glory of a safe landing.

MISS. HOME SECURITY RAPES THE ARABS

1/ 12, 2004

Miss. Homeland Security System was born a bit less than two years ago at the directives of our President. Many have applauded her birth, tossing flowers under her feet, and a few have cursed her while throwing rocks at her. I didn't toss flowers nor have I thrown rocks, rather rushed to the public restroom to puke; I needed to wash it out I was poisoned. Yes, Mr. President and company, I vomit your intrusion on our freedom; you are the worst plague ever descended upon Washington D.C. Through electronic machines you record our names, phone numbers, professions, addresses, birthdates, birthplaces, and points of our departures and arrivals; all in the name of sterile and confusing Security. The majority of us never knew when the level was raised or ended, why, and what to do. Not all is useless, Mr. President, it might secure you a second presidential term. Besides, it serves for many parodies.

Mr. Government, would you mind to address some concerns of an Arab American?

Bring it on, said the- all- daring and caring authority.

The Arab: what's the color of my today's underwear?

The government: Be civilized. We are not invaders of privacy; we're just in the business of coding our multicolored society to save lives.

The Arab: I am a law abiding citizen, as my civil records can prove it. However, I know your Security System has already chosen red as my distinctive color.

The government: As an American citizen you reap the benefits of the green, the blue, the yellow, the orange and the red.

The Arab: Wish you think twice before you project the red on my face. I have not been a member of any terrorist group neither will I be.

The government: We're elected by and for the people, and we will do whatever it takes to protect them from outsider and insider enemies.

176

The Arab: Sounds logical until the logic ceases to sound. Why am I different than others? I've two legs; two hands; all the five senses; a soul and, above all, a heart that pumps blood as red as anyone else's. I invest all of them in America. They all make me one whole American citizen and not a hole in the American heart.

The government: Indeed you're a hundred percent American who has the right to liberty, prosperity and pursuit of happiness.

The Arab: And what does liberty mean? Does it entail the freedom of movement?"

That's obvious.

The Arab: Does it also mean that all Americans are innocent until proven guilty?

The government: That's the law.

The Arab: Are you sure the law embraces all? The skeptical Arab insisted.

The government: Absolutely.

The Arab: But why you keep projecting the color red right into my direction.

The government: Well, and for a final answer: September 11, 2001 has changed the picture; it's all the fault of your race.

The Arab: You're becoming so sensitive to colors that even one word uttered by one of my race on matters of politics can change his green to red. Ay…! Ay..! Is there a doctor in the house, I feel my stomach is going to explode?

The government: what could be wrong with you, have you swallowed a bomb?

The Arab: No. The CIA had wired a bomb inside me.

The government: Don't be so sarcastic; our Homeland Security System will ultimately serve the good of you and your children.

The Arab: Please, promise me that you won't punish them; I'd already paid the price.

The government: You're such a whiner; just enjoy the American security for such a small price.

The Arab: Wow! What a morbid dialogue with the deaf. After all, is there a difference between security and freedom? Now that my destiny is in your hands, America, I still insist to celebrate freedom like any other American. Please let me celebrate liberty; otherwise there is nothing left worth celebrating?"

The government: Now it has become clear to us that you are endangering our national security. Security, add him to the active list; apparently he is not capable of understanding our simple logic.

The Arab: Please, don't… I understand and love freedom so much that I wish it for all, including myself and my race.

The government: Then stop whining, your race is still lucky. It could be worse, just remember what had happened to the Japanese Americans during Second World War. And also forget not the millions of Jews, who had entered the German concentration camps and vanished forever. You Arabs are the luckiest of all; in spite of your heinous crimes… the Twin Towers, the Pentagon and Pennsylvania … do you remember them? The others did not commit any crimes, except being who they are. Therefore, life is still good in today's America for you Arabs. Sing; sing "America Land of the free and home of the brave…"

The Arab: And may I also sing it is the sexy? Today Dr. Sanjay, the CNN medical correspondent, has reported some of the many benefits of sex. The decade- long research has finally established that sex is a strong generator of longevity, an aggressive reliever of pain, a jealous protector from heart attacks and a tender comforter when acute depression strikes… Oh well, it seems that security and sex are such fragile things, the only difference: sex is sweet, security is bitter; but ultimately both bite and poison like boas.

The government: You're rattling now. Since you insist on being so noisy, now you have one decision to make: where do you want to be bitten?

The Arab: Everywhere. After all, I am mortal and mortals must suffer; a price to preserve their dignity. But where is my dignity, if your Homeland Security Advisory System continues to tell other Americans that we Arabs are the ghosts in the house, and that the task of your administration is to chase those ghosts out so that America's children can wake up with smiles instead of nightmares?"

The government: We have already clearly stated our case and that's final; you need to work it out with and for yourself.

The Arab: If that's freedom at its best, then don't bite; rather execute me.

Behold, Lord, I stand mute, not even one word for or against. Too much misunderstanding, anger and mistrust, and all create impasses for the mind. Even, at times, the mind becomes an impasse for itself. Consequently, I have no other support but to call on the classic prayer of Saint Francis of Assisi: "Lord, make me an instrument of your peace .Where there is hatred, let me sow love; where there is injury, pardon; where there is doubt, faith; where there is despair, hope; where there is darkness, light; and where there is sadness, joy."

May we all join hands and hearts to undertake the great voyage to God's heart; our ultimate security and true freedom!

THIS PLANET IS OUR BIOLOGICAL MOTHER

1/ 13, 2004

Today our President unveiled his great vision for America's future after he had messed up its present. I paraphrase: By the year 2020 we will have settlers in the moon. At their turn, the moon dwellers will have their eyes fixed on Mars thus spoke the visionary.

Great! Such a vision surpasses, by far, John F. Kennedy's in the sixties.

Mr. President, for the confusion you have created in my mind, you will never have my vote. Do not accuse me of being anti-progress, you do not know what planet I am dreaming of and why. Yes, earth is the sweetest planet in all galaxies. It is the planet on whose shoulders God rests His head and smiles in infinite affection at His most fertile creation.

Mr. President, do you know what has brought down the Soviet Empire? Yes, the lack of money, a commodity no empires, nations or individuals can survive without. The same fate will be ours, if you keep draining our economy on useless wars and uninhabitable planets.

True, man is born to court the beautiful and mysterious Miss. Knowledge. However, we differ as to how the infinite power of mind must unfold and where its fringes must extend. Certainty not unto the remote stars, for the simple reason: we have it all here and now. This planet is our biological mother because we were made from it through the long process of evolution.

"The earth is literary our mother, not only because we depend on her for nurture and shelter but even more because the human species has been shaped by her in the womb of evolution. Each person, furthermore, is conditioned by the stimuli he receives from nature during his own existence. If men were to colonize the moon or Mars- even with abundant supplies of oxygen, water, and food, as well as adequate protection against heat, cold and radiation, they would not long retain their humanness, because they would be deprived of those stimuli which only earth can provide."- René Dubos in his book: *A God within.*

One looks for a surrogate mother only when one cannot locate the biological one. Yes, this planet is the authentic birthplace of humanity, and man's first honeymoon was in the Garden of Eden. It was and is so sweet that when things went sour between the bride and groom, the Father sent His only Son from the remotest heavens to reconcile with His estranged beloved, man-kind. The Obedient Son, anxious to fulfill His message, did not make even one stop in any of the other planets; so anxious was He to restore the heart of the unfaithful bride chosen by His heavenly Father.

Do you think, Mr. President, we have touched all the curves of the planet that did and continue to move God's mind and heart? Its infrastructures are unequalled, its forests are full of songs that enchant our lonely hearts and its rivers and streams produce music to our ears. Our women enjoy sunbathing on its tender sunny shores. Can the Moon, Mars or any other planets offer better enchantment to those spoiled babes?

We must not sacrifice the limpid rivers of earth, just for a sign of water in Mars. We can't afford exchanging its luminous face with the dusty one of the moon and the brownish masses of Jupiter. If yet we have to discover her most exotic curves, why then must we look at the other faceless planets?

"...the earth with its vistas of breath- taking beauty, its azure seas, beaches, mighty mountains, and soft blanket of forest and steppe is a veritable wonderland in the universe. It is a gem of rare and magic beauty hung in a trackless space filled with lethal radiations and accompanied in its journey by sister planets which are viciously hot or dreadfully cold, arid, and lifeless chunks of raw rocks. Earth is a choice, precious, and sacred beyond all comparison or measure," wrote the physicist and theologian William Pollard.

The love of earth is only the beginning and not the end of the human bewilderment. For that deeply rooted love in our hearts, we've created technology so sophisticated that we can estimate the ages of the fossils of humans, animals, birds and insects. We can register and interpret the sounds of dolphins, whales and other fishes that inhabit the depths of its oceans and seas.

Apparently we have become bored with the most beautiful bride. But boredom is the characteristic of infants. A wise man is the one who lives in constant curiosity and wonder about his environment and himself.

You may play the devil's advocate by saying: also there is as much, if not greater mysteries and beauty in the other planets. Besides, we need a larger living- space.

Is it not the same notion that had pushed a mad Hitler to a war that has left fifty million dead?

Mr. President, still we have so much to do here in this planet. Let me support my statement by mentioning some of our urgent needs: Why not work harder together to improve the science of plastic surgery; I am sure the aging Hollywood artistic population will be very supportive and appreciative of the endeavor.

-- Have you heard of that photo a mother has sent on her birthday to her morbid ex-lover, who had murdered her only son? On the back of the victim's photo, she wrote: "I'm always thinking of you, I will never forget you, happy birthday, Mom."

--And that twenty- one year old Palestinian woman, who has blown herself up to kill as many Israelis as possible. Consumed by a raging revenge, she did not care to leave behind two small children and a husband.

--And that four –year old Iraqi, who stumbled in his blood; a bullet fired by an American soldier had landed right in his head. And you still are proud to shout: "Mission Accomplished!"

--Have you seen the bodies of Lacy Peterson and her unborn baby pulled out of the San Francisco Bay?

Mr. President, guide us to take care of the mess we all have created here on earth before we venture to another planets. Although many are the crimes of her dwellers, still Mother Earth remains the kindest of all. With great tenderness she nourishes us, although she slaps our wrists, at times.

Sad to think that some entrepreneurs amongst your far religious right might be contemplating to sell us parcels in heaven. In fact, my ex- Chilean girlfriend's grandmother, in cooperation with an old priest, had long ago started the enterprise, just to survive the financial hardships created by the Augusto Pinochet's regime. Sure, the prices of those parcels depended on the closeness or remoteness from the Lord's throne and the buyer's favorite Saint. How tragic! They've forgotten that God dwells in a pure heart made of the earth's mud and dreams.

All men of goodwill must preach the unrivalled delights of this earth. It is in this, for this and to this earth God has made and continue to make us through an endless process of evolution. Let's celebrate our Mother Earth; only from her breasts flows the everlasting life, a dream of all the mortals. However, Mr. President, if you do insist that earth is no longer your dream planet; please take your first ship to outer space. You may go to any planet you choose. We might send you Christmas cards but do not expect any on Valentine's Day. Keep on bewildering in the outer space, home of those who have become unworthy to suck the motherly breasts.

MERCHANTS OF POISON

1/ 14, 2004

"**Give** salt and dry bread to Zorba's soul and a fat roasted chicken to his flesh," wrote Nikos Kazantzakis in his book: *"Zorba the Greek"*.

Yes, he is talking to you all the diet-freaks. What could have gone wrong with you? You have allowed the greedy vitamins manufacturers to play with your minds. Every sunrise you have a new menu telling you what and what not to eat. You call yourselves health conscious and I call you health yoyos. Those criminal profiteers preach you the benefits of vitamins made in their laboratories, instead of eating the food offered to you by the tender hands of Mother Earth. They convince you to question the safety of the food produced from earth; so they can sell you the poison prepared in their labs. Could poison have a higher and safer nutritional value than what a tender loving mother offers, tampered with additives as may be?! You attend their seminars after anointing your faces with her gifts, and they succeed convincing you to buy their bottled sweetened poison. You look at those thieves as if they were life saviors. Do not believe them, rather in a gesture of repentance kneel down before the kind Mother and ask for her forgiveness. Once you receive forgiveness, open your mouths wide to her motherly breasts and avidly suck her milk, she is the genuine nurse; anybody else who claims to nourish you is a dragon supplying you nothing but venom. Wake up, do not just smell the coffee, rather drink and delight yourselves with every sip you draw into your throats. How could those deadly chemicals excite so much your appetite?!

181

My heart becomes laden with sorrow as I watch my daughter Nafré rejecting the motherly nourishment to indulge taking- in- your poison. Wish I could convert her to my diet- philosophy. It is quite simple: swallow the earth, so you may live healthier and longer. Behold, I lay under my palm tree and open my mouth, I dream to swallow the sun, the dates, the gentle fresh air and the whistling wind; I am one with Mother Earth, and anyone who attempts to separate the child from his/her mother is a murderer. Life is assimilation and not rejection, after all. Our youth walk pale and our adult stumble, they need to reconnect with Mother. Eat what you desire and desire what you eat; this is the diet of all diets. If you still insist to embrace the death-diets, don't forget to reelect Mr. Bush; he will send you to a remote planet. There you will be starving, a faster alternative to end your life.

KING'S BIRTHDAY AND THE MEAL TO DIE FOR

1/ 15, 2004

It is a victory for all men of good will. It's Dr. Martin Luther King's birthday. Yes, he is still alive and well in spite of the heavy stone weighing on the mouth of his tomb. Happy birthday, Martin, death is the lot of those who wanted to silence your voice of justice. How foolish to have thought killing you; any force that attempts to kill the spirit will eventually collapse. Blessed are those who cry for justice; it will run to them, embrace them, and weep of joy in their arms. I have finally found a home for me thus the oppressed will moan. Martin, today all the voices that cry for justice in the world celebrate your birth. As we celebrate your birth, we discover the connection between time and eternity. Through their alliance, God became man and man became God. What a fantastic union!

 --Today John Kerry has won the Iowa Caucuses by 38 percent. I heard the man shouting in his squeaky voice: "I'm tired of those who speak of the family's values and don't value the family." Yes, Mr. President, he was talking about you. For so long you have been frequently speaking to us about those values and, indeed, you have failed to value the family. How could you claim to be the guardians of our values, if you are robbing us of the basic rights? Yes, it is a basic human right to receive decent medical care, fair trial, good education and perhaps a rewarding job. It is equally a crime to speak of settling in remote planets and give up on earth. If you do disagree with this view, again, please pack up and leave with all the members of your conservative party. There you will be closer to your elusive God of whom you have always been dreaming. We, the Democrats, have found our God in the ghettoes of Chicago, New York, New Orleans and in every corner occupied by the disadvantaged. We've found our God dwelling in the chests of the forgotten millions of elder women, men and helpless children. We've found our God amongst those falling heroes who have given their precious lives for your vain earthly gains. Last, but not least, we've found our God in the humiliation of those you have stripped of their civil rights, all courtesy of the blind arrogance that nourishes your sick self-righteousness.

Rejoice, Mr. President, the- all- knowing and- all- caring Rush Limbaugh, "the Who is watching out for you of Bill O'Reilly and the 700 Club of Pat Robertson and their likes, all admire and propagate your madness.
I have read: *The Meals to Die For.* It spoke of the last meals ordered by the condemned to death. And their prayers! Those too will be a subject of another book, thanks to your policy of electrocuting instead of rehabilitating those who have committed heinous crimes; and that is another shot into the heart of justice, a cause for which Martin Luther King had given up his life. Happy rebirth Martin; justice never dies; rather it transforms itself and others into a realm beyond time and space. I have disappointing news for the assassins: Assassination is the ultimate act of despair, helplessness and defeat.

THE TRIAL OF A THIEF

1/ 20, 2004

I have seen you, Martha Stewart looking frightened as you were painfully climbing the stairs of justice. Do not despair, diva, there are half a dozen of sympathizers shouting from below:
"We love you, go girl, go."
How small is the number of your supporters compared to those who have shouted freedom to Michael Jackson after a long trial that had pronounced him innocent of child molestation. To celebrate his innocence he climbed on top of his limousine and danced. He was not as graceful though as he was in the eighties.
-- Clear up the stage for that infamous drunkard driver Bill Junklow, the South Dakota Congressman. He has killed a pedestrian and left the scene of the accident. The day he has escaped the cage of justice, a chimpanzee in the Los Angeles Zoo has escaped the cage of injustice. May God bless the escaping monkey and punish the- hit- and- run arrogant powerful. After all, what crime could the monkey have committed to be caged? It was about time to fight for his right. Bravo, Mr. Chimpanzee, at least you have given it your best shot to regain your freedom, a noble route the escaping congressman has lost because he was a slave to alcohol and arrogance of power.
--Although the dishonesty of the majority wounds the human decency; it remains cherished by the few. Yes, today I salute you the Greek ambassador in Baghdad. Your kindness has invited that four-year-old Iraqi and

183

his family to Athens to pull out the American bullet that had entered his head as he was playing. That tragedy occurred right after the chief of the greatest army had declared: "Mission Accomplished." Mr. President, we have accomplished nothing as long as there is a bullet inside the skull of a child or a tear running down his cheek.

--In spite we lose faith in man, so often, animals and birds have the power to restore our lost faith. I salute you, Charlie, the parrot. For many years you have never failed to squeak twice a day, "evil Hitler." I know you and your great master, Wilson Churchill, were angry at that monster. I wish you were still alive; you would have vented out that same anger at all the today's tyrants.

THE RINGMASTER

1/ 23, 2004

Three days ago our President traveled from the White House to Capitol Hill. This short but grandiose diplomatic trip got the attention of the whole world. Yes, he had an important message to deliver. No, apparently he had more than one. Ok. Mr. President, tell us more lies or recite the oldies. However, you must worry: although made in time, lies, like any human thoughts or actions, remain timeless. As you were slowly marching toward the presidential podium, you shook hands and distributed faked smiles. To embellish your image of an impersonal president, you have grabbed a little black girl from her father's arms to rest her in yours for a few seconds. But beware; a co-opted photo with an innocent child can't give an angelic face to a Circus Ringmaster.

Soon as you stood behind the podium, a powerful wrinkled man shouted: "Ladies and gentlemen, I present to you the President of the United States."

The applauses became louder; Madame Politics was then dressed up in her most colorful garment of hypocrisy. As you stood stern behind the podium, applauses heated up for a few moments, then died out; it was time to give you the floor. You opened your mouth and lies flew every direction like wasps whose nest had been disturbed by a gang of mischievous children. Having acknowledged the dignitaries, domestic and foreign- without forgetting the citizens- you discoursed. I paraphrase:

…Our deep gratitude to the Armed Forces. Because of your sacrifices now we live in a safer world.

--You have enumerated the steady economical recovery thanks to your tax cuts, a relic from the disastrous Reagan's era.

-- We have gotten ready of Saddam Hussein and brought freedom, security and peace to the people of Iraq.

--The economy is on the way of recovery, and we will have a better health care- thanks to your policy of multiple plans.

-- You have reaffirmed the sanctity of marriage between heterosexuals.

--You have preached that athletes must stop using steroids to be role models for our children.

--All those accomplishments will become obsolete if we fail to renew "the Terrorist Act," you have emphasized.

Wow! All sound great until one puts the dots on the letters. True, we've won the war against Saddam. However, where is the peace for Iraq? Mr. President, a preemptive war does not produce genuine peace; rather it promotes itself. A safer world! Mr. President, force never can guarantee permanently the safety of anyone; rather it prolongs a temporary- rising insecurity. Peace will come later; you have been constantly preaching us. My reply to this: war has only one face, the face of destruction. Peace we have not given to the people of Iraq, nor will it come to them soon; we have ultimately created deeper animosity between its ethnic factions.

Thanks to your invasion we have lost some of our European old friends and gained new enemies amongst the Arabs. Should you still insist to call it liberation; I call it a barbaric aggression and deadly adventure for all. And your claim about the recovery of our economy! Well, Sir, prosperity in Wall Street cannot be the measure of a good economy for the nation. The Fed and Wall Street are counterfeiters, after all. Bad economy is depicted when a high percentage of the nation's population wake up in the morning and have no jobs to go to. Or worse: having jobs that cannot cover our basic needs for survival. Mr. President, eighty percent of us live on such a thin budget that a few dollars spent to meet the unexpected will deeply disturb our zone of materialistic comfort.

As for your new initiatives in the domain of health care: It gives the majority of us a stiff neck; rather than a boost to our pockets. If you do not believe me ask the millions who have no pockets to store the imaginary gift of your generosity, O false Papa Noël.

Some of us might appreciate your modest offer when you have promised $250 million for our junior colleges to create job training. However, Mr. President, there are no jobs in sight and hence there is no immediate need for training. Could we put the allocated money to a better use, such as sending it to Pat Robertson's 700 Club? With this amount, the holy man can issue 250 million one- way tickets to hell for the nonbelievers.

--To please the holy masters of yours, you have reiterated that matrimony can be concluded only between the opposite sexes. In parting with a segment of population, you are dividing a nation known to be united under God. May God continue to bless all, the straights, the gays, the lesbians and the –in- between! That is the

185

blessed America. Mr. President, exclusion is the ultimate insult to the One who sits on the clouds while blessing the earth, planet of the stones that evolved into bones. And thanks to good-willed men, those bones will become wings of angels.

 As for your noble crusade against using steroids on the sport courts, please pump me up with a high dosage of those steroids; I need a moment of strength to break down the cage you and your conservative bodies have built for my soul and flesh.

--Mr. President, through your "Faith- Based Initiatives" to assist the poor, you appear as a man of grace and redemption. You may live your illusion to the contentment of your heart. However, please don't invite me to the banquet of the anointed, I am not ready yet, I am still in ecstasy biting my forbidden apple. Sir, the mixture of religion and State has been and always will be an effective prescription to impoverish the masses rather than to help them. Since when and where have we seen caught fishes escaping the fry pan, even if water added to oil?

In my humble opinion: Religion is an opaque mask of righteousness to bankrupt people, economically and spiritually.

In sum, you have recited to us a long litany of your achievements that have ultimately left us, so far, with a trillion dollar deficit; besides having spent the saved $500 billion your administration had inherited from the Clinton's years. It might not be a bad idea to be a playboy; it can serve some of us as an energizing force for a greater good that can benefit all.

Well, if you think that you have heard it all from me, wait until you will hear it from my children and theirs, I pray for your longevity.

You have closed your speech with the traditional invocation: "May God continues to bless America!" Your wish is God's will. In spite of it all, America's heart has been and always will be after His. However, Mr. President, please do pay close attention: We must be light to the world, not missiles. Do remember, O great warrior, once the sword becomes dull, the pure heart remains man's only weapon of self-defense. Certainly, a prayer from Pat Robertson will not give purity to your heart. When the heart is truly pure, then God's doves will perch on the palms of our hands to sing a song of peace for all. God is the security of all securities.

In your pompous entrance, you have received the child between your arms. As you exit, may you be pure enough for the child to receive you in hers and that is redeeming grace.

THE BOMB IN A SILVER BOX

1/ 27, 2004

John Paul 11, dressed in his white garment, sat on the Papal throne shining with the sculptured face of St. Peter. His Holiness was in audience with Dick Cheney. And I wondered what the two leaders could have in common!

The Vice President, dressed in his executive expensive suit, looked cheerful and warm. Why not, we have grabbed Iraq from the mouth of that most ferocious lion called Saddam and soon oil pipes will pump up the dark gold. And he who has the black gold has the earth as his inheritance.

At the end of the audience, the Vice President gave a dove to the aging Pontiff; apparently it was of no use for the donor. A dove is a symbol of peace and peace is no friend of the Vice President. The gift was a gesture void of any hope for peace. Bring it on; we will whip the asses of any enemies, real or unreal. We are the country of smart bombs that travel through peepholes, cried the voice of the most violent Vice President America ever had.

Anyway, the Pope has accepted the gold plated dove that was caged in a thick metallic box. Dick, your gift is of no use for the Pontiff; he has the Holy Spirit, the ultimate dove of peace. You should have kept it for yourself, it might serve you one day, somehow; the Lord is still in the business of miracles making.

-- His Holiness is not just a man of peace, he also enjoys rap dance. Two days prior to your arrival to the Vatican, the aging lion of peace had delightfully witnessed a young catholic spinning his head in the courtyard of the St. Peter's Basilica. The breakdancing gave His Holiness hope for peace no politics in Washington could offer. Yes, Dick, we must be close to this earth with our heads and hearts. If we put it afire, where then can we rest them? It's true from its woods a cross was made for Jesus; still without that cross redemption would have remained an elusive dream.

Dick, twister of the arms, and young man, spinner of the head, may you be equally blessed, in spite of the difference of the merits of your twisting and spinning.

"His Holiness, may I dare…?"

Please, do, my son.

"Where Dick's salvation lies?"

"In letting out the wolf within him," said the Pontiff with a smile spreading all over his gracefully aging face. May we all spin our heads and hearts on the foot of the cross and this is sure salvation.

MAN'S STRIFES AND INEQUITIES

1/ 28, 2004

We pray for peace; we keep getting ferocious wars. We pray may the motherly wombs carry our babies to the happy shores of life; still we abort over a million of them annually, just in the good USA. We pray for the chastity of the young; still our youth mate with such a passion as if God had directly spoken to them: Multiply, you are in a race with the savage rabbits of the jungles. We pray may our politicians conform to the norms of ethic so we all can grow in God's fear; still they keep robbing us and send us to wars to enrich themselves and their masters, the lobbyists. And we pray for a thousands of other needs, so may earth find its balance, still we wake up every day to find ourselves riding the same roller coaster.

So I decided to separate myself from the herd to live in a smaller and more manageable world. I do not pray for my Mexican mango tree to give me healthy fruits; rather I wake up in the midst of the freezing nights to water it in the hope to soften the effect of a brutal freeze. I do not pray for my children to display good citizenship; rather I hold their hands and guide them to the court of contribution. I do not pray may my heart and that of my spouse become one; rather I carve my heart for her on the rocks of our marital problems so that my love becomes visible to her. I do not pray that may my car run, I steadily keep it fueled and tune it up from time to time. I do not pray that may peace come to the world, I am in a constant chase of the Saddam within me, so may my soul become agreeable to all those who care to travel toward it. Ah, the kiss between heaven and earth, the passionate union between the soul and body! The body is not the humble beast of burden pulling the royal carriage, the soul. Rather, both the carriage and the beast are in a journey toward the Creator of all things in the universe, seen or unseen. And now that I am atop of the mountain, I laugh before the strifes of man and all his inequities.

STYLISH ASSASSINS

1/ 29, 2004

Thank God, the circus is over. For more than two weeks now I had been watching the Iowa and Massachusetts Caucuses. It was as self-inflicting pain. Thanks, Mr. the sadist within me. It was worth it though; I needed laughter and I received tenfold. Yes, I saw that great clown, Dr. Howard Dean flipping steamy burgers and distributing hot coffee. The populace enjoyed the service. They swallowed the burger even at the risk of being the meat of a mad cow. Well, why am I so hard on the cattle industry? We are the original mad cows; we mutually poison one another.

The MD politician was not the only infamous clown of the circus; Leslie Clark, the General, John Kerry, the Senator, and other less prominent clowns have rivaled him. Suddenly all have become our humble servants until they get our votes. Once we grant them their wish, they will give us the upright finger, devoting their hearts and minds to the lobbyists, the thieves in expensive suits, fur coats, shining ties and leather shoes. Just think of the thousands of animals, besides ourselves, that have been offered on the altars of those most treacherous gods.

 One might say: is that not democracy at work? Not at all, rather that's the kind of democracy needing a serious values- revision. It is simply the prostitute dressed in a nun's habit. Maybe we should undress the false nun, even skin her off to unveil the false god she is worshipping. True in many other nations, and I'm particularly thinking of the oppressed countries of the Middle East, politicians don't flip hamburgers; nor do they serve hot coffee. Rather, they send their agents to the voting booths: Vote for me or my agent will shoot you on the spot.

Well aware of the Western notion of freedom, I do not see how its treacherous civility is superior to the violent behavior of the Middle Eastern dictatorship. In spite of his ability to reach the stars, modern Western man is still the bird of the iron cage, the mass media. In the industrialized nations, democracy is often hi-jacked by false ads, courtesy of the dollar power. In the underdeveloped nations, democracy is constantly hi-jacked by gunpoint, courtesy of the tyranny of their politicians. We the people of the West and East, North and South must be vigilant and valiant enough; freedom is a gift worth dying for; a treacherous commercial ad or a menacing gunpoint must not mislead or frighten us.

MYSTERIOUS ARE HIS WAYS

2/ 1, 2004

Today my son Amon has sealed a $15000 deal with "the Sandal Condominium Association." And here you are in the Espiritu Santo Church, kneeling piously as if you were a John Bosco. You might have prayed: Lord, here is my last dollar, let it be the smartest way of any dollar I had ever spent. I know your infinite wealth. Yes, Lord, $15000 is but a drop in your vast ocean of wealth. You have ended your prayer, kissing the Pharaoh cross you had sculpted in the left arm.

Well, it is quite appropriate to reflect upon a few of God's many ways of hunting man: Lord, you are the

189

cleverest fox who knows how to penetrate the hens' house. Once there, you pick up the fattest of them and feast on it, without failing to share your banquet. You are the snake, whose venom can cure all our maladies. You are the only fishing rod able to hook the biggest whale by a hair of its jaws. You are the great sorcerer whose charm no human can rival or resist. You are the vulture whose wings, once extended, cast a shadow that overpowers its preys, big and small. You are the groundhog that never fails to announce to our cold hearts the arrival of spring. You are the light that touches our eyes so we may see through the infinite darkness of space and time. You are the most skillful surgeon who operates on our souls without anesthesia, just a bit of discomfort. You are the huge bell that tolls from the icy mountaintops to announce the rise of a burning sun. You are the gentle wind that touches every flower without breaking one single green stem or detaching a blooming bud. You are the great general of peace who instructs his warriors to lay down their arms to experience the mighty power of prayer. You are the great sculptor who knows how to forge peaceful faces on the iron gates. In sum: You are kind to all, in spite of their wicked intentions. Yes, Lord, you knew of my son's unholy intentions, still you have welcomed him to the holiness of your house. You have accepted his disoriented prayer as well as his meager dollar; both invested for the descent of your mighty blessings upon him.

Your generosity does not stop where ours ends, you always give more. The following week as my son was rushing to church for more of your wealth, you have sent a sweeping wind that blew away the last $50 of his wealth (one of his car wheels had blown up). You wanted all, so you can give it all back to him in tenfold. Look at you and your smartest tactic in wheeling and dealing; it defies our human logic. I know why though, you want to remain faithful to your promise: Those who want all must give it all away.

Having learned my lesson, I surrender to your mighty seduction. Through my meager donation I dream to feast on your infinite generosity. You are ultimately the invisible spirit that pulls the carriage; so help us to hop on your wagon without asking the mistrustful question: where are we heading to?

DON'T HAVE A LOVER IN THE FLESH, JUST IMAGINE ONE- MISS.LAURA

2/ 2, 2004

America the beautiful, where and when have you lost your soul? A man is imprisoned; his ex- wife had accused him of beating the family dog that was then at his custody. After his release they fought for the dog's custody and the fate of the children mattered little, if any at all, for either. Due to the alarmingly rising violence in relationships, Miss. Laura has created this ad in the You Tube: *Do not have a lover in the flesh;*

just imagine one.

She went on to explain in details: s/he will be sweet to you and never attempts to aggravate your life.

For only $100, you can receive, through e-mail, a daily message full of affections for a whole month. Fifty

dollars more will guarantee you an unforgettable erection executed by and shared with yourself, just through

thinking of your imaginary lover. $25 added to the above amount, you will receive a box of assorted chocolate

at the end of the month. A renewal of six months or more will give you 10 percent discount.

And I must say: this inventive idea of pleasuring yourself will spare you the need for a partner who, if waking

up on the wrong side of bed, might beat or even kill you for having had failed to take the family dog out for a

walk. Well, enough of God's grace shining upon our nests of love. Just do remember Nietzsche's words: "Let

man fear woman when she hates: deep down in his heart lays the conviction, man is merely evil, while

woman is bad." -*Thus spoke Zarathustra – on little and young women.*

--The ongoing emotional war between woman and man affects their children as well as their pets. Poor

dependants! But don't worry, happy days are ahead; pharmacists and psychologists are working hard to keep

you alive, by taking anti-depression drugs to avoid suicide. But if the human ingenuity fails to cure your acute

depression, you will welcome death with the song: Happy days are already there. However, since I am an

addict skeptical: to overcome acute depression, I have put my ears against the icy hole where the groundhog

hibernates.

"When the spring will come to me?" I asked the blessed one.

In two weeks, exactly two, emphasized the visionary. I then laughed at the snow and began to plant in my

garden flowers of many colors; I wanted to welcome the-soon-coming spring. Once my flowers are in full

bloom, I shall harvest them and go to the icy mountaintop to distribute them to its inhabitants whom the snow

keeps imprisoned. I wanted to take the spring of my valley to the icy mountaintop. Yes, it is my firm belief

that for the spring to come in nature, the ice of indifference must melt in the heart of man. So, here is a red

rose to you my heartless Colombian wife, despite you had hidden the chocolate box in your son's room. The

brutality of your exclusion has planted the rose of forgiveness in my heart. Sorry for having had told you that

I wanted you out of my life. No, please stay, I must struggle to achieve victory; running away from problems

is not a safe route to take. Like a brave soldier, I must swallow the bullet of your indifference while caring for

the flower of love I had initially planted in my heart for you. And when it blooms, I will bow down before

your feet and say: dear, here is my rose; would you take it? If you would refuse, I will subscribe to Miss.

Laura's site, or even a peek at the video of Janet Jackson's bare breasts might revive the dying pleasure in my

solitary imagination. Janet, dear, don't worry, a flash of your voluptuous boobs, even in an occasion other than the Super Bowl, will always get you the undivided attention of a large audience. As for you Miss. Laura, I just big you, could we compromise: Take the dog, the children, the house and the rest of all my imaginary wealth; just spare me the appearance in judge brown's court; he is a man's hater: could it be that father had taken the dog and walked out on the family when the judge was a fetus? Sorry judge, your justice stinks; I had been in your divorce court.

THEIR SUPER TUESDAYGAVE ME DIARRHEA

2/ 4, 2004

Yesterday was the Super Tuesday for the Democrat Candidates; seven southern states were up for grab. Like the majority of my fellow Democrats, I will vote for the most electable candidate. The reason is simple: my discontent with the Bush Administration. Could that be out of prejudice or envy? Please spare me the light of the day; I have little regard for the worldly possessions, including fame. Prejudiced! Not at all, I just despise this administration that promotes deception. This settled; let me spend some time with my notorious brethrens, the aspiring Democrat Presidential candidates.

Forgive me Miss. Carol. Braun; I am unable to reach a fair evaluation of your candidacy.

John Kerry, I have affinity with you. True, you had killed many Vietnamese, but you came back with profound sense of guilt; you had murdered humanely. Wish I could detect the same sorrow in the President's eyes. Do not worry, Mr. Bush, you are not that bad, Saddam's fall embellishes a bit your savage image.

Leslie Clark, a good general must be able to detect the majority, if not all the tactics of his enemy. Please, General, do not defame the ingenuity of the USA. Army, you must know how to read the maps of your war. But first, you need to study well the map that leads you to your own soul. Truly, have you drawn it yet? No, you can't. First, you need to have a soul; that's why you're having a hard time drawing the line between war and peace. Can the swing of a yoyo win a war for peace? General, first know who you are, then you will be able to define your opponent. Enough of enlightening you about the basic political tactics!

John Edwards, certainly I like to grind up my limited sacks of grains in your father's mill, but sorry, Sir, my donkey had consumed them, thus leaving me with nothing but empty sacks. Do not worry; I might dispel the next acquired sack of grains under your feet to honor your future presidential parade. This is not a definitive promise though, because I am planning to steel that sack from my neighbor's barn, and I have no previous experience or personal talent for the enterprise. Besides of the foregoing legitimate excuses, I have a trial to attend, they had accused me of raping a southern red hair babe. Therefore, I definitely choose to cut ties with you; meaning: I will never march in your parade as long as you hold high the confederate flag.

Dennis, pardon me I have more than one reason for note voting for you. First, you remain obscure to me. Second, you are too short, and third because of my utter ignorance of the Slavic languages, I can't pronounce properly or spell correctly your last name; ignorance is a shameful thing. It is misfortunate, have you been called Dennis the Menace, you could have received the attention of a greater audience. Anyway, this is ancestry, and man must live and die by whatever legacy his ancestors would have left him. Now I must move on to reflect upon my two favorite unpopular Presidential candidates.

Al Sharpton, I have heard you speaking against the conservative movement made primarily of the religious right. Although you are a minister, a man of religion, you have despised them and rightfully so. For that I admire your sincerity.

"If Jesus were living on earth; He will refuse to be a member of any of their churches," you have stated. Certainly hypocrisy is not your cup of tea and for that only I would like to become a member of your church. Al, you have my vote in whatever other arena, politics is a laboratory for the art of deception; don't burn your hands with the acidic solutions in this lab of evil.

Joe Lieberman, I have followed you all along your days of bewilderment, trying to carve a Presidential image for yourself. Your goals were honorable and patriotic, and contrary to the opinion of the mass media, I submit that you have expressed yourself fairly well. However, your integrity has been the bullet you have used to shoot yourself in the foot. That is okay, Joe, better to be lame and walk on the path of light than to have wings and hover over darkness. Joe, you are still my hero; that is, as long as you continue to walk in the light. Yes, do not let the flashy firework of worldly successes take your eyes off the remote stars of ethics. Congratulations, Joe, You had entered the race with great integrity, with the same integrity you have withdrawn from it; and that is the measure of a great statesman. Goodbye and good luck, you are still one of the few true servants of the people.

Now let me move away from the man to the machine. Dr. Howard Dean, please do see a psychiatrist at your first convenience. After all, it doesn't do any good to possess the world and loses one's soul. Glad for having not been one of your Patients, nor will I ever cast my vote for you.

Finally, I must shoot with great sense of equality. You all had been clever and astute beggars soliciting our votes. Would the winner amongst you, be noble enough to repay us back, O great sorcerers and clowns of the treacherous times we live in!

FEELING WELL ON THE DAY OF THE PRIMA DONNA POOCHES

2/ 10, 2004

It is the day of the prima Donna pooches, the -top- hot dogs show. They have come from all over the continent in the company of their proud owners who dreamt of a moment of fame. I carefully watched the canines as they were performing on stage. They were not at one another's throat. Rather, with civility they competed for the top- prize. Well- groomed, they performed, to their best abilities the tricks they had learned; trusting the world to judge their performances. My direct question to you humans: Have you tried your best? Yes, I must remind you that subjugating others to terror cannot guarantee you the winning of freedom. Rather, man's true freedom finds itself as an integral part of that of his fellowman. If you don't believe me, keep on killing one another, no longer shall I mourn your destruction. Many of you have passed on their hatred to their children. What a shame! You could have done a better job. Still I will continue living in hope. From the ashes of your moral laziness and greed for the worldly acquisitions and fame, the gentleman will rise; it's the law of reclamation of the lost goodness within.

Congratulations to all the gracefully racing dogs; there are no losers in a competition conducted under the auspices of civility.

FROM A DICTATOR TO ANOTHER

2/ 11, 2004

Our great orator has delivered a dangerous ultimatum to North Korea for the sake of the world's safety, so he claimed. Mr. President, is it possible that North Korea, through its nuclear program, is trying to overcome the terror we had subjugated its people for over half a century with our own atomic bombs? One cannot prohibit to others what one allows to himself. Weapons of Mass- Destruction are the pie all nations love to have, poisonous as it may be. Let's all surrender to a holy fast; only when the flesh is deprived can the soul find its salvation.

Mr. President, you have claimed that you wanted to save the world from the danger of the deadly poison. If sincere, why are we still raising so high this cup of poison to others? Behold, I see you standing on the mountaintop of arrogance and shouting: Do what I say, or I shall unleash my poison that will kill you, your children, wives, brothers, sisters and your beasts. Because of such a serious menace, many nations want to acquire the same cup of poison to toast it back to us whenever we will toast ours to them. It may be not a bad Idea for North Korea having nukes; it will serve us as an effective deterrent whenever we are tempted to send

194

our agents of death. You want the whole world to hear your voice, because it is the voice of reason, so you claim. It is the voice of madness, I challenge you. Let me tell you about the ultimate barometer of an effective voice: it is that of a gentle heart. I wonder, Mr. President, if the heart has any role to play in conducting your diplomacy. With our unrivaled arsenal of weapons we are able to annihilate this planet one thousand and one times in a matter of hours. Still you want to promote the Star Wars Program; meanwhile denying others from possessing weapons of a far lesser power of destruction. Why is that? Aren't we motivated by fear, to say the least? If so, why can't you understand that others, too, might be living under this curse? Are we the only humans and the rest of the world are robots? But even robots have their own fears. So, Mr. President, if you truly want to promote peace throughout the world, you must negotiate in good faith or else heaven will pour anger upon us. Would you please stop preaching and say a silent prayer of mercy on Albert Einstein's soul; such a prayer might help saving ours as well. I know before death he has expressed some regret for having had fathered that terrible child, the atomic bomb. I am inclined to think that he wished to have had been a Mozart or a Beethoven.

Mr. President, I pray that you would have time to listen, now and then, to the sounds of the musicians' redemptive creativities. As for Albert Einstein's bomb, I hope and pray you hold tight to its keys. However, if your hands are shaking, please do ask Pat. Robertson to hasten the day of rapture; it is a lot safer to be surprised by God than by man.

WE ALREADY HAVE AUTO ZONE, WHY NOT MAN ZONE?

2/ 13, 2004

American cloning scientists went to South Korea after having been challenged by the far religious right. The science of cloning is the latest chapter of man's longing to become godlike. Yes, forever the human intellect will pride itself to have the power of unveiling mysteries, self- creating and life promoting throughout the universe. Ultimately, all the universe's mysteries can be unveiled through the infinite process of evolution, biological be or intellectual.

The hardcore evolutionists have echoed the belief that the universe is not created out of nothingness, contrary to the -long- sustained traditional religious belief. It all started seriously with Darwin, who has preached that this ever- evolving universe is the God the monotheistic religions have dreamed of. The generality of such a theory has seduced a few from the religious sector. I can particularly think of Pierre Teilhard de Chardin, the archeologist Jesuit priest.

In his book *Hymn of the Universe*, he wrote: "Blessed be you mighty matter, irresistible march of evolution, reality ever newborn, you who, by constantly chattering our mental categories, force us to go ever further and further in our pursuit of the truth."

Through its long and tedious process of love, the universe unveils God, the prime energy of love, the energy behind all energies. God contains all; and none contains Him at any given time and under any given circumstances. He is the circle that contains and encircles all circles. It is the kind of relationship that binds streams with their river.

Ultimately, evolutionism gave rise and legitimacy to cloning.

Since through cloning we can manufacture organs in our labs, soon trucks (engineered to preserve the organs' vitality while travelling) will be crowding our national highways, along with those of the May Flowers that transport our furniture and other goods. The business of exporting and importing the human parts will also crowd the national and international skies to meet the expanding urgent need of replacing the parts damaged by the process of wear and tear. Consequently, cloning will have sharper teeth to bite on our religious rituals, if not beliefs. The power of producing human parts will rival, if not will put out of business, the candles industry- since many saints will be losing their jobs as the only and most effective intercessors for the cure of the sick. Worse, it is a serious challenge to the belief that only God can give and take away life. This domino-effect will ultimately shake the faith of many traditional believers. Consequently, the ultra- zealots among them might raise Peter's sword to cut off the ears and necks of those who will be working in and promoting the cloning industries. I worry not about those lunatic zealots. However, I am interested to know how God would react in face of the fierce rivalry of modern man:

1. Would He feel sorry for Himself for having lost the- long- held title of being the sole Creator and sustainer of life?

2. Would the snake of rivalry creep under His throne to shake His Self -confidence?

3. Would He feel betrayed?

4. Would He strike a new deal with the modern rebel? Or would He forsake him, sending him to disintegrate in the wilderness of confusion?

For a narrow- minded creationist all the foregoing grievances are true spears aiming at God's heart. Therefore, He will have no other alternative but to send the rebel to the wilderness of confusion. Then and only then the Lord of the Lords can sigh with relief: At last, I do not have to deal with the madness of modern man, who is constantly consumed by his self- absorption; let the fool be drowned in the sea of his false grandeur.

Contrary to the paralyzing panic of the creationists, I see in evolution God's heartfelt joy and self-satisfaction, self- fulfillment. The universe is not the outcome of a theory; rather of a performance of infinite love that work to alleviate the human sufferings. It is love at its purest and most powerful form. The universe was born out of that creative infinite love of God and the responding finite love of man. It is God who became man, so that man may become godlike. Evolution is nothing less than God's love in its most creative, binding and engaging power.

"The most telling and profound way of describing the evolution of the universe would undoubtedly be to trace the evolution of love…Driven by the forces of love, the fragments of the world seek one another so that the world may come into being," Teilhard wrote.

In the words of André Gide: "The world is divinely, supernaturally natural."

How sublime and dynamic is the God of evolution as opposed to the God of creationism, a theory that presents Him as a stagnant and weary Creator, and eventually deemed to disintegrate along with a fragile and incomplete world He had created in a moment of a depressing boredom. Through our loving deeds we participate in the creation of the forever- evolving universe. However, through our evil deeds we slow down, and even detour its march toward its finality, God. Builders will reach and live in God's heart, and destroyers will be thrown into the abyss of nothingness. So, let's cooperate recreating, through love, a harmonious world for all; a creation that ultimately will honor God and rest us in His Sacred heart. To cooperate in creating and preserving the world is the highest honor and moral obligation God has entrusted to man; it is morality at its holiest dynamics and highest stake.

SCREW MOTHER GENEVA

2/ 12, 2004

The 600 prisoners, the coalition forces had caught during the fighting against the Taliban, will not receive the rightful treatment the Geneva Conventions gave to war captives.

The Bush Administration said and continues to say: They are combatants for the cause of al- Qaeda, therefore; they must be held until terrorism ends.

I believe that the Administration has gone wild, if not barbaric, by keeping them caged until the end of terror. What kind of a twisted logic is this? Terrorism has no foreseen end, unlike any conventional war. We just cannot randomly pick up adults and teenagers, as in this case, to indefinitely detain them under the label of being enemy combatants. What happened to the basic legal code: everyone is innocent until proven guilty; a code the civilized world greatly prides itself with? Are we now abdicating the basics of the human rights and falling victims to the paranoia of fear? Today America has an important decision to make: to live up to its responsibility as a civilized nation or cave into the pedantries of paranoiac fear, malady of a confused mind. When man becomes confused, he begins to see enemies everywhere. As suspicion begins within; he sees even his own shadow running to crush him. This is the madman looking in the mirror and beats what he sees. America, you have never been so powerful and yet so fearful. Are you going to shoot rockets into the air because you fear the stars in the sky might fall unexpectedly and destroy our civilization? Who is that thug who had stolen your self- confidence? You are falling victim of your own fear, and no other power on earth can shake you up. Sadly, today I see you laying flat on your stomach, hands stretched out surrendering to the deadliest malady. Beloved America, you have turned your power of fighting to an imaginary enemy called fear of the other. This other is your fearful self, thus abdicating to your real self, a self that had so strongly and gracefully forged you during your long years of optimism, self- confidence and self- building. America, you are telling me that you are fighting a heartless enemy called terror. Let me tell you about the real source of terror: In the soul of individuals, as well of nations, cohabit two opposing forces: the force of good and that of evil. Could it be that your weakened goodness has been paving the road to the victory of evil within you? How could you allow the wings of evil overshadow those of your mighty eagle?

Free, free, America, the innocent or at least abide to the international laws by bringing them into the court of justice. I know well that you want to become the unrivalled warrior in valor before all nations. Truly, I say unto you: valor must be proven only to oneself, by doing the right thing. The greatest war one must wage is against oneself; all other wars are but a showdown of weakness rather than strength.

Still the legitimate question persists: Must we punish our enemies? There is no quarrel about it. The challenge is to rightfully identify who those enemies are.

We, the liberals, are trying to slow down your advance on the muddy roads of tyranny. But if you do insist, be reminded, dear America, that those neo-cons are plucking your feathers thus depriving you from flying high above those muddy and ungodly roads of fear, caprice and revenge.

"You become fearless when the love of God comes so near you that you not only trust in God, you dwell in God."- The blessed Yogi Bhajan.

A BOW FROM A CHINEESE SERVER IS ALL WHAT I NEED

2/ 14, 2004

It is Valentine's Day, may love and peace be unto the world said the dreamer. As I looked around I have found everything but love and peace. Apparently the madness of modern man is endangering the planet. Still let's call it a less troubled day, even a day flavored with kindness. Although savage amongst the savages, today I have rubbed my cold nose against Marla's in a reconciliatory gist after having abstained to look at her face for over two weeks now. She had treated me unkindly, or so have I believed. It is wise to embrace a truce on the Saint Valentine's Day. Courting the beast, I gave her a $200 watch, in the hope that one day she becomes vigilant enough to bring her out- of –steps march to the marital path. The apes may stand on different trees; still they often throw bananas at one another, after all.

 I also led Marla and her son Javier to the Oriental Supper Buffet on Gulf to Bay, Clearwater. I was hoping for the performance of some bows from a Chinese female server, just to show my wife that revering a man is a custom still alive and well. How I wished leading her to a tent where the harem breathe only for their man. High is the price a male Arab, like myself, must pay to live in America. At times, I even have to show involuntary submission to a wife whose stature didn't much exceed that of the stem of a wild flower. Indeed, the power of the Western woman does not lie in her physical stature; rather in the status the law gives her. And I wondered what happened to the old Book that said: from the cliff of the mountain he will pull your ankle to bring you down to submission. But the contrary has happened today. So quickly the mighty powerful Marla has tightened the rein in my mouth to pull me back to her hellish heart. Returning home, after a nourishing meal, she presented me with a card on which she wrote in acrostic:

No olvido aquel altardecer cuando te conoci.

Andando solitario te vi.

Gracias a Dios quien te puso en mi Camino!

Un gozo nuestra vida tiene divino.

Entre llanto y tristeza, desilusion y alegria,

 Hoy, y no se´ hasta cuando, mi vida junto a la tuya esta´ unida.

Te amo,

Translation:

I do not forget that afternoon when I have known you.

 Solitarily walking I saw you.

 Thank God, who put you on my path!

 Our life has a divine taste between weeping, sadness, disillusion and joy.

 Today, and I do not know until when, my life is tied to yours.

 I love you,

Marla.

In the evening she went to her English class, I journeyed to the Espiritu Santo Catholic Church. There I attended the mass celebrated by a skinny priest whose voice squeaked like an engine that lacked oil. Father Tom was of a medium stature. The texture of his facial skin revealed a man in his mid-sixties. The fact of being a Jesuit priest, besides, a talent of words, gave him the undivided attention of his audience. I identified well with him; our educational background was quite similar. And strangely enough there was great resemblance of our biological features. Anyway, let's listen to the man of mission from God.

"Good evening," he greeted the audience.

"Good evening, Fr.," responded the herd in one powerful voice. That gave him great appetite to preach God's word. I paraphrase some points of his sermon:

My dad in his late years has lost his hearing. God took it away from him because he didn't use it anyway; thus he started his homily.

I began to wonder whom I was listening to, a preacher or a whiner!

Fortunately, Fr. knew well where he was heading to.

You're so much more than what is outside. It's that love of God upon which your faith must be grounded, he said. Then he went on to explain how every one of us can have a personal relationship with God. However, two obstacles stand between the Lord and us:

1. It is the feeling of guilt for not loving enough.

2. Depression, for not being loved enough.

He went on to explain:

A personal experience with the Lord will nullify the poisonous feeling of guilt transformed to us by the doctrine of the Original Sin and endorsed by the erratic whipping of our sadistic educators, the nuns.

It was refreshing to hear a catholic priest speaking about the paralyzing power of the Original Sin and condemning the sins of cruel nuns.

To come alive from beneath the debris of the Original Sin, we need to trust God's grace. We can find salvation only though His grace, despite all our transgressions. Jesus is not our prosecutor; He is our Savior; He holds no grudge against us. So much He has loved us that He did it in a way to elevate us to His divine rank, he elaborated.

We find God in our lives, not through perfection but through our struggles, was the core of his sermon.

It was quite exalting listening to him, in spite of his apparent inability to overlook the cruelty of his father, who had always made a big scene out of his shortcomings; leaving unnoticed his accomplishments. And I wondered when the religious leaders of the world would stop screaming at their followers: You're good for nothing until you do whatever we say.

At the end of mass, a young man sang:

I believe for every drop of rain that falls a flower grows ...

I believe for everyone who goes stray someone who will come to show the way...

I believe that even in the darkest life a candle glows...

"Good morning everyone, I'm Frank's son, please when you see the man, give him my filial regards," thus the young introduced himself at the end of the song. The small stature singer, with the grandiose voice, was the son of a well- known figure in the community of the Espiritu Santo church. That day father had some important business to attend to, so one of the parishioners has told the son.

I felt instant pity for the father and the son. The son lived in Los Angeles, California, and the father in Clearwater, Florida, a mile away from the church. Why could not one of them have initiated a face-to-face encounter? What a lousy relationship they might have had. Thank God for the warmth of my nomadic fatherhood.

THANKS AMERICA FOR THE HOTDOGS

2/ 18, 2004

Today Paul Bremer, the American administrator of the post-war Iraq, has delivered a long speech outlining the many accomplishments his country and its coalition have achieved to prepare the embattled Iraq embracing the responsibility of self-governing on the 28th of June,2004. From the many cited accomplishments, I recall the following few:

1. Water and electricity are now flowing everywhere in the –once- was dry and dark country of Saddam.

2. Millions of children are going back to schools with books that don't mention the tyrant's name.
Indeed, students and teachers are finding their faces reflected on the mirror of the new freedom crafted by the- all-skillful American diplomacy. And I must add: let's not forget the millions of hotdogs Mother America will be serving free to those already starved children. What a beautiful song to sing to their sensitive ears. After all, children are the world. Yes, Paul, sing it along with Mike. Ah, if the Iraqi children could just forget their dead parents, siblings, relatives and friends.

3. The majority of Iraqis will have good paying jobs, thanks to the billions their oil will pump to their new economy, sang the provisional governor.

And let's touch another class of the helpless who will greedily benefit from the American intervention. For centuries, Arabs have undermined women's rights. It is about time to forge for those poor creatures a face endowed with all the human rights. Yes, no more veils, from now on they can wear high heel shoes and tight blue jeans. They can twist their hips to force the old monsters, men, to salivate. They will hold high and low offices. They even can have breast implants to speed up the climbing of the ladder of social success- in imitation of their Western sisters. And thanks to America, they will have the right to divorce their husbands, claim equality in dividing the conjugal properties and put legal fight to take custody of the children and even the family dog. They can drive cars, ride bicycles and roll on bladed skates, thus inviting the fresh breeze of the Euphrates River to caress their wavy hairs. And soon their sisters in Egypt will twist their hips as they walk hand in hand with their lovers to enjoy the moon reflecting its golden light on the Nile. And the cool breeze of the Tunisian green mountains will caress the silky dark hairs of the women of this earthly paradise. To continue the dizzying dance of freedom, they will be able choose their future partners through the internet. Why not? If you offer the cup full, you must expect it back empty. In other words, it is all yours; drink it to the last drop.

Now let's visit the losers' ward. Yes, I am speaking about and to you, Arab men. From now on you must go to schools of communication; you need to learn how to listen to voices other than yours. For so long you have been roaming the jungle carefree and inattentive to those snakes that crawled under your feet. You might even have to stay home caring for the children and pets while your wives are vacationing solo. They need time to reflect on their marital status, meaning: should they continue to bear their families' burdens or run with those bachelor gentle mailmen, who smilingly greet them in the morning while stuffing their mailboxes with piles of ads that inform them about the latest fashion in clothing and make- ups .

Also, Arab men, are you prepared to accept the Nays that will be thrown unto you from your children, instead of the Yeas you have been, for so long, accustomed to hear?

Yes, brethren you must be prepared to listen and bow, sweeping is the voice of the American democracy.

  Many of you might ask: but what happened to the voice of our Holy Scriptures, whose fire our ancestors had kept burning for centuries?

And I reply: Time for America is now or never, and space is here or nowhere. Yes, democracy has entered your tent anchored in the sand of tyranny; don't deny freedom to your wives and children; or else you and your values will be speedily buried alive. You must struggle to hold unto life, in spite of its roller coaster- twists. May your, your struggle be not led by weapons, rather by intelligence, the most powerful weapon of all! Your old security found in emotional flaws is over; it is about time to start building fortresses of reason.

Now that I have communicated with the weak, time is right to say a few words to the powerful: America, your exported democracy is but the dance of a butterfly drunk from the dripping nectar of a poisoning flower. Only when the solid tree of life drips blood, then freedom will fill up the cup of the oppressed. Don't kill the butterfly in whose wings a true freedom grows slowly and mysteriously. Democracy is not a blanket that covers man's inequities, rather a seed that must grow in the gardens of his heart and mind. You must remember, beloved, man of the jungle lives by the law of force; force of the law transforms man of the jungle. In sum: History repeatedly instructs us that freedom is a flower that grows steadily on the hard rock of the human sufferings.

GOD, WHERE ARE YOU?

2/ 20, 2004

I watched on the TV screen a dead boy tightly held between his father's arms. Head down and tears flooding his face; father was searching for a safe hole to bury his son. Sadness weighed heavily on my heart and I angrily shouted:

"My God where are you?" Uncontrollable tears ran over my cheeks.

"That is my question to you; a gentle mysterious voice answered me."

Unwilling to communicate, I closed my eyes and dosed myself into sleep. Shortly after, I wake up screaming: "it can't be."

"Yes it can be," the same voice answered me back. I felt I was hallucinating.

I left home and went to the neighborhood park; I was seeking reaffirmation from its frogs, birds, and snakes that life was still worth living. There I sat on a wooden bench and saw two birds kissing passionately. For a brief moment I enjoyed the tenderness of the scene; then they flew away. I became depressed again.

"My God, why did you not create me as a bird, so I can fly and be free like them?"

"You are a bird that has lost its wings; you can fly and be free when you grow wings again."

"My Lord, should I then wait until man perfects the science of cloning, my wings had been eradicated; no longer I am a bird; they'd reduced me to a reptile?"

"Right now you can become a flying bird, just make the- two- minute walk to home. Get your wife Marla and walk back to the park while holding her hand. You will feel the warmth of a true reconciliation (I held a degree of rancor against Marla because of her coldness toward me).

"Once sitting on the bench of tenderness, listen carefully to her heartbeats and soon both will be flying, just like those two birds. Yes, child, out of your heart's good disposition grow the wings that will carry you to the purest sphere of all, to my own heart... I, too, was watching that ugly scene on the TV screen. I cried with you, you didn't see me, you was high on despair. I followed you to the park and installed myself between those two kissing birds. In fact, it was the sap of my love that flooded their throats with tenderness. I wanted to get your attention and I succeeded. I will do the same when you will draw Marla to your chest to kiss her. Yes, I will be the nourishing source for you as well. I do it all to convince you and the 6.5 billion other people that life is worth living, under all circumstances. But promise to be more lovingly attentive to me; I want you to participate in the tedious redemptive process of this world. Frighten be not, my child, I hold this world on the tip of one of my fingers and America or any other power can't take it away from me. Their weapons are full of evil; mine are fully charged with goodness. And evil can't prevail over good; certainly not on my watch and you know I don't sleep."

Having imagined that dialogue, I felt peace and joy I had never experienced for quite a while; and that was freedom in its purest form. I went home, picked up Marla and walked hand in hand back to the park. We skipped; it was l'élan vital, that divine sap already running through our veins and preparing us to fly. On the same bench, where I had just watched the kissing birds and heard the mysterious voice, we sat, kissed and I felt flames emanating from Marla's customary cold lips. I then understood that the Lord is constantly speaking to us, especially in the midst of the human sufferings and doubts, and we can understand Him only when we tilt our hearts toward His redeeming grace. He never asks us to surrender to Him through our minds. The mind is incapable to understand; or too arrogant to listen and in either case it is useless. America, may you start listening to God's voice with pure heart. Through the ingenuity of your mind you're capable to produce only guns whose smoke suffocates the planet; and that's slavery in its cruelest form. And to the Bush Administration : please don't count on the shallow effect of the aromas of the multicolored flowers you rest on the coffins of our daughters and sons wrapped in the flag- as a token of homage to them and sympathy for their families. You've killed them in the name of a false patriotism. True, the country belongs to all and all own loyalty to it. However, when it becomes a humble servant of greedy industrialists, then it loses its holiness to become gold mine for the few and death trap for the many.

And last, but not least, dear America, stop bragging about your powdered milk and processed canned food sent to the millions of orphans you have created throughout the world.

THE CNN CROSSFIRE

2/ 21, 2004

I sternly sat on my old couch; I was attentively listening to the today's guests on the CNN *Crossfire* program.

As usual, Republicans and Democrats were plucking one another's feathers. The Republicans were bragging about the forecasting of the creation of two million manufacturing jobs in the upcoming year. That's a big lie, the Democrats challenged them. Indeed, Bush was apt to create only lies; and all knew it. However; the infirm needed to change side in attempt to endure the pains of a long night.

And what a better way to please the neo-cons than to warn the fags and lesbians of the nation?! Yes, if those unrighteous don't stop demanding to elevate their unholy union to a marital status, the President will push for a constitutional amendment that will protect the sanctity of marriage. Marriage is, and must remain, a contract valid only between members of two opposite sexes, preached the holy one, just to please his patrons, the neo-cons.

The rightists call San Francisco a city of sin, equal to Sodom and Gomorrah; the leftists call it the city of love. I simply call it the city of humans who, experiencing crushing loneliness, as they travel the tedious paths of life, are seeking companionship. Let's not forget that history has taught us that intolerance is a paralyzing force. Therefore, if we can't wave a hand of sympathy, we must abstain from sending a bullet to those who embark on a road other than ours. After all, we are all travelers in the dark; guided only by our vision of the journey's luminous end. Your path, certain as it may be, does not give you the right to curse mine. One thing remains sure: God awaits all the travelers at the end of their various roads.

Holding unto the crime of arrogance, you may insist and reiterate that your God is holier than mine. To this false pretense, I reply: Brother, God is bigger than your righteousness and my wickedness. Therefore, would you please be humble enough and let God be God? O prince of mud, do not spoil the jewel.

Jerry Falwell ended his discourse against homosexuals with these words: "The yesterday's union of those three thousand couples of homosexuals and lesbians is sinful and they need the blood of Jesus Christ."

O keeper of righteousness, I must remind you: God's loving grace has covered all our sins. However, if you do insist to smear His face with sin, even that smear will brighten up this Holy Face. Now you might challenge me by saying: What is then the use of the Holy Scriptures?

I reply: Yes, they contain messages from God to man; they are the sources that nourish us with His spirituality. However, absorbing this spirituality is man's journey recounted to God in various tales and God loves every tale told by any of His children. They are all cute in His sight when they tell, no matter how silly and mischievous they might be. They become ugly only when they condemn. Therefore, Jerry, please stop judging others, rather let God be the ultimate judge of any man's behavior. I will be willing to jump on your wagon to travel your road, if you would honestly answer this question: who is more sinful, the stubborn arrogant who appropriates righteousness to himself; or the humble who admits his weakness till God's grace bring him home?

Reverend, please don't feel obliged to answer, I turn you to God; He is the ultimate judge. Do not follow me, I am as lost as you are; I just hope that one day you would say the same.

CONSERVATISM IS ANOTHER NAME FOR SOCIAL DARWINISM

2/ 25, 2004

It was Ash Wednesday in the Catholic tradition. Like thirsty sheep, the flocks rushed to the spiritual fountain, we were seeking forgiveness for our sins. As I was walking to the church, I almost got run over by a devout. He was racing another for a parking space; while feasting on my wife's well- rounded breasts. Jack, that's O.k. You may run me over; I know you will be remembering me in your prayers. You might even try to find what hospital I would be at to send me a bouquet of flowers. And in case you would go to my house, during my hospitalization, for a cup of coffee with my beautiful wife, do not be surprised if upon your departure she would ask you to take the garbage out. That will be her way of saying thanks for dropping by. If still pleased to be in her company and plan to re-visit, she might ask you to fix our terrace's leak that has left the white walls of the laundry room with many yellowish stains. Ah the rewards of false ecstasy!

--Speaking of ecstasy, let's not forget that hallucinatory drug our genius researchers discovered. It can oppress the post- traumatic stress, they claim. Did we need to waste time and money to create such a drug? A small dosage of opium can do it; and the new Afghanistan grows millions of tons of it. Yes, the production of this great tranquilizer has tripled since America had occupied that poor country. Thanks America for keeping the world dosed up!

--I have problems not only with the far religious right, politicians and scientists, but also with our economists. Yes, I am talking about and to you Mr. Alan Greenspan. I have lately witnessed you turning into yellow. Indeed, your mind has long ago lost its youthful vision. Wish you would have succeeded becoming a musician; your growing old in creating music would have enchanted many hearts, old and young. Let's take a close look at your latest policies of economy. Yes, I am protesting your proposition to cut our social security to contain the national deficit. Sir, your lack of common sense will create many ulcers in the stomachs of over fifty million senior citizens. The social security for 50 percent of us is in the range of $600 monthly. Could anyone live on this amount in a society that sells everything, included the stars of heavens? It is needless to mention that the price of bathroom tissue has doubled since last year. Well, Sir, worry not, tree leaves and smooth small flat rocks will do. After all, bathroom tissues are a commodity to which only the rich are entitled under your austere economy.

Sir, still the complaint against your latest policies remains legitimate because of their domino effect. In reaction to your drastic proposition the airlines industry is contemplating new ways to earn more money; it is unsafe to count on the federal government's rescue. Therefore, it is quite reasonable to expect the following policy: a small rear will cost $85, medium $150, large $250 and $350 for an extra-large. They might even amend: All of the above ticket prices are valid fro and to any State of the Union until further notification. Under tighter austerities, the tickets will eventually be priced by a fixed- rate per pound.

But to any darkness there is a silver line. Due to the squeeze of our social security, besides the reduction of our medical benefits and the rising cost of living, we the poor senior citizens, will soon have small buttocks; only abundance of food makes big ones.

But even a silver line has its darkness: such miscalculated travelling policies will force the majority of Americans to revive the golden age Horse- drawn carriages. And that will affect not only the airlines industry but also many other related industries as well. Worse, the panic might branch out to other unrelated industries. In fact, such a trend had already taken precedence in some of our barber shops; as the cost of a haircut depends on its length. And that prejudices people of curly hair as barbers need to apply hair softener to estimate its length; another extra expense for the poor like myself and the millions of my dark skinned brethren and sisters-I had been already a fatality of this trend. If this trend in the haircut industry continues, we will become a nation of gurus with long beard but no piety. Unfortunately, it wasn't our choice to grow long beards, and that will allow nostalgia to bite us; we are known to be a well- groomed nation because long ago we had said goodbye to the jungle man.

And forget not, the implementation of such austere policy would force the senior citizens to eat dog food and that will inevitably lead dogs to starvation. Even that will not register a victory for us senior citizens; we need the kind pets for psychological support to fight the stress of loneliness that scars our old age.

And Voila´, Mr. Genius in economics, or economically genius, you have ultimately created an economy of Russian roulette. Sir, if this is hard for you to comprehend; be consoled, the nation is already falling in love with restoring antiques. I mean all kinds of antiques from furniture to the fishing rods left by our beloved forefathers to help meeting our basic needs. Because of this economic attack on the helpless, today I raise your color from green to red.

Mr. President, since the buck stops at your office, would you please consider firing Mr. Greenspan and give a chance to Madame Silvia Brown; her crystal globe predictions might save the country from this chaotic economy. If you find no merit to my suggestion, don't worry, Sir, I will tell my children to tighten up their belts to survive the upcoming lean fifty years. But may you remember: pulling it all to your wrong way is never the right way.

The infamous proposition uttered by the Chief of the Fed, may give rise to this question: "what would you give up to save your financial independence and where will you be travelling to celebrate the feast of Resurrection this year?

And I reply: Thanks to the doom and gloom created by our great leaders, I shall give up on humans and seek refuge in a jungle. There I shall apologize to its beasts for the many transgressions of the past, and thank them for accepting me as part of their herds. Thereafter; I will start the long and tedious journey unto myself, and that's the true celebration of an eternal feast of Resurrection; no more menace of hunger and hammers.

In spite of all the- above-mentioned social ailments, America, we, the people, love you and have great confidence that tomorrow you will do better than today. Yes, darling, you are still a beacon of light and hope to a world full of darkness and despair.

MAN, THIS WHOLE CITY IS A BIG PRISON

2/ 27, 2004

Miss. Bianca stood smilingly on one of the platforms of the New York's subways. Young and optimistic about the future, she was happy to have had secured herself a job, as a secretary in a law firm. Although trained as educator, she had given up on education; nowadays teenagers are quite restless. The subways morning- lights, dazzling into her face, have left her in an existential ecstasy. She even shared her smile with that homeless man, who had just passed in front of her. "Too bad, he walked so fast that I didn't have time to open my purse and pull out some change to give him," she thought. It was her way of giving thanks to God who had given her a job in the crowded city of over four million people. "Those who are in a better position are entrusted with greater responsibility," she remembered the words of her Italian grandmother.

"If I would see him again, I'll make it up to him," Bianca said to herself. A few moments later she found herself down the railroad tracks and there was an upcoming train in sight. She screamed: "O my God! O my God! I am finished." Suddenly her voice died out, she had suffered epileptic seizure, an occurrence she hadn't experienced for the last two years. Lying unconscious, while foaming at the mouth and eyes turning up, suddenly she felt two strong arms. They were the arms of that two hundred and fifty pound Jeremy, a black man from Harlem. He was carrying her back up to the railway platform. At first, he could not understand the force behind the agility with which he had manipulated his heavy body as he was rescuing Bianca. Then he remembered: "A light soul can move a mountain," his black grandmother used to say whenever little Jeremy came home crying for having had been teased, because of his obesity, by his peers at the Martin Luther King elementary school. Slowly Bianca opened her eyes on Jeremy's comfort. He was kind and gentle while trying to calm her down as she was trembling like autumn leaf.

"You will be fine," he said and she tightly held his hand as if to say: Thanks for having saved my life. She then begun telling distortedly what had happened during those few seconds that seemed an eternity as she saw the train approaching.

"…I clearly remembered one thing though: I didn't want to die."

"Thank God you're safe," said Jeremy, caressing her cold face; she was still shaking.

Suddenly she started hallucinating and screamed:

"The train of death is coming; the train of death is coming."

The train of death was none other than that homeless man she had regretted his passage without giving him some change for a cup of coffee. A policeman has led him handcuffed to the accident site; after he had confessed his crime. Counting on the presence of the subway cop, Jeremy pressed Bianca's hand and went his way smiling. As he was riding the electric escalator to go home, after ten hours of night shift as a security guard, he thought into himself: "I didn't know why I had risked my life to save a stranger, but thank God I did it." Suddenly he remembered that woman he called "the white angel." Thanks to her guidance, the –now-middle-aged Jeremy had been reformed thirty years ago from a life of a troubled teenager. That "white angel," was none other than Mrs. Giovanni, Bianca's grandmother.

"Yes, officer, I had to confess my crime. True, my body has no home but my soul has a mansion in heaven," said the homeless as he stood remorseful before a frightened looking Bianca.

"I've pushed her down because she looked like that woman, who had left me for another man, ten years ago. I loved that bitch very much… See, officer, love is a force that can take you up to heaven or take you down to hell… Do you understand; or should I go on explaining better myself?" He took his eyes off the officer to fix them on Bianca's. "Miss., I am sorry, so sorry. I would hope that..." A few tears escaped his- booze- reddened eyes as he bent down to kiss Bianca's forehead.

"That's enough; I have no time for your street- acting. Forcefully pulling him away, the officer shouted: "Now tell me exactly why you did it?"

"Man, you're just as heartless as any train that runs in the New York's subways…I just told you. Have you ever been hurt? I wanted to hurt someone to ease up my long suffering."

"Still you're a criminal who needs to be taken off the street, you belong to jail."

"Man, this whole City is a big prison…Again, forgive me, Miss. I didn't mean to hurt you; hurt comes naturally to me." Dionne was a holder of a bachelor degree in English from City College.

"Do you want to press charges against this man?" asked the policeman.

"No. Let him go, God has been good to me; I don't need to revenge."

"This is not revenge, this is justice," reasoned the justice's representative.

Bianca looked at the homeless, smiled and opened her purse: "Here are five dollars, go get yourself something to eat." The police pushed away the hand that was extending the five dollar bill, and dragged the handcuffed away. Dionne turned around to bow his head as to say thanks and goodbye to Bianca who, at her turn, did not fail to let out a timid smile. "…Forgive our trespasses as we forgive those who trespass against us. Amen." She mumbled those words as she sat in the train, still a bit shaking. In a matter of five minutes the train arrived to the station that was three blocks away from the office of her new job.

Homeless man, I salute you, your moral standards put to shame the director of the government bureau of ethics. After a long investigation and denials that clown has been found guilty of tax- fraud. You confessed your crime; he denied his. And you Mrs. Giovanni, goodness you had sown, goodness your grandchild has harvested and the blessing will be bestowed upon your offspring to the seventh generation; praise be to the divine justice!

THE FOX THAT ATE THE CHICKEN, AND MADE A HAT OUT OF ITS FEATHERS

2/ 29, 2004

Dr. Charles Camborne of the University of Minnesota reported that 70 percent of Americans become gays after twenty years of marriage. Whatever the reason behind his conclusion; gay marriage has become a big political dilemma for you, Mr. President. To balance your- long- held adversities toward the gay community, larger than you had ever thought, you are presently asking the Congress for over $1.2 billion to protect their rights. Well, Sir, your unexpected kindness has angered the far religious right. But don't worry, at the final account they will forgive you; you are the fox of the hills and the flats.

Since Dr. Camborne's report didn't exclude any group, it's fair to conclude that many of those right- wing Christians are gays, too, and that their loud voices against homosexuality are but a cover- up. Indeed, the Holy Bible obliges; but so does the human nature. Politicians promote or demote whatever plays well in the political arena. Mr. President, you are not alone; most of us want to ride the mule, but refuse to feed it. However, the few truly righteous ones raise high their hands to pray: Lord, give us rain; give us pain and give us moral courage without stain. As for you and your conservative brethren and sisters, let God hear yours.

HEAT IT NOT BEAT IT

3/ 8, 2004

Today is the birth of the post- war Iraq's constitution: All citizens have equal rights, but still the Iraqi women must be happy with one fourth of the number in the new parliament. That is quite generous of a culture that believes one claw of the jungle's king is worth one hundred mice. Congratulations to the Iraqi people! I must also extend my congratulations to President Bush as well; he was the one who had snatched the victim from the strong jaws of a ferocious lion called Saddam. Having fairly distributed my congratulations to the right and to the left, to friends and foes, I must restrain overstretching my generosity. After all, a lavished optimism is but the ineptness of the mind to read the future. I warn that Iraq's new constitution will not please all. The remaining few pockets of thugs will see freedom of the others as assault on theirs. For good, for bad, the constitution was born with the mark of the beast, the human madness that hungers for power. Just think of what has happened to ours; the most loved and admired constitution that had been working effectively for centuries. Yes, "the Terrorist Act" has hijacked it mercilessly. Constitution or not, man's survival will ultimately be decided by the disposition of his heart and not by the logic of his mind. That said, I am not calling upon the mercy of demagogy or fatalism; I simply meant we must not ignore that God has first inscribed His laws upon the human heart. Constitution, O Constitution, you are but man's elusive tool of protection when he fails to protect himself from himself. However, once gone wild, he becomes like a worm desperately climbing a fence to seek nourishment, after having lost connection with the underground, its natural habitat.

"Beat it. Beat it...", thus sang Michael Jackson, over two decades ago. Today I have a new song for humanity: Heat it. Heat it. Yes, I am speaking about the heart. Yes pull it out of the ice of selfishness and it will warm up a whole empire, a whole universe and ultimately God's own heart.

But the heart has so many voices, one might object. Indeed, it does. But those voices, like the strings in a guitar, can produce a sweet melody, if God's invisible hands were to tug them. So, men of laws and preachers of pews, silence your ugly voices. Let the true God speak and then we all will have the Mother Theresa's heart, a divine heart. My fellowman, do not try to impress me by reporting that God is in your heart. That is the vanity of a lost soul. Rather, I celebrate you when I learn that you are in God's. Ah how do I long for the day when the lamb will lay tranquilly next to the wolf! Do not accuse me of being a dreamer; rather I have a

211

greater faith in God's grace and man's ability to respond to this grace. Just repent and God's grace will transform you far beyond all your dreams; you are no longer human, you are divine.

Constitution, you are but an agglomeration of dead and deadly words until God breathes on your makers and your followers; then you become a source of salvation for all. So, introduce me to your God; and I will be able to tell your future. Man finds his ultimate freedom in God as he struggles against himself and not against others; the failures of others are but the scapegoats of his own.

BARBARIC

3/ 15, 2004

Today Spain's unpopular Prime Minister Mr. Jose Maria Asnar woke up to find himself ousted, a payback to his conservative party that had blindly allied itself, against the people's will, with the Bush Administration going to war with Iraq. The naïve political analysts have attributed the ousting to the attack that took place on the eleventh of this month during the Madrid's morning railroad rush hours. It was the work of the most demonic organization, al- Qaeda, reported the mass media. In solidarity with the human race, I found the killing barbaric, regardless of who did it and for what reason(s). It is sad to see man killing his own breed; ultimately he is killing himself and God. The only way to eliminate such a sad parade of tragedies is when man finds himself in God's heart. God avoids the path of violence; He is governed by a holy respect for His greatest gift to man, i.e., freewill. Yes, God always honors His pact with man. He cannot rightfully reclaim what he had given and still remains God; giving doesn't impoverish Him.

The following question may arise: Could it be that God has stabbed Himself in the heart, or at least in the foot, for having endowed man with this precious gift?

Far from it! Just many of us prematurely fall in despair, believing that God has forsaken them, so they are entitled to commit acts of violence against their fellowmen. Still, redemption that silver line can be found in the darkness of confusion. I even dare to say that man's violence is but the shedding of the snake's old skin. It is the snake's rebirth from the magical staff of Moses- so long the created keeps crawling towards his Creator in order to reach that Promised Land, himself.

You might ridicule me by saying: hurray, false philosopher of the Century. Indeed, you have offered us nothing but a greater dosage of confusion. Now could we feed your dead brain to the hungry dogs?

Please do it without delay; your excessive hunger for sterile clarity is forcing me to eat the dogs. Still, your deadly logic challenges me: Better to eat the dogs than to be eaten by them.

Without widening the disagreement, I humbly state: the journey of man must continue, in spite of the blinding storms and the uncertainties they plunge us into.

Now allow me to revisit the Madrid victims, I want to kiss the ground that received their blood. Yes, I own respect to anyone of my species. Let's abdicate the blind force of the mind; the mind often times is a destructive force. The heart specializes in manufacturing the bandages needed to heal the wounds the mind creates. Man of the future will have to choose the purity of the heart as a sure means of his survival; the clarity of the mind will plunge him into thicker darkness that will endanger any forms of life. I am not dreaming to create an imaginary paradise on earth; I am simply searching for a habitable place for all.

WHO STOLE THE ORPHANS' PIG?

3/ 16, 2004

"It is a wonderful small world," thus sings the Disney World carousel floating on a tiny serpentine canal of water. I wondered if the writer of this song would not have dramatically changed its wording, had he the opportunity to watch Bush and Kerry at each other's throat during their debate racing for the White House. The President has accused the Senator of lacking the will to keep America prosperous and safe. Mr. President, Please do not bluff me. Beside the big mess you have created abroad, I can think of the equal mess you have left us with here at home. To promote your dangerous conservative agenda, you have succeeded to convince the simpleton majority of us that al- Qaeda has a destructive power all nations must fear. Indeed, the organization of the weak has served well your greatest weapon of mass deception. Mr. President, do not feel guilty; many love that policy. Indeed, insanity binds the insanes and wisdom unites the wise.

--Mr. President, you are not the only guilty of denial in the land, the South Carolina's Governor, too, has denied any wrongdoing, in spite of the dozen proven indictments against him. The man had led a luxurious lifestyle, thanks to the generous briberies he had unscrupulously accepted. Mr. Governor, to avoid vindication, would you like to plead guilty of a lesser charge?

I mean: would you be willing to accept the responsibility that you had stolen the orphan's pig, roasted it and ate it alone? Do not worry, Sir, the jury will dismiss the frivolous charge that you didn't say your prayer before devouring the pig; it's just a personal piety and the Redeemer understands.

--And you Martha Stewart despair not; the same Redeemer will not forsaken you; minor is your sin of gaining forty thousand dollars at the expenses of your company's investors. The most merciful One might even overlook the new waves of falsehoods you have launched to embellish your vilified image before the public.

213

You have lined up friends and daughter Alexis to present to the world, through the mass media, the Martha of honesty, compassion, loyalty and kindness. However, some puzzling facts remain:

1. A few of us know of the incident when you tried to run your lawn mower over your neighbor's body.

2. Nor do the many know about the verbal abuse you have often inflicted upon your subordinates.

3. And how about your refusal to pay some pending bills, especially those pertaining to the fueling of your private plane. Shouldn't all those facts smear a bit your face?

Still, rejoice, Diva, at least some fingers were raised to embellish your image; while not one finger was raised against those who had vandalized the image of the Holy Mother. Inspire of our soft morals, we raise fists of iron on whoever touches our financial institutions. That is why the Holy Mother had appeared on one of them (in Clearwater, Florida, two- minute drive from where I live) to warn us of the danger of worshiping mammoth, money. Holy Mother, please have mercy; the majority of us are ultimately victims, in some way or another, of that green plastic paper that bears the print: *In God we trust*. The statement is confirmed by the image of a Pyramid, built at the command of tyrannical Pharaohs whose names history, old and new, still praise tirelessly. Those brutes have overlooked the death of hundreds of thousands of peasants, just to satisfy their greed for an imaginary eternity. Wish Egypt's present government slow down its stealing so that some money is left for social programs to compensate the survivors for the cruel death of their ancestors. Ah, how I wish to join Jimmy Baker in his new version of "praise the Lord's" scam. No difference. An apple is an apple, is an apple; is an apple and not a pineapple. Just call me serpent.

-- Dennis, the Tyco's CEO, I have one word for you: Thief. I know you resent the calling.

How much should you steal before you accept the title? It is a public record that you have stolen $600 million dollars earned by the sweat of your investors. Could then a stolen billion dollar be good enough for you to admit that you are a thief? Well, I know of someone who had served four years in jail for having had stolen a piece of candy from a grocery store. Would you and diva Martha be humble enough to accept a few months in a restricted clubhouse?

Now I must address your poor victims with these few words: dear, I know you have dreamed of a comfortable old age through your investments. Do not despair, in spite you have been swallowed by those vultures of greed; on the other side of the fence of despair there is hope. Yes, according to a recent investigation, pets and birds are capable to heal your infirmities; a responsibility you had heavily laid on the shoulders of the elusive power of that evasive mammoth, the dollar.

The Gregorian chant is another curative medicine, said our modern psychology. Indeed, victory will be ultimately the lot of the little people, thanks to little animals and gentle sounds- if afforded. And if all would fail you, be consoled, the micro- waved popcorn causes lung cancer, so have reported our diet specialists. Eat plenty of it; that will certainly put a speedy end to your many unbearable miseries. Ah the shattered dreams; they were built far from God's auspices.

CROCODILE TEARS

3/ 17, 2004

I watched the controversial movie, "The Passion of Christ." The ultra-dramatic work of the conservative Catholic Mel Gibson has extracted so many tears. The majority of the audiences were so petrified at the sound of the cruel lashes. Oh pious ones, Could it be that your dramatic reaction has been the result of your unawareness of how deeply the Redeemer has loved you? You have shed tears while murmuring: they were merciless toward Him. I do not dispute the extent of His suffering; I despise your tears. Tears! Is that all you could have done to alleviate His suffering after two thousand years and more? I still do see nothing but hammers and nails in your hands. As always, you are ready to pierce the last fiber of His Sacred Thighs through your misrepresentation of His divine intent for man-kind. And please stop crowding His altars with bouquets of flowers, whose aromas fade in matters of hours; your hearts are all what He wants. Now, the most serious question is not how much suffering He has endured, rather why? It was His mad love for all; including the Iraqis whom you are killing today like flies because of the policy of King George whom you had anointed to be the cast shadow of Jesus Christ.

Mel Gibson presented Jews as the villains who had the big hand in torturing Jesus. To give a more terrifying image to their depicted malice, he made the devil follows the rabbis in the day of Jesus' appearance before Pontius Pilate (as if he were their favorite domestic pet).

Mr. Gibson, Jesus' mad love leaves no room for anyone to exploit His suffering for any kind of prejudice, a crime that has the most destructive power of dividing humanity He dreamt to unite.

The conservative critics looked upon your film as the greatest surgeon who has worked on every fiber of the divine Flesh. In so doing, according to them, you have awakened the dormant human conscience. Through this ingenious, but prejudiced, drama I see that you have sucked Jesus' soul and turned Him into a gold statue. Mr. Gibson, the golden calf has not redeemed a sinful world. Run with your fortune of $500 million dollars. Take your ultimate dream and go live on top of Mount Olympus.

A brief message to those who came out of theaters handkerchiefs soaked in tears. Hypocrites, stop tearing and come to the foot of the cross; only there you will find redemption; no ship has ever sailed in crocodile tears.

215

We can have the horizon in front of or behind us; it is only a matter of choice to journey toward eternity or fall into the abyss of one's own self-deception. So please take time to reflect on how poorly you have responded to the Lord's sufferings.

FROM A DISTANCE

3/19, 2004

Today is the second anniversary of invading Iraq. It is a celebration of an act of mercy toward the oppressed say the simpleton. The thoughtful few see things quite differently. True, Saddam the monster had oppressed his people for almost thirty years. The question is: Are the Iraqis less oppressed today? The unfolding events of the past year leave no doubt in my mind that Bush's adventure has created for them more harm than harmony, so far. I explain: During Saddam's regime, Iraq was under the tyranny of one. After the deposing of the tyrant, Iraq has fallen into total chaos that will last for a long time. So, we are left with the choice between tyranny and demagogy. Tyranny and demagogy sleep with the same devil. However, man-kind has a better chance to overcome tyranny than overcoming demagogy. Popular revolt can quickly defeat tyranny, whereas demagogy is a stubborn evil. Tyranny creates leaders of flames; demagogy creates leaders of confusion. It is a lot easier to contain flames than to contain confusion. A tyrant is a defined territory, whereas a demagogue is an entangled jungle. A tyrant nourishes himself (since rarely ever has been a tyrant female, except in bed) at the temporal weakness of his people; whereas a demagogue delightfully grazes at their most sacred hopes. A tyrant walks in darkness and thus he takes the chance to fall in a ditch at any moment of his journey. Although a demagogue might walk in the shine of the sun, his major problem remains: any direction is as good as any other, a total lack of urgency for choosing one direction over another. Consequently, both tyranny and demagogy endanger liberty, with a variance of lesser or greater consequences. Speaking of liberty, what has happened to our Statue of Liberty? For the last two and a half years the authority has closed it to the public to protect it from terrorism, so it claimed (most likely because of lack of funds). Anyway, today as Americans we stare at Dame Liberty from a distance. Don't you worry, our liberty didn't die; we are just sharing it with the Iraqis; they are already dancing on its beat; thus the Bush Administration continues to preach us. But if they have become so high on our exported freedom, why then are they slaughtering, not only our young men and women but also their own? So far, we have lost six hundred precious young American lives, four thousand are wounded and a lot more to come. Unfortunately, freedom hasn't yet flourished in Iraq and it will not for years, in spite of our huge sacrifices. Reason is simple: freedom is not a cargo for exportation. Please do not rush calling me a freedom's hater. I cherish it, at least as much as you do; we just differ on how to

216

achieve it.

By the power of weapons, you say.

By the power of convictions, I reply.

The power of weapons oppresses and that of convictions liberates. In case, you do insist to call me too opinioned, just listen to the uninterrupted wailing of sirens in Baghdad, Kabul and elsewhere. True freedom can't be delivered stuffed with bombs.

Mr. Bush, most nations have unfavorable opinion about your ability to lead America, and far less the world. An important reminder, Mr. President: what is made of iron is subject to rust and consequently to decomposition. "Man can't live by bread alone," said Jesus. And I said unto you: Nations can't live by germs warfare alone. Mr. President, it is about time, to invite Dame Wisdom to the rich table of diplomacy. America is a beautiful young bride and deserves a better groom. How could anyone see her beautiful face in the opaque mirror of your incompetent leadership?!

Amazing! Not even the most obvious evidence can penetrate the hard head of a power drunkard; his eyes can't see farther than his nose. Mr. President, after all the chaos you have created in Iraq, and the worse yet to come, could you still claim that you are doing it for your Idol Jesus Christ, all ad majorem Dei gloriam - for God's greater glory?!

INCREASING PASSION FOR FRIVOLITIES

4/ 4, 2004

The every day's events demonstrate the world's increasing passion for frivolities. Apparently the culture of frivolousness is going to be man's fatal illness in the 21st Century. I am particularly thinking of the pill that claims to have the power of erasing the unhappy memories responsible for causing us the post-traumatic stress disorder. Well, let's briefly challenge the merits of this new discovery of our unstressed great minds: Doctors of psychosis, I don't want to forget the repeated attacks of the family rooster, even at the award of eliminating my past traumas caused by the aggressor. During my early childhood, that aggressor attacked me on a daily basis; often leaving me with a bloody nose. I was not passive. I, too, plucked one or two of its feathers every fight we had engaged in.

Well, pardon me for having trivialized your most miraculous pill. Certainly it has far reaching benefits than erasing the traumatic conflict between a country boy and his family rooster. I know you were thinking of the victims of incest, rapes, unintended killings, machine accidents and other unfortunate aggressions of nature.

217

Still, little gods, please allow me to ask: Can a man be any happier without the so- called negative memories you are trying to erase? Are they not the microscope through which he sees the good ones? In other words, if you eliminate his bad memories, are you not denying him the nostalgia of a lost paradise, somewhere and somehow?! In a concrete language: If you erase my sad memories with the family rooster, meantime aren't you denying me those sweet memories of mother comforting me as well those memories of the family home that absorbed avidly the sun and the joyful cooing of its roosters. So, creators of the curative pill, please allow me to enjoy the memories of the aggressive rooster. As for the most dramatic memories caused by evil humans and brute nature, they, too, have their humane face. To remain challenged, humanity needs all the emotions it can get from whatever sources they may flow; otherwise it will die by stagnation. Yes, I even see beauty in the night sweat of the raped as well as in the remorse of the rapist. The suffering of the raped will eventually refine the cruel emotion of the rapist. After all, if the grass is ever-green, how could it communicate passionately with the rain? If all man's memories are good ones, how could he nourish his dream of becoming greater than his actual self? Yes, roses need thorns to remain roses, and man needs the negative emotions to remain humane. So, annihilators of the negative human emotions, could it be that you have a serious problem with life itself? How could you attempt to eliminate what you are dreaming to elevate? Is it not your ultimate desire to fold up the life's sheet that had been unfolding and continue to do so throughout billions of years to come? I see that your hearts and minds are getting tired watching this vehement unfolding. You want a new start, in the hope to have less challenging paths. Lazy and spoiled children, start riding the wild horse made of bones and flesh, and do not dwell on the memories of the infantile delights found in the merry go round that accommodated your fragile childhood when your parents took you to amusement parks.

And how dare you to pretend that you can decide the innocence and guilt of a man by hooking wires into his brain? Have you forgotten that the emotions of innocence are entangled with those of guilt? Yes, all around us is in a constant entanglement and that binds all what exist in the universe. The attempt to erase any portion of man's struggle is like trying to knock down the stars of heavens just to have a close look at them with the naked eyes. But if the stars were to be taking off the heavens what light would guide us as we travel through the night?!

I even deny to the mind the compliment for having invented the un-manned- guided plane. It is too inhumane of a method to kill. Even in war, to remain human, the killed needs the killer's presence, unpleasant and cruel as it may be. A final word to or a look at the victim might invite the victimizer to see how God's justice and mercy is tightly connected. Conclusion, the absence of adversities in our lives will create the enslavement of

218

the human brain you are dreaming to liberate. We must not abdicate our humanity, turbulent as it may be, to become grasshoppers that devastate the fields without any concern for the dreams of those who had sown the seeds.

I must confess I am too naïve on the matters of physiology. My knowledge in this field is so limited that I am certain only about the five fingers in each of the two hands of man and the five toes in each of his feet. How they function? This remains a delightful mystery to me. Although I gladly credit you for privileged knowledge, I remain convinced that only God can truly pierce the heart of the matter as well as that of the spirit. Don't despair, all human curiosities are legitimate journeys toward Him, and any journey is vulnerable to estrangement. Just keep in mind: It's through living that we witness the temporal expanding to touch the eternal.

HAS THE WESTERN MAN FALLEN INTO THE ABYSS OF MADNESS?

4/ 7, 2004

Has the Western man fallen into the abyss of madness in the name of his passion for originality? 10 percent of the Brits think that W. Churchill is a fictitious character, and 11percent believe that Adolf. Hitler falls into that category. However, 57 percent of them hold the opinion that Robin Hood and Santa Claus are real.
A few questions to the enlightened: what nationality is Santa Claus? How he has met his wife? Did they have premarital intercourse? And what was the name of their firstborn?

Is the redness of Rudolf's nose a birthmark; a result of the slapping of the North Pole's icy wind; a remnant kick from an angry Santa at Rudolf, who might have shown a sign of rebellion as he was pulling the sleigh through a snowstorm or simply because he had desiring eyes for Mrs. Santa?

Only the curiosity of the Western Mind can answer those most serious questions, certainly after taking a high dosage of the post-traumatic Stress Disorder Drug.

Anyway, if a segment of the Brits are confused about history, I am confused about my religious affiliation. I never know what religion I will wake up to. Well, don't accuse me of being a man who lacks conviction; I just believe that all roads lead to Rome, and I am on a long journey toward the greatest Rome, God's heart. And so we all are. As for the factuality of Robin Hood and Santa Claus and the answers to the foregoing questions, I leave it to the ingenuity of the Western Culture that delights itself in fancying facts and finding facts in fancy.

--Ah, the devastating absence of the heart! Today the leaders of many nations have gathered to acknowledge that one million had lost their lives during the one hundred days of Rwanda's civil war. It is the tenth anniversary of that Holocaust, and the world has just noticed its ugliness; cruel and awkward is the human mind, indeed.

--Why go back to the remote past? A few days ago, the Iraqi insurgents had killed and hang four Americans, who were there to purify their contaminated water. The American military have responded in kind, certainly with a more effective brutality. The hallucinatory mind of the Bush Administration is the cause behind this toll of death from both sides.

--Have they yet found the Weapons of Mass- Destruction? Or more correctly, had Saddam developed them? No. However, he was thinking of... was the ultimate finding of the scientific intelligentsia. This is a historical hysteria worth remembering. Under this scenario I see no big difference between those Brits who believe that Robin Hood and Santa Claus are real but not Churchill and Hitler. In fact, there is no limit to the human insanity, so long as wickedness dominates. President Bush had so distorted reality to the point that even Saddam's knives, sticks and his shoe laces have become Weapons of Mass- Destruction.

Our great leader had gathered the nations of the willing to prevent the end of the world. That the world must end is a sure inevitability. However, the fact that our president is seeking to hasten its end, that's tragedy. "Aggression can't stand," is the infamous expression inherited from his beloved father. Honestly, who is the true aggressor?

--And that weird looking bearded young Shiite cleric named Mouktada al Sader. He is just a remnant of that thug called Saddam, and both are thorns in the American spine. Therefore, the young dude must meet the same fate as the old monster. But at what cost! Well, war is costly, and so is the inequity of man. Yes, our true tragedy lies in declaring war against the wrong enemy. Please, dear God, help me not to understand; knowledge is the deadliest of all weapons. But if this is your final will upon me, then help me to embrace the belief that Churchill and Hitler are fictitious persona, but Robin Hood and Santa Claus are real. Could it be that hallucination is the only way to survive the hardships of this gulag, the today's world? Lord, I thankfully acknowledge that you have created it as a castle, but the mediocre architect, man, has turned into a cage. It is not your fault; certainly it is ours.

THANK GOD FOR THE WOMAN OF THE DEEP WELL

4/ 9, 2004

It is Holy Friday. Marla, Javier and I went to the Greek Trinity Orthodox Church to worship; meanwhile to savor its colorful rites of the Savior's death. It was quite a lengthy ceremony with moving scenes. From seven in the evening until midnight, heartfelt repentances and praises accompanied with the exalting smell of scent ascended to heavens. Thank you, O mad lover; you have so much loved us to the point of dying like a criminal, although knowing that the majority will reject your gift of eternity. Be consoled, some still remember your sacrifices, even after two thousand years.

 Four young men were solemnly maneuvering the wheels that rolled your coffin through the church court. Father James, the church Pastor, in his vehement voice chanted in Greek: "Lord and God eternal, O my joy and delight how I shall endure thy three days entombment? Lord, my maternal bowels are sent with grief for Thee."

Behind the coffin slowly marched little girls carrying lit candles. They wore mournful regional folk dresses and headscarves. Adult solemnly followed them. We sang songs expressing the sadness of separation but with the hope of a reunion that will happen in three incomplete days.

We entered the church through the arched entrance. In the tradition of the Orthodox Church, the rite symbolizes that only through death can man- kind arrives to heaven. When the procession came to a full stop, all proceeded to kiss the icon of the Crucified placed in the center aisle leading to the high altar. Some of us shed tears at His holy feet. Indeed, the Magdalene, in spite of her grave carnal sins, remains an exemplary repentant for the many of us. Thank God for the woman of the deep well.

After the lengthy hymns and praises ended, Archbishop Demetrius solemnly stood to deliver his Pascal homily. His white dense beard made him look like the Moses of the Sinai. I paraphrase the core of his homily: Dear brothers and sisters, the death of our Lord is a reminder of His infinite love for us, no matter how grave our sins may be. He is the loving father who stands on the crossroad looking every direction to spot us coming from the land of the lost. He is ready to receive us with stretched out arms. Let's journey to Him in faith to receive the garment that covers all our prodigal days…Tonight as your archbishop; I bestow upon you all the blessings the Lord has stored in my heart throughout the year. May He bless and lead you to salvation.

The final words of his Eminence have left some eyes swallowed with tears of hope. At the end of the ceremony, each faithful received a white rose to rest on the coffin that hid, temporarily, the Holy Body of Christ; but certainly His spirit was still sustaining the world, as usual. We left the church with the memory of the white roses reminding us of His pure love for all.

SALVATION AND THE GAS PRICE HIKE

4/ 13, 2004

If Jesus has suffered for the human salvation, we Americans are suffering from the gas price hike. Some of us, and I am one of them, wished if we were allowed to use horses and donkeys as means of transportation. Unfortunately, it was too late; the codes of a savage civilization had carved the mark of the beast on our hearts and minds. But why lament, from the bad some good always comes out. Yes, the hike of gas prices has served as a reason of jubilation for the environmentalists, who for decades have been accusing the oil industry of poisoning the air we breathe in.

--Often we America bravely fight wars on more than one front. On the religious front, two catholic archbishops have launched ferocious attack against the authenticity of John Kerry's Catholicism. The pro-choice and pro- civil union Senator can't be a good Catholic. Therefore, we must ban him from taking communion. Unfortunately, the prelates have forgotten that Kerry is a politician and politicians are like pelicans, they know how to fetch a fish with the least pain. Indeed, the Senator aspiring for the presidency has found an easy way to feast on the flesh of the Lord through the Paulists Center on Beacon Hill where he worshiped. There he has encountered no opposition from a community he knew well. Rejoice, Senator, Xristos anesti-Christ has risen and you have replied: aliços anesti- He truly has risen. You might even have shouted: my fellow Americans, help me to democratize the church.

Can one be dissident and still remain a true Catholic?

Yes, one can and rightfully so. Once we are baptized in the faith, we inherit all the wealth it stores, including the partaking of the Flesh and Blood of Christ. After all, the biblical father has preserved and acknowledged the right of continuous inheritance for his prodigal son, despite the long years of lust and lost. Father knew well that his son had already spent his initial inheritance on the whores of Gomorrah.

Religion is not a travel-package to heaven, rather a tedious spiritual journey that every man undertakes on his feet and into his heart. In a journey toward any destination, man is expected to stray, fall, reject, modify, eliminate add and finally embrace. Those so- called erroneous steps in the journey are not for the satisfaction of our caprice, rather missteps that ultimately lead to and prepare us for the great dance before the enthroned God. Therefore, man's salvation does not lie in his acceptance or rejection of religious recipes called dogmas. Rather, it consists of his personal encounter with the living God, sometimes along the tedious road. It is the encounter of two hearts, the heart of the saved with that of the Savior. In this journey, the turtle, the sinner, has an even chance to win the race as the Pope. We must celebrate our Felix Culpa, the blessed sin of stumbling, meaning: fighting God as Jacob did. Every man is a Jacob, a God fighter. In sum: we must look at salvation through the microscopes of understanding and compassion. False pastors, I pray that you may hold onto your pastoral staffs. Don't raise them to crack our tormented heads; only God's mercy can cure our infirmities and dissipate our doubts. Instead of beating us, go to Sinai, pick up big stones and beat your judgmental hearts. Repent, repent, salvation is not when God comes to man's heart; rather when man ,through his falling and rising, finds himself in the heart of God. O men of the stiff necks, you must not condemn others for not seeing what you see; their rocky and blurry journey toward God is not a rebellion, rather a tedious search for Him- often blinded by the storms of their human condition.

HUMANITY HAS TAKEN ITSELF INTO CAPTIVITY

4/ 18, 2004

May the Lord forgive me because I have sinned against you my brethrens and sisters! Behold, today I gather all my dreams to put them against a few teardrops of a suffering child; his/her smile outweighs by far my vain ambitions. Lord, I know there are wars declared in all fronts, most of which in your name. Yet, you have approved of none. In so behaving, humanity has taken itself into captivity. Lord, I bless any man's desire fighting for his self-preservation. However, I greatly fault him when he denies others the same struggle.
--Today five cars had exploded in Basra, wounding hundreds and killing seventy people; twenty of them were children. They were going to school to learn about the achievements of their grownups. Lord, they have left us, and now you're the only one in their sight. I wonder what explanation you would give them as to why their lives had been cut short!
--Also, Lord, the explosions in Riyadh, Saudi Arabia and in Gaza strip were quite devastating. How man could be so cruel? Was he born so, or what a dreadful event has occurred to harden his heart? Your love for us, Lord, is so overwhelming. Since we can't continue staring at one another in anger; what road(s) could we take for reconciliation? Whatever road we may take, we hope to meet at the end of our difficult journeys. Then we will bow before one another asking forgiveness, not for what we have done but for what we had failed to do. At that moment, and only at that moment, our redemption becomes reality. Lord, I pray not for the prevalence of one side or the other of the conflicting parties, rather for their genuine reconciliation. Lord, may we have a space in our hearts for one another to build a higher human consciousness. Help us to believe that Peace is not the absence of war, rather when man succeeds keeping sight of the other and to maintain, in the face of hostility, a deep sense of justice and civility toward him. The pitiful philosophy of the Bush

Administration: "break it, you own it" is but the cry of the impoverished heart. We must not break the golden cup, so we may discredit its maker and appropriate the shattered pieces to ourselves. Ah the human madness! Like children, adults cannot lose sight of destruction while building their castles. Lord, today I bend to collect the pieces of the broken golden glass. Once restored, I shall go to my vineyard to harvest the ripen grapes and press them in the mill of my heart to offer the first drink to my adversary. Yes, from the mess our forefathers have left, we must create a pact of a permanent friendship with our inherited enemies.

Away, away from me, O all the vain dreams; the most authentic dream is to embrace my enemy and not to destroy him; on his destruction I lay the foundation of my own. From the rejection of the false dream of forcing the enemy to surrender to my will is born the song of life for both. So, let's rest it all on the high altar of humanity. Lord, may you bless our various journeys towards your sacred heart.

HOPELESSLY DEVOTED TO YOU

4/ 22, 2004

It is Earth Day, happy day, Mother, in spite of our madness. As the environmentalists sing songs to thee, the industrialists become more determined to silence the chanting voices. Mother, forgive their ingratitude. The sweetest voice is that of the children killed in wars. May their blood spread on thy surface wash away all the dirty stains we adults have created! Mother, here are your children, children here is your mother. May we unite to celebrate the eternal day; our madness is but a passing storm. When the sun will rise again, all shall see the eternal light.

Oh, let's sing a song for the most devoted mother, she carries and leads us to the limpid fountains of life. As our destructive neurotic temperament whirls, she prays for our tranquility. When we curse her, she affectionately looks upon us and tearfully begs you: Aba, forgive my children, they know not what they are doing. In spite of all our scandalous brutal acts, I just want to say: Mother, I love you in your spring, summer, in your fall and especially in your winter.

HOW DARE YOU DENYING IT TO OUR FALLEN HEROES!

4/ 23, 2004

The pentagon forbade the photographing of coffins of our falling heroes of war in the name of social sensitivity.

"Adam, Adam where are you?"

Promptly Adam plucked leaves from a tree and covered himself to become invisible to God.

And today the American people ask Mr. Bush and Rumsfeld: where are our children, the apples of our eyes? They are wrapped in the American flag as they lay in mahogany caskets, reply the warmongers. Don't worry we shall deliver them to you under the opaque obscurity of the night, so you may grieve privately.

But why not let the public share the sadness of their follow citizens? After all, we Americans have great sympathy for the human sufferings. To those who suffer we respond with flowers, prayers and, often times, we give them our greatest love, money; just asks the many nations that have experienced tragedies. Our falling heroes are the most worthy of our unfailing sympathy expressed to others. I often wondered why the image of the Crucified decorates millions of chests. If God needed man's sympathy, how could we deny it to one another? Are we stronger than God? Hypocritical leaders, stop insulting the true human sensitivity in the name of a false one. The only thing you are sensitive to is to avoid letting the public know of the harvest of your crimes. You have no sympathy and know of none. You claim to revere the human life. What does it mean to you? Why are you then denying the dead a moment of public respect; and to his / her family a moment of sympathy? The ultimate sacrifice of our falling heroes may curve our great appetite for war. Yes, the dead can teach us a lesson about the ultimate meaning of life. Behold, under the obscurity of the night, I walk to the tombs of the falling heroes to pay them my final respect. There I shall shed tears of sorrow and ask them to forgive your cunning arrogance, hypocrisy and insensitivity. As for their loved ones, I pray may they accept the nation's heartfelt gratitude; the death of their beloved is an act of faith and loyalty to us all. Today and forever we promise our falling heroes a binding gratitude, their self-sacrifice is the greatest gift any person could give to his/her compatriots. May you rest in the Lord's peace and love; fragile are the peace and love granted by man.

STEP OUT OF THIS CAVE AND YOU WILL SEE THE LIGHT

4/ 26, 2004

Lord, for how long, for how long, Lord, can I endure witnessing the sight of destruction? Every morning I wake up to see black smoke hovering over several sites in Iraq. Has man really gone mad? I am quite convinced that war is the clash of two arrogant wills, but there is a third one that is violated: yours, Lord. Yes, when man declares war against his fellowman, he is definitively declaring war against you. Every time I follow the trail of war there is a trail of guilt follows me. War is a missed prayer, a retained smile and a closed heart. It is ultimately a denial of you. Lord, today and forever help me to pray, to smile and to be attentive to the voices of others.

225

It is easy to spot the smoke in the skies of others; but we often overlook our own raging fires. Just this morning I noticed Marla was depressed.

"Don't let the world hold you down," I preached her.

"The world isn't holding me down; you're, you've failed to play the role of a father to my son," she replied in tears.

"It's easy to blame others for our shortcomings," I challenged her with some resentment. Stepping outside myself, for a moment, I realized it was not his fault that he has been such a difficult child; it was mine. Indeed, I have failed to guide him with love and understanding through the challenges of his very turbulent teens. After all, what is fatherhood but a guiding light? Lord, forgive me; I have failed Javier, Marla and myself and you, above all. It is human to run away from the cross but it takes a courageous person to embrace it. May you equip me with the armor of a warrior; I need to defeat my greatest enemy, myself. Help me, Lord, to accept the challenges of the road that leads to my family, to my fellowman, to myself and ultimately to you.

THE WORLD IS A MARKET PLACE

4/ 27, 2004

The world is a marketplace. A few come to it to do commerce honestly; many to steal and a very small category stays at its outskirts, just to watch, wonder, laugh and cry. Raised in a seminary, I was trained to believe, at early age, that man is sinful and only prayer can save him. I did pray then. Today I leave that zone of comfort to resent the arrogant politicians preaching us the deadly philosophy that war can lead to peace. In what jungle have they been raised? If force nurses war, peace has a mother called kindness. How could they favor force over love? Certainly we live in a dangerously absurd world and to face this great danger, kindness is the duty of all responsible men.

--We often criticize the erratic behavior of our teenagers. Unfortunately, our madness surpasses theirs. Here are a few examples: In Chicago, Illinois, employees spent hundreds of thousands of taxpayers' dollar calling prostitutes or consulting with psychic readers. Wouldn't be more beneficial for them and society to concentrate on their work?

--Michael Jackson came out of court as an innocent man after his arrest for allegation of child molestation. He danced on top of his limousine, just to thank his supporters. Why a great singer has chosen to be such a clown?

--Two catholic prelates ordered their priests not to give communion to John Kerry; the Senator is violating the commands of the Holy Mother Church. And I wondered where those prelates had buried the scene of Jesus with the woman at the deep well of forgiveness?

-- In New Jersey, Jayson Williams, the NBA star, claimed that he had accidentally shot his chauffeur; while being under the influence of alcohol. Well, Mr. Star, shouldn't you have known that alcohol is deadly.

--Miss. Porter, a twenty- eight- year old elementary school teacher in Tampa, Florida, ran over four brothers, and took off leaving them dying instead of calling the ambulance. Still her lawyer called her "a courageous young woman," after she has confessed that she was the driver, who had killed two of them and badly injured the other two. She was far from being courageous, an eyewitness had identified her; she was forced to that confession. Should we refine our conscience to become our ultimate watcher?

--The Brits are mad at Americans for having televised Princess Diana's last moments. They even have accused us of being controlled by the power of the all- mighty dollar. Now do hear who is talking! They have forgotten that her brother charges entrance fees to those who go to her grave- site to pay their respect.

-- Scientists lament the -soon- coming end of the males' chromosomes. As a result, say they, we will have a world dominated by females. Well, that's unnecessary worry because if only one single female remains on the planet, still all men will be under the rule of one. To look at the bright side, one surviving stud can impregnate thousands of women. These extensive impregnations will ultimately guarantee a respectable return of the once- was- endangered species. We must not lose faith in the power of randomness; it can redeem the rigidity of science.

--We must, rather, show more of a serious concern for the endangered spotted owls. They have committed the biggest crime against themselves when they had left the security of their caves to nest in our forests, desired zones by the eyes of the greedy industrialists; meanwhile subjugating themselves to Rush Limbaugh's harsh ridicule.

 Let me conclude assuring you that my heart itches every time I see a chimpanzee jumping from one branch to another. It is that freedom of the jungle I am missing. What a curse to have evolved to be a human. I welcome revolution; it is the only remaining chance for man to regain his innocence, a virtue that has been greatly damaged by the process of his steadfast biological, but not spiritual evolution.

THE INDIVIDUAL VERSUS THE STATE

4/28, 2004

Does the President have the right to indefinitely deny, in the name of national security, legal access to the

Guantánamo Bay detainees, alleged to have had allied themselves with the enemy combatants? Two of the more than 500 detainees are American nationals from Islamic ancestry. The nine Supreme justices seemed to be in disagreement interpreting the rights of war prisoners. They were haunted by the three centuries old dilemma: the good of the one versus the good of the many. The British 17th Century Thomas Hobbes and the French 18th Century Jean Jacques Rousseau have extensively dealt with the dilemma. The two great political thinkers have agreed on the same initial status: all men are naturally created equal. However, they veered so far apart when defining the natural state of the human nature, and how to achieve and sustain this natural equality. The Rousseau's society, described in the Social Contract, enable the individual to be absorbed into the general common will without losing its own (will). Hobbes decried man in his natural state as a savage, who is constantly at war with others: "bellum omne contra omnes- war of all against all." To avoid this perpetual war amongst the barbarians, he subjugated their will to the will of a monarch. However, this absolute form of government is restricted. It can't infringe on the individuals' basic rights such as: endangering their lives, confiscating their properties and unjust imprisonment. Under those circumstances individuals have the moral obligation to rise against the unrestricted despotism.

Unfortunately, some of the American pillars of Justices have endorsed the Bush Administration's position that has suspended indefinitely the rights of the Guantanamo prisoners, thus nosing up, not only the old notion of equality amongst men but also the clear cut modern laws of the Geneva Conventions. To justify their endorsement, those Justices cited the case of the confinement of the Japanese Americans during World War II.

I must bring to the attention of those scholars of legality: the Japans' confinement was and is a historical shame which no decent American should be proud of.

We must mourn, our God's given right has been hijacked by an Administration that holds the obnoxious conviction: freedom is circumstantial and for some people to reclaim it as a universal human right is an endangerment to America's security. Could we embrace today such a shameful position and still sing, "America land of the free and home of the brave?"

Mr. President, you have claimed that the world has changed since 9/11/2001.

In my humble opinion, the world is still the same; you are the one who have changed as fear had stolen the best within you. What happened to the infamous legal code: "Every man is innocent, under all circumstances, until proven guilty?"

It is a code in which the Western World takes great pride. Are you, Mr. President, withdrawing America from the charter of the civilized nations to join the barbarians? Your suspicion of crime does not give you the right to hold American citizens, or other nationals as hostages; the law is not a thug that lingers at darkness to commit acts of kidnapping and torture. Freedom is God's gift to man and no other man can legally retract it as he wishes. Indeed, it is God's gift to man as life is; and whoever attempts to take away the one or the other is a murderer of justice itself.

Yes, government has the obligation to protect its subjects from all enemies, be outsiders or insiders. Individuals also have an equal right to protect themselves from the tyranny of society, under whatever disguise it appears. "…To renounce liberty is to renounce being a man," wrote Jean -Jacques Rousseau. It's the State versus the Individual and vice versa. The rights of the one must not deny, suspend or even diminish the rights of the other. Aren't Americans and others entitled to the basic human rights such as freedom, the right to life, ownership, and fair trial? If this code is applied, there is no justification, whatsoever, for capricious imprisonment.

A true sense of Justice can be achieved only through a due process executed in honesty that rejects all forms and shades of caprice and prejudice; meaning: if you do accuse me of a crime, prove it through the legal channels. Otherwise, you are guilty of a greater crime as you continue to point the finger at me. Mr. President, it is about time to restore justice for all. By denying the legal access to those detainees, although suspected to be enemy combatants, you are intruding on the rights of all Americans. A true justice cannot be self-destructive. It is that ever-virgin bride who sleeps with all men and never loses her virginity to any; her heart is for all. Mr. President, the people have mandated you to protect their rights under all circumstances, meaning: this mandate isn't a carte blanche to do as you wish. Indeed, your legal advisors had given you a deadly advice. Mr. President, may you observe justice for all; that's the only way to establish order, security and peace in society.

Freedom is a-temporal. Suspending someone's freedom nowadays, even temporarily under the umbrella of suspicion to guarantee the safety of the many, is an assault to its modern notion. If freedom is circumstantial; then I wish to leave this world of masks as soon as possible. In the Book of Genesis, God said, "Let there be light," and there was light. This light is that God's given- freedom to man. Unfortunately, Mr. President, such an expression often runs from your mouth as water runs on a rock.

Justice, I salute you whether I am in an imprisonment cell or sitting on the clouds while zipping from the nectar of the gods. May we all wash our faces in your holy tears; suffocating is the odor of caprice.

4/ 30, 2004

To distract us from the never-ending killing in Iraq, the news media has decided to take the political pulse of Iraqis.

"Are you happy to see American soldiers roaming on your soil?"

71 percent replied no, 19 percent considered the Americans as liberators, 10 percent were undecided. Various may be the reasons behind the poll's results; one thing remains solid: freedom cannot be exported; it can grow only at home. Therefore, here is my advice to the Bush Administration, whatever your intentions may be: retreat with some pride. You have been good enough to the Iraqis; you had crushed the snake's head. Now you must give the bitten a chance to destroy the biter's tail.

In my humble view, the Bush Administration has committed the grave mistake of dismantling the Iraqi army; thinking that the Iraqis will have lost love for the butcher, Saddam. But if so sick, then they don't appreciate freedom and they will not accept it; even if one would offer it to them in a golden plate. You can't kill the wild deer and cook it for them; they, too, need to learn the art of hunting and cooking.

 The other grave error was the missed opportunity to use the power of the tribes' Sheiks.

They exercise great power over the insurgents. America must have known that those Sheiks had grown their fat bellies from the sweat of the so- called "thugs." A thug for someone is a humble servant for another. We must not forget that nations are governed by their own cultures, and failing to understand each other's culture can perpetuate deadly conflicts. It is time for America to pull its troops out of Iraq; although order is yet to come to this troubled land. In so doing there is no betrayal, as the Bush Administration does think. Rather, it is an act of tough love. Freedom is a celebration of tough love between adults, and the puppy love of America can't serve as a solid foundation to build a democracy that will withstand the test of times. Let the Iraqis find their national identity; the birth of a nation is as painful as, if not more traumatic than, the birth of individuals. With or without the presence of the American forces, the already aroused tribal struggle for domination will endure for many years. Still, Iraqis must be the ones who will ultimately decide their own destiny and at their own time, costly as it may be.

 It is imperative for the American Administration to welcome all factions in Iraq; to make them feel that the land is still theirs, and that will be the greatest weapon to bend the cycle of violence promoted by the insurgency. I just wish the Bush Administration follows Count Basie's advice: "If you play a tune and people don't tap their feet, stop playing the tune."

America must use more its diplomatic skills and less the might of its weapons. We must remember that humans are like strings in a guitar; too much of implied force oppresses the harmony of their coordinated vibrations. To bring the desired stability to Iraq, Mr. Bush must stop relying heavily on the expertise of the Dicks, the Rons and the Condis. Rather, he must consult with old Mrs. Jones, a black teacher whom I'd the honor to know personally. Yes, she was a great troubleshooter. She knew how to identify the troublemakers amongst her students and convert them to great cooperators of her own cause- bringing discipline into the classroom. Indeed, true victory is won through the winning of the minds and hearts and not through the devastating power of mighty weapons. You can defeat an enemy but you never can destroy him; his forever-lingering humiliated spirit will fight you back, in one way or another, even after a thousand years. Must politicians and military take courses in pedagogy?!

To close this chapter on the failure of the military machine and how to remedy its failure, President Dwight D. Eisenhower's words are appropriate, "…I think you know that I believe we must be strong military, but beyond a certain point military strength can become a national weakness."

LIFE IS A BATTLEFIEGROUNG

5/4, 2004

It was almost midnight when I heard a voice mumbling, "Dad." For a moment I thought I was listening to my own voice, I, too, needed a dad to call on to nourish me with hope. It was not my voice, it was Amon's, so I realized after the second call coming from behind the closed door of my bedroom.

"Come in, Son," I said while still lying in my bed. He slowly entered and painfully sat on the floor (his choosing the floor was a clear indication of some defeat).

"What's going on, Son?"

"Dad, I'm just beat, everything seems to be out of place, life is so hard," he said with tears in his eyes. I stared at his paint- stained hands and noticed that his face looked less youthful. Indeed, he was beat.

"Son, life is a battleground we must fight with great valor to win the war."

"You have a great point, Dad. I guess I'm just a bit discouraged."

"What happened?"

"Well, lately everything seems to be going down the drain. The Sandal Condominiums Association has cancelled its contract of $15ooo to pave their driveways and clean their roofs; due to a lack of money allocations," the association says.

"Son, success is a tricky thing that comes under many disguises. At times it even comes under the disguise of great disappointment and even failure."

"Failure, that's exactly what I'm feeling right now." He looked very depressed. He collected himself and with some strength, he said: "Well, Dad, don't worry; everything will be all right."

"Son, life swings between success and failure, hope and despair. We must be like flowers that swing with the wind. Better swing with the wind than standing still; violent wind can break even steel bars."

Thank God, apparently Amon has found in my words the balsam he needed for his wounds.

"Tomorrow is going to be a better day…I hope," he said with a timid smile.

"Son, today's sorrows become sweet if we could see them through the scope of tomorrow's hopes. We all have our moments of despair. At times things seem to be as if heaven is closing on earth. Still it's far from being the end; rather it's the beginning of a long fight we must win."

"You're absolutely right, Dad. I guess I've no other choice but to be optimistic about tomorrow. I am still young and the fight has just begun. I must keep on fighting, can't afford losing the war."

"Son, great battles are won inch by inch and an easy victory is often a defeat in disguise…"

Suddenly I found myself silent, and Amon, in a very relaxed voice, began reminiscing about the great pleasures of the small battles he had already won in his very young age. Proudly he spoke how he has turned his life of a troubled teenager to be the owner of "the King's Pressure Co.", little lucrative has been, so far.

"…Well, it takes years to build up a business and I'm determined to succeed," he added with some light flashing from his eyes. "I also must be thankful to God; I'm doing very well in school. Besides, I am becoming very selective in choosing my friends."

"Son, with such a positive attitude you can only succeed."

"Thanks, Dad, your good advices always energize me…. True, it takes a man to understand a man… For instance, Jacky, (his girlfriend) doesn't pay attention to me when I talk about my problems; nor does my mom."

"Son, seek sympathy from a stone before you seek it from a woman or a child. They like to hear only the good and sweet side of life, leaving the bitter one to the devil, man." We laughed; we needed laughter to cope with our depressing present realities. After a moment of silence, I confessed: "I, too, have my serious Problems with Marla. In fact, at times I think I am nothing to her but a mere commodity. I may be wrong; still this raging feeling keeps playing with my mind. Anyway, Son, wrong or right, one must learn how to win the big battle inch by inch."

"Wow! Thanks, man. Now I must go to bed, I'm tired… By the way, Dad, could you wake me up for the seniors' breakfast at 9 a.m. at the Radisson Hotel, Clearwater Beach."

"Certainly, Son, I will."

"Good night, Dad," he said, letting out a light smile.

In the morning I woke Amon up. A big smile spread all over his face. Why not, a gourmet breakfast was waiting for him.

Quickly he got ready and walked into on my bedroom to say," Thanks, Dad, for waking me on time; I'm ready to leave now."

"Enjoy the bacon, the eggs, the pancakes and any other fruits Mother Earth offers you. But don't forget to use your utensils. Man is a sophisticated predator; he hunts his prey with a spear and eats it with utensils."

"O.K., Dad, I will do," he said, letting out a light smile.

Unconsciously I found myself murmuring, "May the days ahead will be good to you!"

RIDING THE TRAIN OF ALIENATION

5/ 6, 2004

For over a week now the TV media has been bombarding us with the ugly photos of the mistreatment of the Abu Gharib prisoners. Nothing is new; throughout history the strong have always tortured and humiliated the weak. However, the most shocking news is modern man's claim to have overcome the savagery of his ancestors. He hasn't; rather he has succeeded creating art out of it. Instead of calling it torture, he calls it softening up for interrogation, the big moment to find out the truth. Ah the truth, that mythical treasure of humanity! Indeed, modern man has perfected the art of deception and never before has he been so remote from truth. Is America's ultimate ambition to fulfill God's dream for man, meaning: to know the truth that will liberate him? Or simply is she dismissing God on whose altar all man's dreams must rest? To answer this question, I must follow her most recent step taken in the tedious rocky land of the Mesopotamia.

Could we call the dragging of a prisoner, attached to a leach, a step toward freedom? For whom the bell tolls, the dragged or the dragger? Certainly for neither! How could we be free by humiliating others?! Yes, I am particularly thinking of that Iraqi we sat on as if he were a stall in a beer house. Afterwards, he was dragged on the concrete floor. To that young pregnant soldier, Linda England, who has performed both ugly acts, I put the following question: what would you tell your child in ten years from today?

You have sat on and dragged, afterwards, a man on the floor with a leach attached to his neck. Could you, under this circumstance, justify to him/ her that better to be born than to remain in the world of nothingness?!

And you Sergeant Sivist, looking back, one day, to all the atrocities you have committed against those prisoners, would you honestly say you have honored America that prides itself to be the guardian of the human rights?

Well, why pick on little people, like you and Private Linda. After all, your leaders, the Rums, the Meyers and the Karpinskys have misguided you.

A year ago, the Secretary of Defense declared that the Geneva Convention Accords have nothing to do with the treatment of the Iraqi prisoners. Even this voice is a victim of another voice of a greater arrogance. Yes, it is that of Mr. George W. Bush who, before the break of war had proudly stood behind the presidential pulpit to shout: "The UN is irrelevant."

Those arrogant voices that have shouted the irrelevance of the world, today the world is shouting back at them; and you, too, are irrelevant to us.

That's all what you have achieved: complaints and complaints, you might say.

"I am not complaining, rather, this brief but violent period of history has taught me the following lesson: The struggle between evil and good is a fictitious one. The true struggle is that of the good against itself. That's to say: when good fails to be good, the mythical monster called evil pops out. Evil is the absence of good, i.e., the good has failed itself. That said, I am not adopting the sterile optimistic view that man is born wrapped in goodness, whether on his own merits or through a gift from a generous benefactor. Rather, I postulate my thesis in the following light: All are born with a fat account of goodness that the human experience has left for everyone. Our obligation is to invest this capital in a firm called humanity. When we fail to properly invest our inherited fortune in this firm, by choosing to spend it erratically or capriciously, we exhaust it. Result: we become impoverished. Since the account of our accumulated human goodness has dried up within us, we desperately deliver ourselves to acts of robberies and brutalities. As we do rob and brutalize others, we bleed to death those others, as we had done to ourselves.

Mr. President, a dead cannot raise the dead. You may continue to pretend, but pretense never can deliver. Concretely speaking: yes, you have captured Saddam and caged the beast. However, by abusing those whom you claim to have had spared from the monster's jaws, you have created millions of the likes; just look now at the ravages of the new monsters.

One wonders what else was in Cleopatra's egg basket. Yes, the venom of violence can kill not only humans but also the gods themselves. God has created an orderly world, and the Bush Administration is seemingly is working hard to sink it into a total chaos. All is done in the name of the false pretense of wanting to free the oppressed. Mr. President, your exported freedom to all, offers freedom to none. To free others, one must be

234

free from the instincts of arrogance within oneself. The simple question is: America, are you today truly free from yourself or have become drunk on the might of your guns? We can't be liberators of the oppressed, if we continue to graze in the prairies of arrogance and confusion.

Freedom has not come to, nor will it dominate Iraq as long as we continue to impose our own will upon its people. Although freedom is an absolute concept, like any other human value, it reveals itself (in this case to the oppressed) through a slow and painful process, meaning: we must respect the culture and psyche of those we want to liberate. Humiliation and torture cannot serve freedom; rather envenoms it. We must not kill what we want to save and must save what we do not want to kill. However, if we continue to embrace a culture of moral confusion, then killing and saving become two facets of one reality called alienation. Following this erroneous path, all will end up in a bottomless pit.

THE CURSE OF RACISM

5/ 9, 2004

It is prom night. Amon returned home from work at 7:30 p.m. He looked quite tired and the pain of the manual labor was shown through his stained clothes.

"I'm late; I need to be at Jacky's by eight," he said rushing to shower. In a few minutes he reappeared dressed in a tuxedo.

"Dad, please do me this last button."

I struggled for a moment doing it because of its narrow opening.

"Thanks dad, wearing a suit is a bit uncomfortable."

"Son, does a moment of looking civilized really discomfort you?" I asked, smiling.

"I haven't worn a suit since my graduation from kindergarten."

"Well, enjoy the special occasion and do remember: no drinking."

"I will, Dad. Thanks for the advice." He then got into his car, leaving behind a suffocating aroma of cheap perfume. Suddenly, I heard a knock on the door. I thought Amon had forgotten to take along an important article such as: a gift for Jacky. Surprise! My good friend Gary stood in front of me and immediately started talking how his constant backache is making life boring for him. He then became nostalgic about his agitated, but exciting, life of a gangster in Chicago. After a long moment of silence he asked, "Akhmed is God a male or female?"

"What do you think?"

235

"He must be a female, just think of all the tricks women play on us."

"And what kind of tricks did God play on you, since you don't give a damn to women?"

"Well, He told me that once you're born you will start your journey to paradise. Life for me, so far, has been nothing but a journey to hell."

"Gary, life is what one makes out of it."

"Is it my fault that I have this constant nagging backache?"

"It is not God's fault either; it is just the human condition. We all have those aches of old age. We must be thankful though; they show that we are still alive, and being alive is better than being dead."

"Wow! Rejoice oh my ears now that you've heard it from the great philosopher of Del Oro Groves Estates"- our neighborhood.

"Would you rather be dead?"

He broke into his customary silly giggles.

"Well, Gary, you need to control your drinking habit; it gives you such bad mood swings." I thought he wanted me to drive him to the neighborhood store to get a pack of icehouse, his favorite beer.

"I don't need beer, rather the big dance of a slaughtered chicken, would you...?"

"Are you asking me to kill you?" By now I knew how to interpret his style of talking.

"Why not...? We are friends, and friendship obliges."

"Gary, only God who gives life has the right to take it away."

"Oh well, since I can't talk to you, holy preacher, I am going next door to raise hell on that old prick. Yes, he deserves my utmost anger; I am but the unfortunate outcome of a horny moment in his damn life."

"You really don't like your father."

"Never did nor will I ever; he's a pain in my ass." Gary looked upset as he spoke about his father. I felt consoled, I might have done something right; my five children love me, at least so I believed.

After a long depressing conversation I had to apologize to Gary; I didn't want to miss the Anderson Cooper's program on CNN. Race was the topic. He reported about that prom's event at a high school in Alabama. It was celebrated in three different locations on the same premise: One location was for the white, a second for the black and a third for the Latino students.

"Until I receive a new order, I'll continue to implement the school board's policy," said the principal when interviewed by the news media.

And I thought to myself: here is the happiest night in the life of those poor youngsters and look what we have led them to. Adults are criminals; they work hard to stain their youths with hate and prejudice. Race in itself is not the tragedy. Only when we add to it the 'ism', it turns to be the saddest of all. There is no place we can hide, and our only alternative is to be accepting of one another. We cannot be separatists because of the pigments of our skin. It is just a color and all colors are subject to mix. Therefore, we must be rejecting something deeper than skin color. Even that something, whatever it may be, cannot stand a chance to win against the fact of the melting pot America is made of. In other words, as Americans we must all eat from the same pot, or else we will starve; it is the only manna heaven offers us.

Lord, help me to see my face in all the other faces, different from mine they may be. Lord, teach me that my life is meaningless as long as I remain unwilling to integrate others into it; they are reflection of you in this human garden. How can I refuse to see you in them and still hope to inherit this paradise? Lord, when I am tempted to close my eyes before the sight of any human being, nourish my heart with enough kindness to accept what my eyes may repulse. Only the heart can see; the eyes are but organs of illusive visions. Brother, give me your hand; with the joining of our hands we can build the ladder that reaches God. And when the great light embraces us, we shall forget the darkness of prejudice on this earth. Lord, may tonight's dance of my son with his Jewish girlfriend be a sign of a soon- coming big dance of peace between our peoples in conflict! After all, where there is encounter, there is joy; hate is but the result of a poisonous indifference diluting the goodness in our hearts.

HELL IS PAVED WITH GOOD INTENTIONS- ANONYMOUS

5/ 12, 2004

Lord, I thought I had seen it all. I was mistaken. The beheading of the twenty- six -year- Old Nick Berry by the Islamic militants made me dizzy. However, there is a bigger underlying reason that keeps my head constantly spinning: violence has become spiral. Has humanity drowned in despair?! Lord, I know despair is the result of man's inability to communicate lovingly with the world. Once this force of love is absent, he becomes like a moth that dashes itself into fire to perform the dance of life; whereas, in fact, death is awaiting it. Admirable is the seeking of light, however, it is tragic to blindly throw oneself into it all at once. In so behaving, one rejects the light, rather than embracing it. The reason is simple: light is pure and purity can mix only with purity. We need a long process of purification to dance in the light without being burned. It is the dance around the light that will ultimately put us into its heart. When we learn more about the light's nature, we melt into it gradually and naturally, unlike the brutal consequence of being thrown into it all at once. We must understand the light's powerful nature or else we shall perish. Yes, I am specifically thinking of America wanting to democratize the Arabic world. America must seek to catch that strayed with imperative caution. It is kind to give medicine to the sick but overdosing him/her is an act of homicide. One cannot expect a bountiful harvest, if one would have sown the seeds without regard to the conditions that favor their growth. Let's grant America the good intentions. Still, good intentions cannot prevent the devastating consequences of forceful and unwise adventure. America must pay a close attention to someone's saying, "hell is paved with good intentions."

Nothing is more remote from democracy building than the logic of military power. Surprisingly, great understanding of reality requires a return, or at least an attention paid to mythology, at times. I exemplify: A few years ago I bought a pomegranate tree from an old Greek man. Thus he instructed me, "Plant it in the full moon and then dance around it twelve times after watering it…that is if you want it to give you abundance of healthy fruits," he emphasized.

I laughed at what I then considered a mind full of superstitions. I carried the infant tree in an earthen pot. Soon as I arrived home around sunset I planted it. Putting the hose in motion to inject water into the heart of the dug soil, I retreated into the comfort of my sofa. It had been a decade now and the pomegranate tree never carried at once more than ten blossoms whose lives were cut short by the wind. I started to seriously think that my failing to follow the old man's directives was the cause behind my fruitless tree. Could this be applicable to what America is now going through with the Arabic world? Arabs perform the dizzying Dervish Dance- the revolving dance around oneself; while Americans love the Tap Dance- the dance of the competing nails that shake the ground under. Intoxicated on their own dance, they begin shooting at one another from a distance too close for comfort. When the minds and hearts become alienated, we fail to understand and appreciate one another's steps; then despair of- ever- meeting grows. When despair grows, the other becomes irrelevant. The feeling of being irrelevant engenders rebellion and rebellion begets violence. Like cancer, violence spreads and ultimately leads to death. In the words of Pearls Buck, "to eat bread without hope is still slowly to starve to death."

So, let's keep hope alive for our survival's sake. "There are no desperate situations; only they are desperate men who render desperate the situations," said an anonymous. To avoid rendering desperate the situation, conflicting parties must engage in honest dialogue. Like any other grandiose virtue, honesty requires self-criticism more so than criticizing the other. It also requires genuine respect for that other. Americans call Arabs terrorists, and some conservative talk -show hosts have used crueler words, calling them sub- humans. Arabs think Americans are ruthless and ungodly people. I must prompt to say that each party has more than one reason to insult the other. However, they have forgotten that exchanging insults and acts of murder cause at the end of the day serious devastation for the victim as well as for the victimizer. To escape this iron circle, goodwill is required. Only an act of faith is capable to create a milieu of sincere mea culpa, atonement for sins we would have committed against the other. It is hard to say I am wrong, but its effectiveness is vastly rewarding; open wounds begin to close as a result of this humble, not humiliating, attitude. The process of healing leads to trusting hope. The birth of hope effaces despair, cause of all hatreds and killings. Ultimately, hope is peace standing on its most solid foundation. And when peace is born, cooperation is born. When cooperation is born, the dance of life begins and hatred becomes remote from our children's memory. We must embark on this road; we own them safe passage. In sum, to achieve peace between two opposing cultures one needs, at times, to become mythological. It is just a lesson learned from the heavily laden pomegranate tree of that Greek old man, and that sterile one of mine (because I had failed to perform the dance of hope around it). O all the parties in conflict; allow me to introduce to you today the dance around the tree of hope, a force we all have valiantly fought to kill. The arrogant powerful and the desperate weak must keep in mind that we're winners through our concessions, strong through our hopes and immortal through our mortality.

WAITING FOR THE TRAIN OF HOPE

5/ 19, 2004

It is the graduation day of the Dunedin High School, class of 2004. My son Amon was one of the 300 hundred graduates. What a happy day for him; he has gotten the undivided attention of his divorced parents and siblings as well. The music played while the graduates were proudly marching toward the stage. They all looked happy and victorious as they slowly moved to receive a certificate that testifies s/he no longer belonged to the camp of the illiterates. Some of them chewed gum, the last sweet taste of a carefree life. They were quite conscious that soon they will be thrown into the muddy world of greed and treachery. Not even the commencement's flattering voice, "you are the hope of the world" could have convinced them to trust the mad dog, the world. Over forty years ago, I myself had heard this same voice. Still I am waiting for the train to take me to that wonderful land of hope. As long as there are CNN, ABC and NBC news, my waiting will be longer and my hope will become thinner. Still I must continue holding onto the spider's whip. How can one lose hope and still have enough energy to travel through the thousand zigzagging dark paths of this jungle called life? Once born, we have no other choice but to hope. Hope is our guiding light.

The ceremony proceeded in a joyful atmosphere. A few of the black graduates presented the ultimate taste of joy as they performed their wrap dance (certainly the solemnity of the white boys and girls did not intimidate

239

them).

Some adults find a peculiar way to express their joy. Jacky's mother belonged to this category. Many tears have escaped Orly's eyes as her darling was advancing to receive the- long- awaited diploma. Elbowing me, David whispered in my ears, "Now that my wife has warmed up, she is able to shed tears for a whole village." "Thank God for women, they give different taste to any occasion," I replied. We exchanged a light smile and continued to watch the happy parade.

All rejoiced for the graduates and applauded their achievements. After the two- hour ceremony, families parted to celebrate that special day in the life of their children. To celebrate Jacky and Amon's, the Levys and the Abdous took Juliet and Romeo for a branch at the Adam and Eve Paradise restaurant, located in a small plaza at the eastside of Dunedin. Many of the old customers stared at the young graduates with nostalgia. Why not? Even the thirties, the depression decade, deserved a moment of nostalgia. After all, man is a nostalgic animal, no matter how horrible the times were.

That morning the Abdous ate from the delights of Adam and Eve's Paradise, while dreaming of the evening's banquet at the Cheesecake Factory in Tampa. It was the siblings' gift to their baby brother. At dinner, the graduate ate as if it were his last meal. How often he had such an elaborated dinner, anyway? His mother had excused herself and her absence served us as an opportunity to talk and joke freely, a choking environment to a religious fanatic. After dinner we decided to go to Clearwater Beach. There we walked under the stars on the sound of giggles and tranquil sea waves. Was it a good life or just a passing dream?! Whatever it was, it could not have happened without the magic of the family. Indeed, the family members are the stars of heaven shining upon one another.

A TOUR OF MEA CULPA

6/ 4, 2004

Today George Bush has begun touring Europe to distribute his mea culpa to the old Allies, who had initially opposed his dangerous adventure in Iraq. Was it a true atonement, or just the fox's ruse to find a way out the hole dug by its own claws?

Our struggle against terrorism will save the Western Civilization, he reiterated his old lie.

Mr. President, your preemptive war in Iraq is rather leading the world to a new form of barbarism. You have taken the wrong road. You wanted freedom for the Iraqis and, perhaps, for all the people of the Middle East. That is quite noble of you. However, Mr. President, failing to draw a line between a dream and reality can

240

turn both into nightmares, and nightmares you have gotten, so far. Could even a genuine mea culpa redeem your unwise option for war?

There is no definitive answer to this question; history is the march of the blind toward God and here lays your potential redemption.

-- I have heard of a Californian man who had gone through many plastic surgeries on his face, just to look like his happy and loyal puppy. What an insult might conclude the human logic! However, the right answer does not lie in our logic; the dog's behavior was the ultimate answer to our embezzlement. To the owner's disappointment, the canine has stopped wagging its tail as before. Rather, it led a constant crusade of barking at the master as if he were a total stranger, and perhaps a thief. The lesson this dog wanted to teach his master and all: we are in peace only when we accept our differences of existence. That said, I am not denying freedom, justice or any absolutes. Rather, I am opposing the belief that those values are recipes to be delivered at the head of missiles, rather as gifts that must be gradually and gratefully received. They are realities that grow through great discrepancy of time, depending on the disposition of the minds and hearts of those who need and seek them. In the words of Albert Camus, "Rebellion is one of the essential dimensions of man; it is our historical reality"- "*the rebel.*"

In other words: the liberator must not hasten the birth of liberty through inducement; this is abortion and not birth. Michael Mandelbaun's new book: "*the Meaning of Sports*" contains many parallel for successful teams and countries.

In Iraq's case, only the Iraqis can win the game of freedom for themselves. "America's greatest role in the Middle East is to give a tilt," in the words of Thomas L. Friedman, the man who understands quite well the psyche of the region.

Mr. President: touring Europe may recover a lost sympathy between you and some of the- initially- opposing old Allies. However, this political reconciliatory gesture cannot bring a soon peace to Iraq. Again, I must remind you: All men dream of freedom but they must exercise their own means to attain it at their own timing. This is a sacred path; do not alter it or else the vision will disappear. A misplaced dance is an insult to the audience. Mr. President, you had chosen the dance of death and today the world can only offer you its condolences.

THE DEATH OF A DINOSAUR

6/ 6, 2004

Early this morning I've learned of Ronald W. Reagan's death that had occurred yesterday. Like millions of

Americans, I was saddened; in spite I despised his two-terms' presidency. Could a man be separated from his deeds and still continue to claim genuine existence?

This question has ignited a duel between two competing philosophies:

The scholastic philosophy that declares: every entity has criteria, properties, essence that makes it the kind of thing it is and not something else.

The existential philosophy identifies a man with his actions.

Young and naïve, I had embraced the laziness of the first system of philosophy. As I matured, I have divorced that docile sterile woman to embrace the indomitable but fertile one, existentialism. So why then was I moved by the death of the dinosaur, although I had despised his deeds? Well, humanity is a tree whose leaves are made of everyone of us. Each falling leaf, dried as it may be, leaves a rancor in the heart of the other leaves. It is the human sympathy, our existential entanglement in its utmost vitality and kindness.

--Regan's death came with the sixtieth anniversary of the D-Day, a day in which the Allied Forces stormed the five beaches of Western France. That date marked the beginning of pushing the Nazis out of the Voltaire's county, and later out of the entire Europe. What a success! The memory of such a success has constantly brought tears to the eyes of the living old soldiers, the great warriors of yesterday. Watching their tears, I shed some of my own; the human sympathy is a unifying force, like that of self-sacrifice. It is not the transient life that unites us, rather the imminent death that hovers over all.

As the Veterans marched in their military uniforms, they looked happy, although worn out. It is the dawning death, and not the victory, they were celebrating (after an authentic life of self-sacrifice to their families and country). That thought forced me to reflect on the elusive achievements of Reagan's short life, long as it might have seemed.

Some historians attribute the fall of the evil empire to his political endeavors. They cannot be more wrong; communism had long dug its own grave, a task which only it was capable of.

The history of men is no different than that of nations. Both, men and nations are subjects to their own internal law of self-destruction or endurance. Therefore, I discredit Reagan of being the man behind the fall of communism in Eastern Europe; he was just a key witness of the fading Russian empire. On the contrary, I credit the man of having erected a social Berlin Wall between the American citizens. Over that high opaque wall, a few were capable to jump and many others remained behind, suffering the cruelties of social separation. For that separation, may God forgive you, Mr. dead President! After all, it wasn't out of malice; rather your short vision- a vice your admirer Mr. George W. Bush has proudly embraced. Both have seen a few parts of the tree; you could not see it in its entirety, a work of men of imagination, intellectual capacity and big heart, qualities you both have lacked. Your sight has become myopic by the selfish philosophy of conservatism, a reminiscent of the Darwinian Theory: only the fittest survives. Darwin died, survived by the worms that were eating him up from inside. Lesson learned: share with me your bread, soon or later worms will feast on your opulent flesh that has eaten my share; your greed has only enhanced their appetite.

THE FREEDOM OF TO BE

6/ 18, 2004

Exactly at 7:30 p.m., the Indian born Maestro bowed before looking tired audience. Joining hands, the seventy three-year- old man piously rose up his shaved head for a brief moment asking the universal spirit to impregnate the agitated planet with love and harmony. Then he dignifiedly sat, after collecting the fringes of his long and wide snow- white robe, so no human feet could stumble over them. Gently he revolved the round table to pick up a flute that was out of his reach; many other musical instruments laid there waiting for his divine touch. The meditative music of Maestro Sri Chinmoy filled the air with joy, a relief from the heavy daily stress. The free spiritual concert has offered inspiration rather than entertainment, a break away from the poisonous Western materialism. We all were charmed as he played his flute, piano, guitar and other musical instruments I could not name, due to my gross ignoramus of music. O holy man, would you please play the flute for me one more time. It reminds me of that old pastoral flute my father used to play while leading his flock to the family home; darkness had fallen. How joyful we were then! Even the mud- walls used to be moved by that melodic tune.

Attentively we listened to the Maestro who played heavenly sounds from the mystical land of India. "The people who come to listen to my music are also doing something most significant; we are all trying to bring about oneness and transcendence. It is teamwork. We are all in a boat sailing together toward the destination." With those humbling but exalting words he closed his concert.

Ah the oneness! Why cannot humans acknowledge, accept and live it? No sheep can find salvation outside the flock, after all. Yes, we are brothers and sisters. Our diverse affiliations with Moses, Jesus, Mohammad, Confucius, or any of the righteous ones, who had gone before us, must contribute in sailing the big ship toward the destination that lies within the universal soul.

Oneness! Oneness! For your sake, today I put on my shining armor of forgiveness. Yes, I need to forgive that greedy man who had charged me five dollars to park my car. If the tow- hour concert was free, why cannot earth join heaven, for a moment, in a melody that celebrated the freedom from *to have*? Is there any melody of

243

a greater enchantment than the freedom of *to be*? To be or not to be that is not the question, rather the answer. As the concert concluded, the audience warmly applauded the Maestro. With genuine humility, he bowed to acknowledge our admiration and quickly disappeared in the dazzling light of the great hall; his genuine modesty has forced him not to dwell in the vanity of the human compliments. Indeed, he was free from the tyranny of having to enjoy the grace of being. May the Universal Spirit lead all to their most worthy destination!

SADDAM THE JOKER

7/ 25, 2004

Glancing at the pages of the St. Pete Times, my eyes caught the word Saddam. Hurray, he is dead was my initial thought. No, unfortunately, he is not; he is writing poetry, gardening and reading the Holy Qur'an. What a loser! Had he gardened the love of his people, by now they would be writing poetry about him, instead.

Was this a new ruse of yours, Saddam? During your long political life, you have discarded the teaching of the Holy Book. Rather, you have listened to your diabolical inner voice: Oppression is the only way to rule them. Tyrant, you have lived by the law of humiliation, this same law will soon lead you to your mortal fate. Stop deceiving yourself, certainly poetry, gardening or reading the Holy Qur'an will not come to your rescue. You had your great opportunity and you have missed it forever. God's mercy can cover any of the sins born out of weakness but not those committed by malice. Your heart never knew mercy toward your people, God's children. His divine mercy cannot embrace you today; mercy and love come to those who have faithfully observed them. In his life, the blind Ray Charles sang, *"Georgia on my mind..."* It was the pride song of his life. In spite of his rapture by death, he is and will be on Georgia's mind.

Tyrant, those who live by the law of sword, die by this law, and those who observe the law of love, will forever live. Just remember: one harvests what one would have sown. So, fox of the desert, be assured of our lack of sympathy. Poetry of deception makes the deceiver and poetry of love makes the believer. Your deceptive poetry is nothing but a heritage of the wind and what the wind carries away, no man's heart can retain. Saddam, you are a foolish moth, your whole life has been nothing but a dance of death. Almost a year and a half ago, people toppled your bronze statue erected all over the country; today do not try to rebuild it in their hearts through empty words. You have been a false idol and forever your memory will so remain.

244

THREE DAYS OF CIRCUS

7/ 26-29, 2004

Three days of circus! O Lord, have mercy on my frivolous inclination for amusement. Although, I am a Democrat, for a lack of a better party, I feel nauseated by the false promises my party has offered us, so far. "Help on the way." "Hope for tomorrow,' repeatedly screamed John Kerry. What more political jargons should my ears suffer? The most depressing aspect when the populace has sung those empty political slogans. Who did they think our leaders are? Are they drunken Santa Clauses, who will sell their red garments and pluck their white beards to buy us the most dreamed of toys?

Mr. Kerry, throughout your well- orchestrated speeches, you have promised good health care, excellent education, higher wages and, above all, a safer America. All the aforementioned promises have earned you the ephemeral love of the populace. They have even sung your name… "Go Johnny, go."

But where to, brothers and sisters, do you dream this clown would take us? Farwell, herd, please do not blame me if I have refused to accompany you to the barn; I am the estranged sheep that loves to be nowhere else but in its own skin. In this natural habitat, I shall receive the holy four elements of earth in the highest form of passion. And when my flesh, soul and heart will mix with the sacred elements, I shall fear no humans or beasts; I am no longer opponent to any of those earthy entities; I am in the heart of each one of them. And when you're a part of a whole, then peace is born; it's the prize of integration. Those who preach division are but false prophets. Listen to them not, death and destruction they are preaching. I dream of that day when Democrats and Republicans will go to the same bathroom without cloaking their noses before the sight of one another; all deliver the same…

LIVING SINATRA'S WAY

8/1, 2004

At the end of their short vacation at the Paternal home, the Abdou's children have called for an emergency meeting. Two major concerns dominated the call. First: we must cast our votes to the Democratic Party. The second concern was to discuss the future of the old man. No, no, it is not what you might be thinking; he is still relatively young for confinement in a nursing home. Rather, he must look for a part job to escape the boredom of retirement; meanwhile supplementing a meager social security income; after having had brutally subjugated his long- past years to the caprice of a lucrative writing. Still writing was the only passion the aging Papa has ever cultivated with so much love. Since his early childhood, he has exhibited no genuine interest for any other paths. Even in that institution where he had spent almost a decade and a half of his prime years dreaming of the red, the vestment worn by the Catholic Church's prelates, he wrote more than prayed. And when the day of rapture descended upon him, specifically falling in love with the mother of those four firstborns of his, he worked to the minimum measures to meet the family's basic needs; devoting his high intellectual energy for writing. Such a dreamy path has greatly affected his children's comfort- zone; so they have chosen action. Thank God for the children's different paths.

Although trained from early age to believe that not all birds like to migrate to the warm south, still they worried about dad's insistence to stay in the North Pole, the cold poverty. But is there any urgency for a man greater than to follow the call of his own heart? Is it not the only road to salvation? A chosen road of damnation is more worthy than a road of salvation one would have been pushed onto. And when death will come, the aging gonzo can rightfully sing Frank Sinatra's infamous song, *"I did it my way..."*

"So, dad, what's your plan for tomorrow?" the anguished children asked in one single voice.

"Well, kids, my plan for tomorrow is no different than the one of yesterday," affirmatively replied the stubborn old man.

"Dad, you have been dreaming for so long, it is about time to wake up to reality," said Nailah, the Ph.D. psychology candidate.

"Does anyone of you have a memory of hunger?" I asked a bit irritated.

"I do," responded Nafré the vitamins' swallower.

"I don't remember that has ever happened... And suppose it did, it might have served you well, you're all doing fine; no one of you has failed to succeed and for that you must be grateful."

"Dad, we're happy to have found our paths, still we're worried about yours," said Tameri.

"The future doesn't worry me a bit; I'm strong enough to suck water from rocks, if thirsty. And in case of hunger, I'll be content with earthworms on my table."

"Dad is entitled to live in whatever land he finds himself comfortable. That's okay, Dad, don't worry, you have five kids who will take care of you," fervently said young Amon. "...By the way, dad, I just want to remind you that my college registration is coming in a week, I need money," the hidden One added with mischievous smile.

"No problem, son, but I hope by now you all realize why I didn't save one penny for my retirement."

"Sorry, dad, we're not exactly the two hundred children of Ramses... still we thank you; we always had shoes on our feet, although they were not made of leather," said Tameri.

"Who cares, we shouldn't have shoes at all, nor should we ask for too much clothes; all those greedy desires bleed nature to death," commented Babafemi, the environmentalist.

"At least, father, just pay more attention to the house. Try to repair the leaking roof and keep the yard well groomed. It's the esthetics of the neighborhood you must bear in mind," suggested Tameri, the recently elevated planning supervisor for the renovation of the Westside of Los Angeles.

"Also, dad, it's about time to change your diet, you're no longer young to eat a lot of red meat," advised Nafré, the health freak.

"Kids, let's eat dinner and then take a stroll to Safety Harbor Pier," I suggested.

We sat around the dining table to eat avidly from the variety of dishes Marla's hands had lovingly prepared. As for Papa's uncertain future, it has been secured by a historical oral agreement that stated: The children will take care of the aging lion. And he amended: or they will have to face the Japanese civil law, meaning, incarceration. Amendment was approved by all, and his heart could not be more filled with joy.

A HIGH DOSAGE OF MALICE

8/ 09, 2004

The CNN news delivered to me the day's high dosage of malaise. How could I be not annoyed by the frivolousness of the United States Congress debating to carve Ronald Reagan's face on Mount Rushmore (as if it was more urgent than to implement the recommendations of the 9/ 11/committee report to prevent future acts of terrorism).

Yes, nations must honor their leaders, who would have governed them with just for all. But what Reagan has done to the natives, to say the least? In my humble opinion, the only way to fulfill God's justice is to return the Mountain to them. After all, it was their sacred Mountain from whose top their ancestors spoke to the gods and sought their guidance. Apparently, those gods did not give them the right advice- having failed to warn them of the evil intentions of the white man. Anyway, as a compromise, why not carve Jimmy Carter's face. It could be more agreeable to the Indians than Reagan's. Reason is simple: Carter has built huts and houses for the poor, and Reagan courted the rich at the poor's expenses. I just hope that next morning I won't wake up to hear the right-wing politicians suggesting the carving of George W. Bush's face. Please, Lord, do spare my sanity; I don't need to see the face of another injustice. Great conqueror of the Mesopotamian valleys and mountains, rivers and swamps, you are needed to act in more than one drama. Yes, Mr. President, Keep shaking the hand of Ahmed Chalabi, the thug you thought to lead the new free and just Iraq. You have considered him as its future savior. So quickly your dream has turned into nightmare. Today you woke up to the news that he is a thief. If you don't believe me, ask your ally, the King of Jordan. He will not hesitate to tell you that thug had milked two million dollar of his Majesty's impoverished kingdom. Conclusion: Mr. President, you are just unwise like me, always embedding the wrong partner.

The depressing news did not fly only from the American soil.

-- According to the latest investigation about social behaviors, the majority of the British women prefer to have a hot cup of tea than to have sex with their men.

-- The Dutch women have asked that the head of a man. He had sneaked in and sucked their toes while they were sunbathing on a private beach, and he must be brought to them on a platter. It was a bit unfair on their part, though. Had they given up bathing in the nude, that sex maniac would have just been happy to fantasize about them from a distance.

--Well, not all the news were depressing; Oprah has accepted an offer of 600 million dollar to continue doing her most popular show for the next five years. Was the good news a genuine confession of mea culpa to the-long- oppressed black community; or just a ploy of White America to perpetuate a shrewd policy of self-interest? Indeed, it all amounted to this simple logic: Oprah, your worth is based on defending our interest; and who could do a better job than you, the queen of talk show hosts?!

Anyway, Oprah, my gal, congratulations for the fat sum! I am sure you will be remembering the hundreds of thousands of your black brothers and sisters who are occupying the dark cells of America's prisons.

-- In spite of all the aforementioned depressing, and somewhat confusing news, I remained enchanted by the conclusion of the latest investigation about the benefits of soybeans. Although there was no definitive proof that they can prevent women's breasts cancer, as had been stated in previous scientific Investigations, still soybeans have the power to make women more pleasant and less neurotic, thus confirmed the most recent one. Ah, I welcome the good news! Now at least I have the hope that my erratic Marla will not murder me while I am sleeping. Thank you, Lord, for the soybeans' power to calm the rising tempest of the feminine anger. Certainly sacks full of them will be stored in my house. Just please, Lord, let your most merciful heaven to rain on me a few extra dollars; soybeans are quite expensive. Certainly my life is more precious to be taken care of first before repairing my leaking roof. Lord, I will always remember that the human life in your book is worth all the treasures of this earth. But, Lord, don't forget to remind George Bush and all the industrialists of the same.

AGRESSION IS THE HURRICANE OF ALL HURRICANES

9/ 29, 2004

It had been a month of violent meteorological destructive activities. During those four consecutive major hurricanes, I watched how people had reacted so frantically. And here I'm this evening enduring the violence of the fifth hurricane: the first Presidential debate between the incumbent Republican president George W. Bush and his opponent Democrat Senator John Kerry. In spite of their debated differences on how to navigate America through the imminent violent waves of terrorism, it remained clear to me that we must not fear any of the outside enemy forces; fear is the result of our shortcomings. Yes, for peace and security to come to us, we must work diligently to create harmony for ourselves and others. Man-kind nowadays is choked by the crimes of greed; violence; tyranny; hypocrisy; and confusion. All those negative forces are heartless executioners. At the end they assassinate us mercilessly; the only difference for us is to choose our assassins. I would hope that you take responsibility; the laziness of your heart and mind hastens your assassination. However, please do not rush choosing me to be your ruler, spiritual director or your teacher; I, too, will be an equal- opportunity's assassin. So we must keep on searching our way to true freedom. In fact, let's stop searching anywhere else; our ultimate freedom lies within and it is a matter of awakening that giant.

Every man has two Images: the one he perceives himself who he is, and the one of how others perceive him to be, based on his self- sharing and empathy with them. The closest the resemblance is between those two images, the more authentic of a human being one is. One can see the full portrait of oneself only through others. This self- sharing doesn't impoverish the person; rather it serves him as great source of enrichment; since it forces him to go through the tedious process of self- releasing. However, the grace of self- releasing, self- challenging, and ultimately self- sharing, requires a higher grace, the divine grace that nurtures its subsistence. In other words, only a godly self –sharing can reveal the true identity of a human being as he releases, unfolds his full potentialities that inevitably benefit others; rather than absorbing them (using them as objects, commodities) or being absorbed by them. The more a human being travels through life in union with others; the more he affirms his solid reality, his God within.

"The I is real in virtue of its sharing in reality. The fuller in sharing, the more real it becomes," wrote Martin Buber in his book *"I and thou"*.

Could hurricanes be reminders of those services and sympathies we had failed to offer to others to alleviate their sufferings?!

After a long agony diving into the state of our changing nation and the world, Lord, forgive me for having had criticized many. My sincerest apology goes especially to President George W. Bush; I had failed to see the heavy load he was carrying on his shoulders. You know, Lord, I don't have a grain of hatred toward him; I was just upset about the war; still unkind words hurt. Also, I sincerely apologize to anyone else I might have offended; deep inside I believed they weren't bad people, rather weary and confused. As for my lingering resentment toward the fanatics and tyrants of the world, Lord, may you work on my weakness!

"…I don't know all of your purposes. All I know is what we can do in this earth: love one another." Bob Edgar in his book: *Middle church.*

Thank you, Lord, for giving me the breath to pour my soul and heart out; may all be for your glory. Lord, hold my hand and lead me to the mountaintop, where I will await the sunrise to watch in your presence the ice melting. There at the mountaintop of your mercy I want to reconcile with the high and low. And now, Lord, that I am reconciled with all and to all, let me die in peace; I have seen the lamb walking side by side with the wolf, and both were consumed by your presence. Praise to you, O mighty God, you are the only One who can draw all to your most Sacred Heart. Indeed, you are the- ever- blowing wind that drives the universe unto its right path and no other force can alter its course.

www.ingramcontent.com/pod-product-compliance
Lightning Source LLC
Chambersburg PA
CBHW071336280526
45787CB00001B/114